AMBITIOUS MEN

AMBITIOUS
·MEN·

THEIR DRIVES, DREAMS, AND DELUSIONS

SRULLY BLOTNICK

VIKING

VIKING

Viking Penguin Inc., 40 West 23rd Street,
New York, New York 10010, U.S.A.
Penguin Books Ltd, Harmondsworth,
Middlesex, England
Penguin Books Australia Ltd, Ringwood,
Victoria, Australia
Penguin Books Canada Limited, 2801 John Street,
Markham, Ontario, Canada L3R 1B4
Penguin Books (N.Z.) Ltd, 182–190 Wairau Road,
Auckland 10, New Zealand

First published in 1987 by Viking Penguin Inc.
Published simultaneously in Canada

LIBRARY OF CONGRESS CATALOGING IN PUBLICATION DATA
Blotnick, Srully.
Ambitious men.
Includes index.
1. Executives—United States—Psychology. 2. Business-
men—United States—Psychology. 3. Success in business.
4. Ambition. I. Title
HD38.25.U6B55 1986 658.4'09'019 86–40274
ISBN 0–670–81061–4

Printed in the United States of America by The Book Press,
Brattleboro, Vermont
Set in Electra and Trump Medieval
Design by Susan Brooker/Levavi & Levavi

ACKNOWLEDGMENTS

No work of this size and scope is the result of the effort of just one person. As with past projects, I am grateful to the hundreds of research assistants who helped gather the data on which this book is based.

For nearly a decade now I have had the invaluable and often brilliant counsel of *Forbes*'s editor Jim Michaels to help ferret out those findings which weren't all that surprising from those that truly were.

Viking Penguin editor Gerry Howard was of major assistance at every step, offering a series of insightful suggestions. I have worked with second-rate editors at first-rate book publishers and first-rate editors at second-rate firms. But at last, I had a first-rate editor at a first-rate publisher. That has made all the difference in the final product.

Jay Acton, my agent and an attorney, helped resolve a number of problems that stood in the way of the completion of this project, the most important of which involved ensuring the confidentiality of the people about to be discussed. Because he had the courage of his convictions, all went well in the end.

CONTENTS

AMBITIOUS MEN

INTRODUCTION

THE DREAMS
OF THE DRIVEN

People with power aren't supposed to have problems. With all the resources to reshape the globe at their disposal, it is commonly assumed they have the wherewithal to better their own condition.

The problems of powerful men are rarely simple; neither are the solutions. If they aren't making as much money, being promoted as quickly, or winning admiration as widely as they anticipated, or if their own business isn't growing, their first impulse is to use the approach that worked before, this time more energetically. Should that too fail, they are willing to try a slight shift in direction. Through it all they remain convinced that their general strategy is still effective and that a minor course correction will result in significant improvement. They have good reason to think this, since the formula worked well enough to bring them their present level of achievement. If that formula is modified, its effectiveness seems likely to continue, carrying them at least to the next plateau. But what happens when it doesn't? What should a man do when a tried-and-true formula for success, one that actually worked for him in the past, no longer does?

During more than a quarter of a century of studying these questions I have found that most ambitious men live their lives from day to day, hoping for great things but reacting to more immediate pressures. Their high expectations for themselves make them take setbacks personally and hard. Each agonizes over missed chances without realizing that there is a distinctive pattern both to the setbacks he experiences and the major opportunities he overlooks.

These conclusions, and numerous others, emerged as the result of an ongoing examination of the lives of more than six thousand white- and blue-collar workers. (How my staff and I selected and studied these men is described in the appendix on methodology.) Most of the conclusions that I had expected to find turned out to be false—for instance, that the object of a man's ambitions would remain largely the same throughout his professional life. The changes in goals turned out to be a fascinating story unto itself, one that is discussed in chapters 9 (Early Success), and 12 (Fame and Fortune). Some of our findings about other topics have already been published. In *Corporate Steeplechase: Predictable Crises in a Business Career* we described the hurdles that the majority of men and women can expect to encounter on the job in the various decades of their work lives. In *Otherwise Engaged: the Private Lives of Successful Career Women* we examined the experiences of a large group of driven women. Now we want to see what happens to ambitious men, and why.

How do we know if someone is ambitious? As the word is used in this book, five criteria determine whether the term is appropriate. First, he has to have a desire for *more*. More what? Someone is considered ambitious only to the extent that he wants more money, fame, prestige, or power. Notice that if he states that he wants a happier life, the public—whose attitudes we have quantified and then used as criteria in our study—does not view this as evidence of ambition. Happiness doesn't qualify, in their eyes, as an appropriate goal, and neither does romance. Sex is another matter; it qualifies because aggression is involved. So does strength—the power to move things or people. The four goals that are considered suitable targets of ambitious individuals aren't independent, since, for instance, the attainment of fame or fortune in and of itself gives its holder a certain amount of power.

Second, in judging whether someone is ambitious the public doesn't care about "quality," they care only about "how much." In monitoring audience reactions to film clips and written profiles of various people's lives we noticed that, to the audience, "ambition" is a quantitatively oriented word. It was irrelevant to them that the person was having a good time each day or a bad one; all they focused on was the amount of something—say, social status—that the person had accumulated.

Third, they were not inclined to give him forever to accumulate the amount. If someone in the film they were watching said, "I want to make $100,000, but I don't care if it takes me thirty years to do it," they didn't see him as particularly driven. To be adjudged ambitious he had to be in a hurry—and the more of a rush he was in, the more ambitious they saw him as being. He had to want the "big four"—money, fame, prestige, or power—right away, not later than 9 A.M. tomorrow morning.

Fourth, his quest had to be open-ended. Someone the audience heard say, "Once I make a million dollars, I'll never work again, just lie in my hammock and smile," they considered more goal-oriented than ambitious. If the word were truly to apply, they felt the person had to be willing to strive virtually till the day he died.

Finally, the person had to seem somewhat ruthless. To the extent that he was concerned about other people's feelings, to that degree they downgraded the level of ambition they saw him as having. Unless he gave the appearance of being "out for himself," many were reluctant even to use the word. In short, only a person who wanted a lot more money, renown, social status, or power, and who wanted it just as soon as he could possibly get it—without caring about much else—was seen as being genuinely ambitious. From studying the views on this subject of more than ten thousand people, by testing them in a variety of situations over the past twenty-five years, we know that the definition of the word in the minds of most Americans has remained unchanged during this period. The one thing that has changed is that people look on the word more favorably now than at any time during the past quarter of a century. In fact, both men and women see themselves as somewhat defective if they can't comfortably claim to be ambitious.

From our studies of audience reactions—to determine whether its members felt that the people they were watching on screen were ambitious, and if so, to what extent—we learned that the public has a picture of "success" that is quite limited, and one that differs significantly from that of "ambition." Someone on film who says that he is happy is viewed as successful only if he has also attained a substantial quantity of one (or perhaps all) of the big four. "Success" is a very performance-oriented word; people who inherited their wealth, renown, social status, or power were generally not viewed as being successful, since they hadn't done anything to get where they were. (Those who added substantially to a fortune they inherited were an exception to this rule, for they were thought in some sense to have "started over," though from a very high level.)

Interestingly, while quantity mattered every bit as much in the minds of an audience assessing "success" as it did in the case of "ambition," speed was no longer important. Whether it took the person ten, twenty, or thirty years to move up made no difference to audiences anywhere in the country. All they cared about was "how far" he had come, not "how fast." Similarly, the degree of ruthlessness he had displayed during his rise was now irrelevant. They focused only on the end, not the means, and even adjudged some pretty shady characters "a success" if each had done well enough in his particular line of work.

In measuring ambition and success we always used a relative scale. Unlike temperature, where water freezes at 32° Fahrenheit and boils at 212°, there is no absolute level at which driven people boil over or their success bumps up against a ceiling beyond which they cannot go. Some people are indeed almost infinitely ambitious, in the sense that all they think about morning, noon, and night is the ever-expanding dream they are pursuing. Similarly, no sooner has someone made a billion dollars in his lifetime (which at one time seemed safe to adopt as the upper end of the scale) than somebody else makes ten billion.

So when we say in forthcoming chapters that someone is very ambitious, we mean that he wants to attain more—and have it sooner—than the typically driven person does. Success, on the other hand, is easier to measure and is more stable; for, instead of looking at emotions (which vary from minute to minute), in this case we examine a person's net worth, annual earnings, life style, the number of people who know him, and the positive or negative opinions of this audience.

Although the American public has a strong tendency to see success in terms of financial and professional accomplishment, we've had to extend the meaning of the word a bit in this book because we also care about the personal lives of the men in the sample. The phrase "successful marriage" should therefore be taken to mean that the couple not only stayed together, but—and this is a crucial test—would marry each other again if they were currently single and had the opportunity. Another criterion for the phrase to apply was that the two were sufficiently satisfied sexually over the years to not be looking constantly for other erotic relationships to make up for what was missing in the one they had.

THE DIFFERENCES AMONG MEN

In studying contemporary American men as they are affected by contemporary pressures it is useful to look at analyses of earlier periods as well. The popularity of a work of fiction in the past can be seen as a kind of public opinion poll before such measures were as widely used as they are now. Looking at such works is particularly important if we are to get beyond the monolithic and usually negative picture of "men" that has been prevalent in the media (especially movies, magazines, and TV) during the last fifteen years.

For the purposes of our study, differences among males are every bit as important as similarities. The works of three American novelists earlier this century help alert us to the fact that not only do the differences exist, they have been in existence for a very long time. The first of these writers, Theodore Dreiser, wrote about businessmen in a largely positive and realistic light. In *The Financier*, published in 1912, he gives us a picture of a man who, when asked, "Well, what are you interested in?" replied proudly, "Money!" Far from being a dreamer, the young man, Frank Cowperwood, is aggressive and openly ambitious; the minute a better opportunity presents itself, he seizes it. As the author states, "He had an uncanny faculty for getting appreciative hearings, making friends, being introduced into new realms." As many moderns might suspect, Frank is anything but tightfisted. "It was not his idea that he could get rich by saving," Dreiser tells us. "From the first he had the notion that liberal spending was better."*

Anyone who was raised in a small town or major city has met a man like Frank, but there are other significant types. F. Scott Fitzgerald, in

---

* For the purposes of this book, Dreiser's *The Financier* is the most illuminating choice, although *An American Tragedy* is far more widely read today. Part of the appeal of *An American Tragedy* is that it describes ambition in a disturbed individual, which gives it artistic power, but at the same time deprives it of general validity.

The Great Gatsby, depicts a man who is interested above all in social success. To him, money is little more than a ticket of admission to an elite and eminently public circle of which he wants desperately to be a part. It is hardly surprising that Daisy, the woman to whom Gatsby is attracted, appeals to him precisely because she seemed to be "gleaming like silver, safe and proud above the hot struggles of the poor." Although the novel is indeed a love story (and that is how more than 2,500 people we polled who had recently read the work categorized it) what Gatsby also wants very much from Daisy is to stabilize his own social position at a high level.

Hemingway provides the third and final type of man we should keep in mind: one who has great distrust of "literature" and fancy terms. As Frederic Henry says in *A Farewell to Arms*, "I was always embarrassed by the words 'sacred,' 'glorious,' and 'sacrifice,' and the expression 'in vain.' There were many words you could not stand to hear and finally only the names of places had dignity." As a British critic, Walter Allen, has stated, "Hemingway's vocabulary must be the smallest of any major writer, and the restriction was deliberate. His criterion of truth was almost what could be assessed in terms of physical impact. It was the one thing he could be sure of. It was both his limitation as a writer and the source of his power."

While the material world is much on the mind of such a man as Hemingway created, and often forms the basis of his livelihood, we shall see that what matters most to him is self-reliance.

"LET ME TELL YOU ABOUT THE VERY RICH"

It is no accident that these three works were widely read at the time of their publication and have become classics. For the types of men they portray are examples of characters to be found not only in the authors' era, but also in every decade from then to now. Modes of dress and speech may vary from one period to the next but there is an important continuity beneath the surface. While the appearances of such men may be different in the Roaring Twenties and the late 1980s, the main drive of each is recognizably the same.

It was not the aim of our research to categorize men by type. What interested us most was which ones would do well, which would do poorly, and why. Nevertheless, as the years went by, it was fascinating to see that the men whose characters Dreiser, Fitzgerald, and Hemingway found "larger than life" the contemporary world also did. There was no escaping the fact that there were thousands of such men in every large city. Their looks and manner changed from decade to decade, yet in many ways they were descendants of the main characters described in these classic works more than sixty years ago.

During our study we also found that there is a vast difference between literature and social science. For instance, in *The Financier* Dreiser has Frank Cowperwood stumble upon what, to him, is a great insight. After watching what happens in a fish tank between a lobster and a squid, in which the former finally kills the latter, the author writes, "The incident made a great impresson on [Frank]. It answered in a rough way that riddle which had been annoying him so much in the past: 'How is life organized?' " Now, at last, Frank knew. "Things lived on each other—that was it. Men lived on men."

Dreiser's attempt to characterize what goes on in the mind of someone who is out to make a fortune as a broker, trader, or middle man is accurate, but only somewhat. To an outsider it may seem that what takes place in the world of business and finance is merely "dog eat dog." However, in more than twenty-five years of looking, we were able to find very few men who became wealthy with this as their dominant attitude. What worked far better, and was far more frequently found, was that the person was truly involved with his work, not just the money-making. In fact, he had to become caught up, thoroughly immersed, and ultimately an expert in his field; otherwise he was unable to distinguish himself sufficiently from his competitors to earn the sizable sum he was seeking.

Similarly, a famous passage of Fitzgerald's says, "Let me tell you about the very rich. They are different from you and me." This sentence appears in his 1926 story "The Rich Boy" and millions of people who have never read any Fitzgerald have heard the line. However the actual passage goes on to state that "They possess and enjoy early and it makes them cynical where we are trustful." After decades devoted to studying groups of men who were comparable in most important respects except that one was rich and the other was from a modest background, we feel safe in saying that it was men in the latter group who seemed streetwise and cynical, while their rich counterparts were, if anything, too naïve and trusting. Over the years of our study, this innocence has gotten them in trouble much more often than the public realizes.

Finally, in *The Sun Also Rises*, Hemingway has one of his characters, Jake Barnes, an American newspaperman, say, "It's awfully easy to be hardboiled about everything in the daytime, but at night it's another thing." Like the words of Dreiser and Fitzgerald quoted above, this one has a "common sense" ring to it, yet the evidence we've collected indicates that the reality is often the reverse. Many ambitious men and women are extremely flexible during their workday. Eager to succeed, they are accommodating and responsive almost to a fault. It is only when they go home that the rubber band snaps back, as it must somewhere, and they act in a hardboiled and uncompromising manner on evenings and weekends with their spouses and children instead of relaxing after the workday's strains.

In spite of the questionable psychological assertions that novelists frequently make many of their insights are invaluable, for they give us a clue about what to look for, especially if a work was not only popular in its time but also eventually attained classic status. As we said earlier, the larger-than-life characters of the past can be seen among us today, if we know what to watch for. In this book we will examine three typical ambitious men; only many years into our study did we come to realize that they closely resembled the characters so resonantly depicted by Dreiser, Fitzgerald, and Hemingway. We call them, respectively, Larry, David, and Bill.

Larry is representative of the many self-made men who become consumed by their work but would admit every bit as openly as Frank Cowperwood that their primary interest in life is in making money. David, the Gatsby of our story, is the most social of the three and has unwittingly groomed himself over the years to be at his best when in the company of those he considers "the right sort of people." Finally, our analog of Hemingway's male heroes is Bill, a man with a working-class background and profession who distrusts even more than Hemingway himself did fancy words and things he couldn't touch.

WHAT FUELS AMBITION?

After looking at men in terms of the three types that we now identify, respectively, with characters in novels by Dreiser, Fitzgerald, and Hemingway, it slowly dawned on us in the early sixties that there was one missing. Too many educated and intelligent males were distinctly different from the three discussed thus far. The kind of man we didn't yet have the tools to describe is more reclusive than the other three, more likely than they to be deeply involved in literary, artistic, or scientific pursuits. It amused us to realize that although we were describing men in terms of the characters in novels, we had neglected to include the novelists themselves. They generally resembled a fourth personality, the representative of which in this book we call Steven.

Using these four types we found it possible to analyze the behavior of the men in our sample in a more illuminating manner each year. That doesn't mean every man is like one or another of the four, or even a mixture of two or more of them. A more accurate way of describing what we discovered is that ambitious men share in varying degrees the main *drive* each of the four embodies. In Bill's case it is a quest for *autonomy*; for David it is a burning desire to have life be as *social* as possible; to Larry nothing is more important than to move up in the world and at last be considered as deserving of *respect*; finally, to Steve nothing equals the powerful appeal of doing something *original*.

These four kinds of quest allow us to look at ambitious men in a more concrete and meaningful manner. It doesn't take many years of monitoring men in their twenties and thirties to realize that four of them may be pursuing the same goal—say, fame—yet each is using a different one of the respective routes discussed above. With this as our vantage point we are able to give more substance to the word "ambition," seen over the course of a person's lifetime, than it usually has. For there is now an overarching theme that links together hundreds of seemingly disparate comments and events in his life.

By viewing men as members of these four categories, we are better able to isolate the characteristics that determine whether someone will succeed or do poorly, both professionally and personally. Once we establish what their basic drive is (though they themselves seem rarely to know), it becomes increasingly clear what the "magic ingredient" is that each has to have in order to realize his particular dreams.

The search for this ingredient—which in reality requires an inner adjustment of a critical but not radical sort—is the main subject of this book.

ANXIOUS TO PLEASE

Much has changed in the lives of American men as the nature of the economy has shifted. Briefly turning the clock back two hundred and fifty years, we know that most worked on farms and that land was their principal asset. Since money was in short supply at the time, people were able to get the diversity of goods and services they needed primarily through barter; it was common to pay one's debts "in kind."

Although Americans have been romanticizing their agrarian past for most of the century, it is important to realize that an economy in which land is the main source of people's wealth restricts the growth of autonomy of the next generation. As Philip Greven, Jr., has stated in *Four Generations: Population, Land and Family in Colonial Massachusetts*, "inheritance constituted the principal means of transferring the ownership of land from one generation to the next. Thus although the great majority of second generation sons were settled upon their fathers' lands while their fathers were still alive, only about one quarter of them actually owned the land upon which they lived after their fathers' deaths. With their inheritances came ownership; and with ownership came independence."

Surprising as it may seem at first, when money became more widely available it served as a basis for the estabishment of one's independence at an earlier age. Whereas previously the only kind of wealth was "property capital," now a new kind, "liquid capital"—cash—moved increasingly to the fore. Family ties loosened, not just in the last two decades, but more than two centuries ago when money—the new, portable capital—began to play an ever more prominent role in the economy.

As the United States became increasingly industrialized in the late nineteenth and twentieth centuries, another significant change began to occur in the world in which men had to make their way. While liquid capital was still important, "intellectual capital"—embodied in a profession for which one had trained in a college or university—gained ascendancy and finally came to occupy center stage in the post–World War II period. At this time the economy became more oriented toward services than goods. Although it was many decades in arriving, this shift is a more drastic one than has commonly been recognized. Farming and manufacturing were similar in a variety of ways that also make them very different from the urban-centered jobs of white-collar professionals working in offices.

The service ethic that is part and parcel of these professions made men see themselves and those around them in a new light. Whereas in an earlier era their work was concerned primarily with the physical world or products (such as land, sea, and machines), now a growing proportion of the prestigious and high-paying jobs involved only people. That had the effect of making "personality" more important than "character," as nineteenth-century authors continually referred to it. Since workers were carrying their profession around largely in their heads and needed a host of interpersonal skills to handle the variety of individuals they met daily, flexibility became essential. The steadfast and stolid qualities summarized by the word "character" slowly began to seem ever more dated and limiting.

While life in a service economy certainly seems more pleasant and less dangerous to workers than life in an industrial, mining, fishing, or agricultural economy, our preliminary studies made us suspect that this benefit had a hidden cost. From the start of our study we therefore decided to concentrate on "the anxiety to please." It is all well and good to talk about men fulfilling their ambitions and becoming rich, famous, or both, but the man who pans for gold, hunts buried treasure, or drills for oil is traveling a very different road from the urban professional whose routine involves managing, marketing, or sales. What it boils down to is that in the past, large numbers of ambitious men attempted to extract wealth from the earth; as our study got under way, it became clear that an increasing proportion were now trying to extract wealth from one another.

Our guess was that this new psychosocial environment would involve not only changes in the ethical guidelines workers use to judge the rightness and wrongness of their own behavior, but also in the amount of tension they carry each day. Thrown into a sea of highly individualistic people, in a country that valued this individuality above all, Americans seemed likely to us to spend many years being bounced around emotionally, trying to find one psychological stance that was suitable for all occasions.

In the not too distant past most workers found one face to wear throughout the day. The period before World War I struck many observers at the time, and strikes many historians today, as an era of certainty. In government, science, sex, and manners, it was an age of absolutes. There appeared to be little doubt about what was correct and what was not, both at home and on the job. Then came World War I and the appalling destruction of millions of Europe's finest young men. As William Manchester reports in *The Last Lion: Winston Spencer Churchill*, "He sensed that the terrible slaughter of the rising generation could destroy Europe's world hegemony." That is just what happened, and the United States took its place. "London [before World War I] had the push and bustle foreign visitors began to note in New York in the 1920s." This was followed by the one-two punch of Freud and Einstein, so familiar to us now, so new at the time. As their ideas began to be widely popularized in the 1920s, relativity, not only in scientific affairs but in human ones as well, became the order of the day. Still, it wasn't until after World War II that this trend in science and psychology combined with that of an increasingly service-oriented economy to make most men feel that, to be successful, they would have to depend above all on their wits. From our preliminary studies it seemed to us that the men who were hit hardest emotionally, though not financially, by these powerful shifts were those with college educations working in white-collar professions.

Even in our earliest interviews it was apparent that blue-collar workers weren't being subject to the kind of psychological buffeting, a sense of walking on thin ice, that afflicted white-collar workers day after day. In many ways time had stood still for those who did manual labor for a living. Their workday in the twentieth century had more continuity with what took place in the nineteenth century than did that of the typical ambitious office worker.

This perception had a strange consequence, one which made it essential to include working-class men in our long-term study. While men working in an office a century or so ago appeared to be thoroughly secure and were often pillars of their community, the livelihoods of manual workers were subject to the many vagaries of wind and weather as they labored at sea or on land. Now the reverse was so. Blue-collar workers appeared the more secure of the two, taking into account the amount of chronic anxiety white-collar workers carried. Jobs requiring a college education usually offered higher levels of pay and prestige, so even men who were attracted by a romanticized image of physical work—and many were—found the switch from mental to manual labor a hard one to make. However, what intrigued them also intrigued us: the difference in the emotional tone of the everyday lives of these two groups.

Another compelling reason for not confining our attention exclusively to men who attended college is that the blue-collar world isn't as simple and one-dimensional as it seems, nor was it in the past. In *Poverty and Progress: Social Mobility in a Nineteenth Century City*, Stephan Thernstrom wrote, "The laboring family that settled in the city was usually able to elevate itself eventually into the class of property owners. Hard work and incessant economy [by a worker] *did* bring tangible rewards—money in the bank, a house to call his own, a new sense of security and dignity." Both then and now, the blue-collar world contained many young men who were not only ambitious, but also were quite likely to go on to become self-made successes. We wanted to see which ones did, and how they resembled or differed from their counterparts being raised in more affluent settings.

THE SIZZLE AND THE STEAK

One problem that seemed likely to plague white-collar men in particular was the distinction between "substance" and "style." Workers of all sorts in the past were more involved with the physical world of products, materials, and minerals, and the work was more dangerous and at times even deadly. Yet they had little doubt about what was real. They could touch and feel it. How many college-educated workers can say the same? Often paper is the most important physical product they handle daily. Another is the phone. But a voice on the line and words on a page have a much more transient and malleable nature.

Each year of our study there was a substantial number of men criticized by co-workers and friends for being more concerned about the "sizzle than the steak." However, those criticized could rightly retort that the dividing line between the two had not only grown as thin as a human hair, it had all but vanished. Were they being "narcissists" because they sought to dress well, sound educated, appear physically fit, and radiate enthusiasm? They didn't know, and at first, we didn't either. Since they were carrying their portable profession in their minds, however, and were no longer fixed to land-and-a-house the way their parents were, it seemed natural to them to adopt a different approach. While the typical father of these men spent many an evening and weekend making "home improvements," thereby increasing the value of his most important asset, the next generation felt it wiser to make "personal investments" and thereby increase the value of their most important asset—themselves.

The drubbing such men took from leftist critics, such as Christopher Lasch in *The Culture of Narcissism*, was not only cruel but also old hat, the past flaying the present for having moved on and adopted a somewhat different set of goals and, even more sinful, a new way of attaining them.

What made matters worse was that the principal message the men were getting from their fathers and mothers had changed. Greven, in *Four Generations*, reminds us that nearly two hundred and fifty years ago, in colonial America, John Abbott was typical in giving each of his four sons something different to get them started economically in life. The oldest got his land, since dividing it up would have made each piece insufficient for any of the four inheritors to support himself with; the second son was given a trade—shoemaker—which, the father writes in his will, "I helped him into"; the third was given an expensive liberal education at Harvard; the fourth was given money, to buy land in New Hampshire.

The majority of men in our sample resembled the third son in being given an education, thanks to caring parents who emphasized its importance and paid for its cost. However, the parents did—and still do—something else that wasn't as obvious. From a tender age, middle-class American youngsters are encouraged to express themselves fully, with a high value put on individuality: being different from the rest, and preferably better. Emphasis is placed on developing dormant talents and, especially, creativity. While parents and teachers repeat the message year after year, it is a mixed one, usually laced with reminders to learn a trade or profession in order to make a living, in case the "self-expression" route produces little or no income. "We won't be in a position to leave you much, you know," more than three out of four told their children in our sample. "And with people living longer nowadays, by the time you do get it, you're likely to be in your forties or fifties."

In spite of the inner conflict generated by the effort of taking this mixed message to heart—and without realizing it, millions of adolescents do just that—there is a delightful way out, a resolution of the sometimes painful ambivalence it produces: the best of all possible worlds is one in which an individual combines money-making with being creative. If he continues to do this, eventually he winds up both wealthy *and* unique.

Early in our study it was apparent that most men feel that the way they earn their living has nothing to do with their highly touted "inner self," upon which parents and teachers doted when the men painted pictures at eight, played the piano at ten, or wrote essays at twelve. So much subtle emphasis had been placed on this subject that striving for originality had obviously became an end in itself. Many college graduates who enter the work world and go on to earn large sums of money, therefore, are not particularly proud either of their profession or their accomplishments. They have never quite made peace with the "creative urges" that allegedly sit at their core, yet which become more deeply buried each year, a self to which they swore as adolescents they would be true and are now presumably deceiving. The day-to-day demands of business force a certain conformity on those who spend their lives working there, is what they usually say to themselves as they promise secretly to "someday get around to what I was really meant to do."

It was interesting to see that the guilt these men felt about their "dormant creativity" was likely to surface only once they began making more than $50,000 per annum. At lesser income levels a concern with economic survival tended to push aside such thoughts and make them even seem frivolous. Would the young men in our sample also dismiss, as adults, the importance of many of their own accomplishments because nothing "innovative" was involved? During their formative years they were being exposed to a chronic demand for something "new and different from deep within themselves," all in the name of "personal growth," "self-expression," and "becoming more of a person."

Unlike boys from working-class families who tried to excel in a sport and finally dropped it, the pressure on boys in white-collar families to be creative seemed likely still to be there decades later. We wanted to see if it was, and whether it was beneficial or a hindrance, especially considering that most of the truly original contributions by history's great artists and scientists have not resulted from a self-conscious attempt at being creative. In fact, typically the works—labors of love, really—seemed a bit odd or even controversial at the time and only later were recognized as "pathbreaking." Be that as it may, we found that the pressure on the young men in our sample was indeed there decades later, and in the pages that follow we will see the helpful and harmful ways it exerted its influence.

AN OPPORTUNITY TO SHINE

Excelling at something work-related may be one way for people to demonstrate their uniqueness but it certainly isn't the only one. Another is to cultivate an interest in a subject that clearly has nothing to do with one's profession. Everyone does this to some extent; not one of the men in our sample wanted his job to be his entire life. Even those who spent between sixty and seventy hours a week at it found a different activity to turn to for a change of pace and a chance to unwind. However, the men we're talking about were subconsciously seeking more from such a pastime than mere entertainment. They hoped to have it serve as an opportunity to publicly demonstrate some kind of *expertise*.

Since the knowledge they had accumulated about the subject wasn't work-related, they were doing something that, in their view, was noble. As a volunteer effort, one they weren't being paid to undertake, they considered it deserving of an extra measure of applause. On the job, the main reward they got was money; during their leisure hours, the reward they expected was recognition. For what? For being connoisseurs of wine, gourmet food, film, theater, art, music, travel, clothes, or restaurants—even sports.

This intrusion of expertise into these men's private lives seemed to us a double-edged sword. It did indeed stand a chance of impressing their friends, but it also appeared capable of alienating them—especially the men's girlfriends and spouses, who might admire the display in some settings but resent it in others. We wanted to see when this happened, and what the consequences were. Of one thing we were certain: some ambitious men were going to invest such knowledge—and the demonstration of it—with much more emotion than they realized.

In the 1950s these nonwork-related areas of activity or knowledge were usually labeled "hobbies," and typically involved stamp or coin collecting or puttering in the backyard. However, the world of men like those in our sample was becoming more competitive and affluent with each decade of our study and something that was both upscale and public was needed to "keep up with the Joneses." Spending *had* to be involved, since these were basically consumption activities, in which each wanted to show his friends that he was a more knowledgeable consumer than they. However, this was also an age of specialization, so each felt compelled to present himself as an authority on the subject. Imitating what he had done in school, he bought books and read articles about the topic.

One thing that seemed likely to cause the activity to get out of hand in many cases was, between the 1950s and 1980s, the United States changed the way it viewed credentials and careers. Generally speaking, something is valued only to the extent that it is rare. Where college degrees, the basis of most white-collar professions, are concerned, a conspicuous shift took place during the decades of our study. What had previously been relatively uncommon and hard to obtain became available to an enormous number of people, with nearly a million students a year receiving a college diploma in the 1980s.

Even fields that required graduate education, such as law, medicine, dentistry, and business administration, became glutted. Many who wanted to gain entrance to these professions decided it wasn't worth the bother, and those who were already members found themselves being held in much lower esteem by the public than they had formerly been. Career changes became common as hordes of ambitious men and women did the unthinkable and walked away from a field for which they had spent a good many years preparing. Disillusioned about the degree of distinction their efforts over the years were bringing them, they tried to gain in their leisure hours a feeling of being special that they couldn't find on the job.

Unfortunately, not one in a hundred recognized the powerful psychological forces in operation here, ones that we sensed could easily get out of hand. To make matters worse, in turning a hobby into an opportunity for a public display of expertise, they deprived themselves of a sorely needed vehicle for relaxing and recharging. That had to have consequences of its own, both at home and at work, which we'll examine shortly.

In the next four chapters we profile the four types of men—more accurately, four types of drive—for self-reliance, respect, social status, and originality. We do this by looking at specific examples of men—respectively Bill, David, Larry, and Steve—who embody each of these drives. None of these men is a composite, and their names and a few irrelevant details are the only aspects of their stories that we have changed, to safeguard their identity. By interviewing not only them, but their mothers and fathers, sisters and brothers, classmates and co-workers, over the years we were able to obtain a much richer picture of the four, as well as the others in the sample.

While the general economic and social trends we've been discussing affect ambitious men of every description, they affect the four types in very different ways. Gaining an understanding of the differences not only illuminates the reasons why some men do well and others, equally talented, do poorly, but also gives us a body of needed practical information that wasn't previously available. People who want to improve their performance are right to resist modifying their approach until it is clear why the old style wasn't bringing them the results they anticipated and why a new one is far more likely to do so. By the time the book is through we hope they'll have had ample opportunity to learn from the mistakes of others and find the most productive and personally satisfying path for themselves.

·PART·
ONE

CHAPTER
·1·

PEOPLE WHO NEED PEOPLE—AND THOSE WHO DON'T

Few worlds appear so immediately graspable and yet are as difficult for outsiders to penetrate as that of blue-collar workers. "It's pretty obvious what these guys are all about," is a standard response when men who are college graduates from middle and upper-middle-class backgrounds watch manual laborers work. The burly men often wear hats, everything from baseball caps (with, say, the logo of a beer brand) to hardhats, and that alone would set them apart from businessmen, who in recent decades have abandoned this piece of apparel that was so popular in the 1930s, 1940s, and 1950s.

Nevertheless, something deeper separates the two groups, and it is more psychological than financial. In many fields blue-collar men earn more than white-collar workers do, even if we split the white-collar world into two tiers; an upper one consisting of doctors, lawyers, accountants, teachers, and others with a college or graduate degree, and a lower tier, of people doing basically clerical or secretarial work in an office. A crane operator, plumber, or electrician earning in excess of $50,000 a year is no longer rare, so money isn't the dividing line it once was.

What separates blue- and white-collar workers decisively is their approach to work. In the eyes of white-collar workers, especially those from the upper tier, there is a certain glamour to manual labor. A typical comment, this one from a thirty-six-year-old lawyer: "I don't do physical work for a living, but if I did, I wouldn't have to go to the health club three times a week." His college-educated peers point to other features that they deem attractive about this kind of work—for instance, that it is frequently done outdoors; that it starts and stops at a particular hour, and doesn't spill over into evenings and weekends; that it doesn't tax minds and emotions the way managing a company in an office setting does; and, finally, that manual laborers often seem to be having a good time, laughing and joking with one another *while* they work.

However appealing the laughing and joking may seem, they are there mainly because the men find their work repetitive and boring. It doesn't catch them up and hold their interest. They want—in fact, need—to keep themselves entertained and their spirits high, lest they become inattentive. One slip while they are pushing a beam, as opposed to a pencil, could result in harm both to themselves and the structure on which they are working. The many white-collar managers who envy this kind of work would quickly be disillusioned if they had to do it decade after decade for a living. For it would deprive them of the feeling of being consumed, an emotional state they often complain about to friends but actually prize. Not having that feeling, not finding their work involving, would make them feel they had been cheated.

In stark contrast to such a rose-colored perception, the views of blue-collar men about their own professions are full of resentment and dissatisfaction. To begin with, college graduates can choose to do physical work for a living, but few manual laborers could trade places with a middle manager, much less a top one. Many have the interest, but not the skills. Unless they go to night school (which less than 5 percent of the more than four thousand manual laborers we surveyed in 1986 for a national business magazine indicated any serious desire to do) they know they'll spend many years to come in blue-collar or, at best, low-tier white-collar positions.

What blue-collar workers resent most about their labor is that it is dirty and at times dangerous. Less than one half of one percent of all the white-collar men in our sample had injured themselves on the job during the past quarter of a century, as opposed to more than 38 percent of the blue-collar workers, some fatally. Primarily because of its adverse effects on their well-being, they view comments about the "health-club aspects" of their work as absurd. A typical remark, from a construction worker in New York, voiced sarcastically, "I suppose you could get killed or lose a limb falling off one of those stationary bikes in a spa."

Although the homes of blue- and white-collar workers often look similar, and may in fact sit side by side in the same suburb, the attitudes of the occupants are very different. In our sample more than twice as many working-class as white-collar couples rated their marriages unhappy. Although lacking a basis for comparison, their children couldn't help being aware of this. A comment we frequently heard from the teenage children of manually laboring fathers was, "My parents are married to this house, not each other—my father is always fixing it, my mother is always cleaning it. Without it, I don't think they'd have very much in common."

Given the limited and uncertain economic prospects of such children's parents (both of whom usually accepted layoffs as normal) and the even more restricted emotional world they saw at home, it should come as no surprise that most of the sons of blue-collar families we studied wanted badly to have a better life than their parents did. The parents agreed that this was a goal worth striving for and tried to help make it happen, yet they were more ambivalent about their children's leaving home than were white-collar parents, and friction was common. With less parental assistance than children from upper-tier white-collar families usually receive, most men from such backgrounds were forced to make their own way. They began looking after themselves at an earlier age than their white-collar peers did. Making a virtue of a necessity, they came to value *self-reliance* highly.

NO NEED FOR SECRETS

William Hoyt is a construction worker. When he was in high school, he thought about going to college but the idea didn't appeal to him. "I don't much like school," he told us during his junior and again in his senior year. "You don't learn anything in class that you need on the outside." Most people think of men who become manual laborers as being forced to do so because other options aren't available to them. That wasn't so in Bill's case. He was bright enough to have done well in college and, a few years after graduating from high school, he did attend a community college for a year and a half where he took and easily passed vocational courses. However, Bill's primary interests were manual, not mental. "I like working with my hands," he said at eighteen.

Another common misconception (believed by 73 percent of the white-collar men in our sample) about people who labor physically for a living is that they aren't ambitious. Bill was. It wouldn't have occurred to him to view his job as merely a mindless way to spend his workday, waiting for the evening's fun—allegedly the day's real payoff—to begin. "I want to be the foreman here," he told us a few months after taking his first full-time job. He was a carpenter's apprentice, helping to erect the wood frame-work of two one-family houses being built on adjacent lots. Coming from someone else, the comment might have seemed arrogant, but in this instance it wasn't. It reflected a willingness to wait. "I've got a lot to learn," he said quietly, "but as I do, I want to move up."

The checked flannel shirts and work boots that many men donned on weekends to project a masculine image were Bill's functional uniform at work. At home, in a gray sweatsuit, he looked comfortable glancing through *Electronics*, *Popular Mechanics*, and auto magazines with the genuine interest of a tinkerer. Bill had always known that he would earn his living outdoors. His face usually reflected the summer sun or winter winds. The muscles on his 5-foot-9-inch frame were developed from daily labor, not exercise machines. The broad shoulders, slim hips, and sun-streaked hair were a direct product of Bill's manual line of work and were all the more attractive for their authenticity.

If Bill had a fondness for a particular kind of woman, it wasn't apparent in his early choice of bedmates. Some were tall, others short; a few had good grades, the rest were average; some were virgins, others had "been around," as he described them. There were eleven in all between the summer after his sophomore year and his graduation from high school. His first sexual encounter, when he was sixteen, took place in an upstairs bedroom at a party. Bill was unusual in his circle in not discussing the women with whom he slept. He made plenty of remarks to and about the girls in his classes, and he openly assessed the more attractive ones in terms of the sexual experiences he would have liked with each. "I can just see myself getting into her saddle," he said at seventeen, about a busty woman passerby in her twenties wearing a tight sweater. "I'd like to die there."

Bill's friends shared his attitudes and aped his behavior. Of the five young men in his group, Bill was actually the quietest. The remaining four barely noticed that there were other patrons in a restaurant or other people on the street. The four spoke loudly and uninhibitedly about anything and everything, not caring who heard. For the most part, Bill just relaxed, listened, and laughed in their presence, clearly enjoying their company and nonstop antics.

One noteworthy aspect of the group's behavior was that its members tended to highlight laughingly anything that was wrong with anyone they knew, including one another. They held nothing back. "Hey, Bill," said one of his companions, while they were all having a pizza, "you've got a booger the size of a Buick hanging out of your nose." Reaching for his napkin, Bill replied, "That's nothing. You've got breath so bad it's making my eyes cross." They wanted everything open and aboveboard, not just because of the greater amusement value it had that way, but also because they simply weren't oriented toward hiding anything or keeping secrets. They couldn't see the need and resented having to make the effort, feeling that it prevented life from being truly enjoyable.

"I'M NOT BIG ON SMALL TALK"

When Bill was away from his buddies, he was a different person altogether. Strangers who met him for the first time considered him "remote," "aloof," and "unemotional." Women found him even more so. Those who were trying to bridge the distance to Bill—either to meet him or to get to know him better—found the gap a wide one to cross, while others whom he eventually bedded down with found Bill only slightly more accessible subsequently than he had been initially. Barbara, the first girl he ever made love to, when both were sixteen, had sex with Bill seven more times before high school ended. Although each encounter spawned dozens of pages in her diary, which were filled with detailed descriptions of her feelings and actions ("I put a note in his math book, telling him how much I love him. Will he see it? Will he care? *Does* he care?"), Bill said little to anyone about the encounters, either then or later.

As Bill entered his twenties and his social circle expanded, he started meeting women who apparently appealed to him more. He liked watching baseball and football games, preferring to be in the stands rather than viewing the events on television in his living room. During half-time at a football game, he saw what he considered to be a truly beautiful woman and walked over to her. "I'm not big on small talk," he had told us a number of times, and he clearly meant what he said. He approached the woman, whose name was Lynn, told her he thought she was a "knockout," and asked her to go out with him that Saturday. Instead of being offended, Lynn was pleased. "I liked your directness," she later told him. "It turned me on." She also thought he was handsome and sexy.

What Bill had done was unusual for him. From the time he was fourteen, when we first began interviewing him regularly, until he was twenty-one and approached Lynn, he had never, to our knowledge (or that of his friends), asked a woman out. "They come to *him*," one of his pals commented, in a disbelieving and envious manner. "He doesn't have to say, 'Hey, baby, what are you doing tonight?' All he has to say is, 'I'm ready if you are.' They always are." Yet here, without a moment's hesitation visible, he did what most other men his age have done dozens of times, nervously and awkwardly. Neither of these states was in evidence; "He was as calm as a lake," Lynn later recalled. Nevertheless, we assumed that his new willingness to reach out to a partner in whom he was interested would bring more of his emotions into the open.

It did nothing of the kind. Even while Bill was making an overture, he remained reserved. His attitude, as he expressed it at twenty-two, was that "Every woman loves sex, unless she's a lesbian or a liar." Since the remark sidestepped the question of whether or not she wanted to have sex with *him*, he added, "If I'm not her cup of meat, I'd just as soon find out now rather than later."

This was the base on which his calm rested. Since women were as-sumed to be every bit as interested in him, romantically and sexually, as he was in them, there was no need for him to turn himself inside out attempting to elicit that interest. It was indeed there, as his own erotic experiences during the previous six years had demonstrated to him. Therefore the only issue was whether he and the woman in question were, as he put it, "generating enough electricity" to make it worthwhile for them to go on to the next step. "I don't have to *do* anything," he said at twenty-three. "Either it's there, in the air, or it's not. You can't manufacture it."

This view was applied not only to his initial encounters with a particular woman but also to their subsequent get-togethers. While he definitely became more friendly and affectionate after the two had spent the night, he still maintained an "aloof" quality on which all his partners to whom he spoke commented. "He's a passionate lover," Lynn observed, "but I'm not sure I ever really got to know him before we stopped seeing each other." It took us a while to realize how deliberate a policy this represented on Bill's part.

People who listened to Bill talk candidly about sex assumed that it represented his primary reason for becoming involved with women. It didn't. The words were deceiving. The feelings were there, but in his view it was the woman's job to provide them. At least initially, he would pursue her sexually and she would pursue him romantically; later, both could do both.

Far from wanting to hinder the process, he was trying to aid it by remaining remote. Some women criticized him for seeming so inaccessible, yet he felt that he was actually doing them a favor. There is an important paradox here and it is worth spelling out. Bill was convinced that romantic feelings are fragile, even when two people are right for one another. Since he felt that the feelings were especially important to a woman, and were supposed to be initiated by her anyway, he could help her get them started. How? By remaining a blank slate.

Throughout adolescence he couldn't avoid noticing that the women who lusted after him most eagerly or who loved him most knew him least. After they got to know him better their feelings moderated significantly, an outcome that disappointed them far more than it did him, since he had been a marginal participant from the start. Many complained that they had never gotten to know "the real Bill," but he rightly retorted that he never came to know them either. "They come at me with the top buttons on their blouse open and a head full of preconceived ideas," he said at nineteen, shaking his head from side to side. "You'd think I was a rock star." Small wonder, then, that when the woman doing the projecting was one about whom he truly cared, he considered it valuable, even essential, to let her keep on projecting, even after the two had made love dozens of times. His aloofness was the foundation upon which their prospects for continuing romance stood.

WORDS VERSUS ACTION

Bill's brief replies and penetrating gaze allowed women who became involved with him to see whatever they wanted. It also allowed them to feel that they hadn't yet snared him. Their imaginations *and* the hunger of each for a partner thus remained active, and for some women at least that was an exciting combination.

It would be easy to conclude that Bill had adopted this strategy consciously in order to intensify the emotions of women who were already interested in him. While that was true to some extent, to a much larger extent Bill was making good use of attitudes he had learned in his childhood home. Bill's father, a baker, and his mother, a secretary, weren't used to expressing their feelings around the house. Annoyance was the sole exception. Both experienced a fair amount of frustration on the job and regularly gave vent to it with co-workers. That seemed to them the appropriate audience. Neither rehashed the day's events with his or her spouse during the evening. Bill's father watched television and his mother talked on the phone to relatives or Bill's brothers.

Observers who have had a chance to watch how working-class families behave at home typically state that the main reason the adult members don't air their personal feelings is that these individuals aren't educated and articulate. Since they lack the training and encouragement needed to be able to describe an inner state well, it remains undescribed altogether. They talk about events, not the subtle aspects of their emotional reactions to the events. Intimacy has to be inferred, since it isn't obvious from the words or actions of each spouse.

Raised in this setting (both Bill's parents finished only high school), it is hardly surprising that Bill adopted a similar approach and viewed it as normal. However, he knew that the interpretation given his silence by college-educated observers was wrong. More precisely, it was too negative. In fact, the standard explanation that "the reticence is based on a discomfort with feelings and words" seemed to the many men like Bill that we studied to miss the point totally. (We say "men like Bill" because we never directly discussed this with him.) Instead, what was really at issue here in their minds was "words versus actions." And as they saw it, actions were all that counted. Bill made his views on the matter clear when he was angry, by repeatedly pointing to the behavior of certain others. "There are makers," he said flatly, "and there are takers—people who produce nothing but wind." Words, "fancy terms," were generated by parasites who were using their verbal barrage to mask the fact that they were making little or no contribution to society's welfare. "If they were all dead tomorrow, who would miss them?" he asked rhetorically on a number of occasions. Whereas without people who worked with their hands and with machines, "there would be no places [in which] to live, nothing to drive, and nothing to see when you got there." The people whom Bill considered the most contemptible were those he labeled as being "all talk."

Rather than feeling inadequate and inarticulate, Bill actually felt superior to the millions of white-collar professionals and managers who had gained social ascendancy in the post–World War II era. The greater prestige and income they received bothered him, but not very much. He was better than they, of that he was certain, and it prevented him from walking around in a huff.

With this as his basic view of the world, it would have been difficult and perhaps impossible for Bill to sit around and discuss his personal feelings in depth. That would have made him feel like a fake. Worse still, it would have forced him to think of himself as one of the people he most despised. He did spend hours chatting with his friends, yet it was understood by the entire group that the conversation was supposed to be about events, not people's personalities. Doers could spend hours talking with one another, but only about the actions (or lack of same) of other doers.

When the women he was involved with pressured Bill to "open up," they might as well have been batting their heads against a wall. Had Bill not been raised in a working-class family, he still could have made a compelling case (based on his own teenage experiences) for remaining cool and reserved, much like the characters portrayed on screen by Clint Eastwood. Such behavior inflamed the passions and curiosity of the women who were interested in him, that much he could see with his own eyes. However, since his action orientation made him feel a cut above the millions of what he called "spongers" in society, an attitude he had learned at home, his outlook on the world and on women had an undeniable unity. The central forces in his life—professional, romantic, and recreational—were all pushing him in the same silent but active direction.

Although Bill liked women well enough, he took only the company of men seriously. As he commented at twenty-eight, "You can trust men, but with women—you can never tell what they're going to do." He could truly relax with his buddies, whereas with women he felt it safer to seem one step removed.

He met Nancy Hazelton, the woman who was to become his wife, when she sold him a shirt in a department store. "She didn't come on to me," Bill said later, "and I didn't come on to her." Nevertheless, he noticed her direct, no-nonsense manner and liked it. "She was pleasant, easy to deal with—no 'attitude'—and was trying to do a good job." The two spent nearly an hour going through the various styles and price ranges. By the time they had finished, they had exchanged names and Bill had asked her out. "I was amazed when he did," Nancy later recalled. "I didn't see it coming. He wasn't even looking at me just then. He pointed to a shirt I'd handed him and said, 'How about a different shade of blue and dinner Saturday night?' I told him, 'Both sound good to me.' "

From the time they met until the day they married, fifteen months later, there seems to have been little doubt in the mind of either that this relationship was different. Bill was twenty-seven at their first encounter; Nancy was twenty-six. He had already decided "not to ask a broad out anymore just to get laid. If that's all I want, I've got enough names already." With his friends marrying, one by one, he too decided that it was time to start thinking about settling down. This time around Bill was looking for a more romantic, as well as erotic, relationship and found it with Nancy. "Sex was pretty wild right from day one," she later commented. "We even did it in the back row of a movie theater." However, the two also enjoyed being together without talking. "I want to make him happy," Nancy said, four months before they got married.

A SEARCH FOR ACCEPTANCE

David Hayward is a lawyer. It wasn't something he planned to be. "It just sort of happened," he adds. Nonetheless, it was clear even when he was in high school that there was a variety of fields that David wouldn't enter. For one thing, unlike Bill, he wasn't particularly athletic. He played baseball and volleyball in gym class, and enjoyed them somewhat, but only somewhat. Mainly, he tried to be good at sports because his classmates loudly praised people who were. He never kidded himself, though, and when he dreamed about his glorious future—a normal aspect of adolescence—visions of being a professional athlete (Bill's most frequent dream) were conspicuously absent.

Instead, he usually envisioned himself attracting and keeping the crowd's attention with his oratory. He was addressing a large audience and they were listening intently, and even laughing occasionally. Not too often, of course; he was delivering words of wisdom, not a stand-up comic's routine. "One thing I never wanted to be was the class clown," he told us at seventeen. David was bright, verbal, and at times even a bit theatrical. As he entered his freshman year in college, it seemed fairly certain that he would earn his living with his mind.

Government was the major he chose, and he read political-science texts with the same speed and interest most people read novels. He bought many books on the subject—primarily paperbacks—that hadn't been assigned in class and devoted weekends and summers to losing himself in them. "It's hard to believe the system works at all, with so many competing interests battling it out in Washington," he remarked at twenty, during his junior year. David's intellectual involvement with the topic was not a prelude to a hoped-for career in the political arena. This was a fantasy in the late 1960s of some of his friends that he wasn't sure he shared. "It doesn't grab me at all," he said thoughtfully, "because it's so consuming a career. And rough. Once you're an elected official—and even when you're running for office—it's no holds barred. That would get me down."

Since he didn't intend to go on to graduate school in his field ("I don't want to teach this subject"), and political life seemed unacceptably crass, he made what he described as "the easiest professional decision I'll ever make." He decided to become an attorney. What made the decision easy was that it permitted David to stay in an intellectually demanding field, one that he felt had a connection to his current major, yet also provided opportunities for him to come to terms with the real-world pressures he was experiencing to earn a decent living. "My parents aren't rich, you know. They're paying my tuition—and will do the same for graduate study—but I have to start thinking about supporting myself and a family."

Between the ages of twenty-two and twenty-five, David labored away at law school, keeping up with the material covered in each class rather than just cramming before exams. "I hear some of the students saying, 'This is silly, we aren't going to use most of this stuff once we graduate.' I can't work that way. They're just trying to get by and latch on to a law degree. I think that will hurt them in the long run." David graduated near the top of his class and found a job in the legal department of a fast-growing consumer-goods firm.

Once he'd had the job for a few months, the personal habits that helped define his professional self appeared, and they have been there ever since. To make up for his somewhat shapeless middle, David spent a considerable amount of time and money on clothes. Among what he called his "trade secrets" was the name of his tailor, who knew how to make the most of David's 5 foot 11 inch height and minimize the rounded shoulders he has had since high school. While no dandy, David liked to look his best and wanted to forget about his clothes, once dressed. He had a standing appointment at the barber's every three weeks and wore his brown hair parted and short. The gold-framed glasses he kept in his jacket pocket were used as much for effect as for reading. So was the gold pen he got from his parents for graduation and which he often rolled between his fingers while appearing to consider the problems before him.

David's attitude toward women was the same at twenty-five as it had been at fifteen: anxious, and, at times, fearful. Unlike Bill, who approached women calmly on the assumption that they were at least as interested as he, David wasn't sure what anyone with whom he had contact—male or female—expected of him. Trying to read the signals, paying attention even to minimal cues people might be sending, he attempted to mold himself instantly into the person he thought they wanted him to be.

Meeting someone new was therefore exciting and nerve-racking. He liked the idea of presenting them with his latest self ("I *think* I'm a more substantial human being now than I was a few years ago," he told us at twenty-four), yet he was far from certain that it would be publicly well received. David always accepted the lion's share of the blame when one of his personal encounters didn't go well. In some respects that was a very optimistic way of viewing the world. For it meant that he had the power to correct any interpersonal situation of which he was a part, or have it go the way he wanted it to in the first place.

Since reality didn't always match that expectation, he frequently found himself alternating between anxiety and mild depression. During such moments he would reexamine his own sentences and those of the others who had been present. Somewhere in the interchange lay an error or room for improvement, and he was intent upon finding it. At twenty-seven, visibly uneasy about a conversation he had had with a colleague, David said, "I want to learn from my mistakes," apparently unaware that the intensity of his search might itself be a mistake.

"THERE'S NEVER A DULL MOMENT IN MY LIFE"

Although David did some petting in high school, it wasn't until he was a college sophomore that he had intercourse for the first time. It was with Beverly, one of the switchboard operators on campus. David had gone to the administration building in response to a complaint that he hadn't paid the balance of his tuition (the check had been sent by his father but it had been credited to the wrong student's account). While waiting to speak to the appropriate party, David struck up a conversation with Beverly. She was twenty-nine, recently divorced, and subsequently told him that she had "taken this job until something better comes along—and *anything* would be."

David's personable and chatty manner had made it possible for him to have a number of good friends in high school. The skills he developed there stood him in good stead here, and he found himself exchanging flip remarks with Beverly. During a lull, he noticed that she was eating a jelly doughnut between calls, and asked with a smile, "Stuffing your face for a change?" David explained to us that "since she was thin, I knew she wouldn't be offended." She wasn't, the repartee continued, and a few minutes later he asked her out.

Their first date turned out to be more passion-filled than David had anticipated. "I've never met so wanton a woman," he said a few days later about the evening and night he had spent with Beverly. David had had oral sex a few times with a high-school girlfriend, Marcia, but they had known one another for years, had been going steady for months, and were restrained about it when it finally happened the first time ("Neither of us climaxed"). This was different. "Don't get me wrong," he said, opening his eyes wide. "It was wonderful in a way. It's just that Beverly and I hardly knew each other." The incident wasn't repeated, since she got a job elsewhere soon afterward. He didn't attempt to find out where.

The contrast not only in their premarital sex lives, but also in the emotional tone of David's and Bill's days was striking. David spent a large portion of each day mulling over forthcoming or recent events. The hours he spent dwelling upon his feelings about them occupied much more of his time than did the events themselves. That made his hours on the job and off seem full to the point of overflowing. "There's never a dull moment in *my* life," David said at twenty-two, twenty-six, and twenty-eight. A great deal *was* happening, at least in his teeming brain. Bill, on the other hand, meant it when he frequently said, "Everything is quiet, going along just fine." The comment wasn't to be taken literally, since he liked having a radio playing nearby while he worked. "If I could watch a movie and do my hammering, that would be terrific," he once commented. The visual and aural stimulation that Bill longed for on the job was provided for David internally, in verbal form, by his profession.

It was during dinner at a friend's house that David met Susan Reed, the woman he eventually married. They didn't like one another at first, in large part because they spent so little time together alone. Both were talkative and got lost in what they were saying to the group, each resenting when the other would hold forth. However, when it came time to leave, both were heading in the same direction and agreed to share a cab. It was a cool summer evening and they decided instead to walk together until their paths diverged (they lived three blocks apart).

"The more I talked to her," David told us, a week after his twenty-seventh birthday, "the more I realized how good she was to be with. I liked the others—they're old friends—but when I got home, I recognized that I liked being with her so much more." He called her just as she was walking in the door. Skipping the hello, David began, "As I was saying a moment ago, we should get together soon." They did. Within a few weeks they started being in daily contact, each managing somehow to find an excuse to call the other.

Majoring in fine art at the New England college she attended gave Susan few illusions about her own talent. If anything, it did the reverse. She enjoyed working in various media, but she viewed her own work as "nice, at best, and uninspired, at worst." The next best thing to being an active participant herself was to be around art in galleries, and that was where Susan was working when she and David met. He found her elegant and articulate manner appealing and noticed her long-fingered hands and the gliding walk that kept the upper half of her body almost totally still. While her clothes were simple and muted in color, her eyes lit up when she smiled. Her voice was soft and modulated, well suited to the position she held selling paintings and sculpture to a largely wealthy clientele.

Their first lovemaking session, which took place six weeks after they met, was warm and affectionate. "It was amorous and tender," David later said, and Susan agreed. There were a few physical problems, the most important of which was that David couldn't become completely erect. Rather than reflecting an absence of interest, the condition was the result of there being an excess of it. "I was *too* excited," David told us, a bit chagrined. He was indeed excitable, here as in so many other situations that mattered to him. At such times, he appeared so eager to speak his mind he would voice his words in a long burst, fearful lest he not get them all said before someone else started speaking.

This chronically heightened concern for how the others present might react stood in stark contrast to Bill's approach. Bill said what he had to say, and if the listeners displayed so much as a hint of indifference, he stopped. It bothered him little if at all when his words in a social situation fell on deaf ears or were interrupted in midstream. "He seems happy just to be sitting there taking up space" was how his wife once described it, shrugging her shoulders. Under similar circumstances, David reacted to the disruptions and indifference by becoming increasingly exasperated, eventually displaying his annoyance by using sarcastic or curt comments. He expected to be taken seriously, even during dinners with friends. That left him in a peculiar bind: he wanted to be thought well of by the very people he was most afraid would interrupt him at any moment.

"THE LITTLE GUY ALWAYS GETS SHAFTED"

The basic reason for the striking difference between Bill's relaxed leisure-time style and David's visibly more tense one took a number of years to emerge. Each situation was different, yet the similarities they possessed in tone told the story. For instance, Bill felt no compulsion to start a conversation with a person—stranger or acquantance—sitting next to him, and if one got going anyway, he felt no obligation to continue it. Often he didn't bother to respond when someone, a companion or co-worker, made a remark that could well have called for a comment from him about, say, politics or an event then in the news. The same silence was often there even when questions were asked of him outright. Assembling these and many other incidents allowed us to see that the basic motive for his lack of a reply was Bill's profoundly held belief that "talk is cheap." David's view, on the other hand, was that "talk is contact, and contact is *everything*." Once it was established, he considered it absurd to rupture the emotional connection that he presumed had sprung up as a result of the conversation, no matter how brief.

Since something significant had been created as a result of the verbal interchange, it didn't end merely because the words had. As a result, David frequently agonized more after a conversation than during it because he knew that it might lead to still more conversations—perhaps about him—and this time he'd not be present. "People talk," he said, as the depth of his concern about the subject once again surfaced. The connection in his mind between any specific encounter and his general reputation was much tighter than it ever could have been for Bill.

To Bill, each conversation was "just so much hot air." Therefore, if twenty people talked about him, whether or not he was present, that was "twenty times as much hot air." David, on the other hand, saw people as dominoes. His public standing could be severely compromised by having even one, as he put it, "malicious and gossipy enemy, who might start a chain reaction." That made him continually attempt to placate people of whom he wasn't particularly fond. One of his classmates, who noticed David doing this at seventeen, remarked, "He tries to pacify guys like [the class bully] because he's not a very good fighter. He's afraid he'll get his ribs broken." Perhaps. His desire to avoid fisticuffs and his modest physical strength certainly helped send David down this path. However, as we know from studying boys who were much stronger than he, yet who wound up on the same road, he would in all likelihood have acted this way even if he had been muscular and athletic. His upbringing alone would have made him worry more about his reputation than his ribs. It isn't enough to say that "he wanted to be liked," for that trivializes his whole approach to life.

More to the point, David saw himself as existing in an inherently public network of emotional connections, linked to others even if he had merely exchanged hellos with them once or passed them in a hallway. Even someone who knew only David's name or recognized his face, perhaps from a school or company photo, was included in this extended sense of self. Bill, by contrast, saw his life as being inherently private, and was convinced that nothing of importance sprang up during conversations, especially brief ones, with passersby. The fact that some people he had never talked to knew who he was made him dismiss the bunch as irrelevant. His social sense of self was vastly more constricted, and that prevented him from agonizing—or even thinking about—the opinions of people he barely knew.

Let's step back a bit, to gain a better perspective on these two men. Bill intended to make an impression on the world using his hammer, whereas David intended to make an impact using words. In that sense, David was the more modern of the two. The attitudes that Bill held are valuable in a farming, mining, or manufacturing economy. Muscles and machines are needed to produce goods from lumber, metals, and the earth, and the output of each laborer is readily measured. It is a common and valid observation that the character of a country's citizens and the nature of its economy are linked in many ways, both on and off the job. Bill's personality profile and everyday habits were in harmony with the manual work he did for a living. Given the friends and the wife he chose, a similar harmony was present when work was through.

The same can't be said of David's life, though his approach to people in general, and women in particular, was as much a product of the attitudes he learned in his childhood home as was Bill's. David's father was an insurance broker who owned his own firm ("I represent a range of companies, depending on what people need") and David's mother was a schoolteacher. Both were college graduates. They had encouraged him above all to achieve yet be thoughtful and nice. Bill too was told to be nice but was actually taught to expect the worst. "Someone is constantly out to do you dirt," Bill's father told him repeatedly. "The little guy always gets it in the neck—from big companies, big government—somebody is always giving it to him. You have to watch those bastards every minute. You have to stand your ground."

David had been schooled both at home and in his classes to become associated with, and perhaps an integral part of, the powerful institutions that Bill's father felt needed constant watching. Even when David spoke defiantly about splitting off from the large company at which he was corporate counsel and starting his own law firm, he remained very much a member of the white-collar world he had inhabited since childhood. While the differences between being an employee and being self-employed seemed monumental to David, Bill sensed that the similarities in these two choices for David (whom he did not know) were more important than the differences. "Whatever he went to school to be, he still is," Bill said flatly, after considering the matter for a moment. "And that's all that counts. The rest is just decoration—titles on the door, and that kind of thing."

People with only minimal knowledge of an area may dismiss features that are of real importance to the area's inhabitants, yet the distant view may provide insights of its own. Whether David was working for a large corporation or himself was irrelevant to Bill since David would still have the same profession—that of a practicing attorney—in both settings. However, there is another key respect in which these two contexts for David's business life were the same. In both he would be providing services, not manufacturing goods. The distinction seemed crucial to Bill. "The only thing lawyers manufacture is trouble," he said at twenty-seven.

While Bill may have been talking about legal services, he was estranged from other kinds as well, in what was increasingly a service society. Goods production involved a steadily decreasing proportion of the United States labor force from the 1940s through the 1980s, falling to less than 20 percent by the mid-1980s. It was in this sense that Bill represented the old order and David the new. Not only was the shift from manufacturing to services affecting the lives of both blue- and white-collar workers in our study, but their personal lives were never the same again, either.

A MAN OF SUBSTANCE

One clear sign of trouble in David's case was that he found it difficult to brush people off, something Bill did with ease. If David was in the midst of a conversation with someone he liked, he found it no easy chore to say goodbye and leave. "My feet might as well be stuck in taffy just then," he said, trying to justify why he claimed to be fond of punctuality yet was frequently late. "The conversation usually runs longer than I thought it would." The reason for this, of course, was that David let people go on and on, unable to bring himself to tell them to stop. His wife, Susan, offered the explanation that he did this because "David is very generous of his time with his friends." A disgruntled client of David's told him,

"You're only doing this to let the bill mount up, since the meter is running all the while I'm yakking." The proof that neither of these explanations went to the heart of the matter was that David let people he didn't like who weren't even clients do the same.

A number of pop-psychology authors have written in recent years about how hard it is for some people to say no. What these glib analyses ignore is the tremendous pressure exerted on both budding and mature white-collar professionals in a service-oriented economy to be *responsive* to the needs of others. The whole idea of a "no" misses the point, since it is quite often necessary for such a professional to unearth the "need" in the first place. (Obviously, there is room for error and even fraud here.) This unearthing process is what the professional's training and experience presumably allows him or her to do expertly—far better than the client, who may not realize that the tax, medical, psychological, or legal need exists at all. Once the professional has discovered the need, it would be absurd for him to then refuse to help fulfill it. The client might never find out about the deliberate neglect, but it would undoubtedly bother any dedicated professional.

The difficulty David had in saying no, and letting people he didn't like use up much of his time, was actually a consequence of his highly professionalized approach to life. This was a competent and intelligent man who, from childhood on, had been led to believe that he would be a great benefit to society. "By helping others," his mother told him repeatedly, "you'll be helping yourself." Both of his parents emphasized that he possessed the abilities required to do this with distinction. The implication was that he was sufficiently gifted so that, whatever field he ultimately chose, he would become widely recognized within it.

For David abruptly to turn a deaf ear to the complaints of others merely because his workday was allegedly done would have struck him as coldblooded. Like many other white-collar professionals, his working hours therefore expanded and at times consumed a sizable portion of his evenings and weekends. It happened quietly and wasn't strictly business, inasmuch as these weren't always "billable hours," as his profession labels time spent on legal matters on behalf of a specific individual or corporate client. Instead, this was simply spill-over, a result of his inability to keep a helpful stance—his service-oriented approach—confined to the office.

Bill had no such trouble. He saw lives such as David's as involving only symbols, whereas his own involved substance. Moreover, since his work utilized physical rather than intellectual tools, he could separate himself from his day's labors merely by putting down his hammer and saw. David could rightly retort, "I carry my mind with me when I leave the office and can't shut it off." He and other well-intentioned professionals who have found themselves unhappy at home consider this a reasonable—even scientifically valid—explanation for their marital woes. It isn't. David could have been twice as caught up in his profession and remained happily married, as we'll soon see. His work wasn't the problem so much as his attitude toward expertise.

ANTICIPATING THE WORST

When Bill was polishing his station wagon one Sunday afternoon, a friend came by to pick up some tools that were in the back of it. Finding the rear gate of the wagon locked, he asked Bill for the keys. Bill, who was polishing the hood at the time, simply reached into his side pocket and threw them in the right direction. "Comin' at you," he said without glancing up. The friend wasn't even looking in Bill's direction as the keys sailed toward him. Upon hearing "Comin' at you," he turned around and stuck out his hands just in time for the keys to land in them.

A few weeks later Bill was visiting a friend of his named Ken, who asked Bill, "Do you want a beer?" Bill replied, "Sure." Ken said, "Help yourself, there are some in the fridge." Bill got one and, with his head still in the icebox, shouted, "You want one, too?" Ken replied, "Yep." Bill walked into the living room, taking a swig of his, and gave the other an underhand toss twenty feet across the room. "On its way," he said, as it headed toward Ken, who caught the can with both hands.

It would never have occurred to David to do such a thing. If a friend wanted something, he was likely to walk over to the person, carrying the object himself. Even when he was transferring it, he seemed uneasy about whether the recipient was holding it firmly. "Do you have it?" he would ask about, say, the drink. "You sure you've got it?" Only then would he let go.

Bill wasn't part of the service economy and didn't want to be. The ethic among his pals had long been, "You have to look out for yourself, because no one else will if you don't—they're too busy looking out for themselves." In his view, far from being insulting in throwing them a can full of beer, Bill was actually doing his friends a favor. For he was helping them to stay alert. He was also giving them a chance to practice their hand-eye coordination, and, finally, he was giving them the drink for which they had asked. This combination of actions signaled that he was a member in good standing of his group.

When David handed someone a drink, he surrounded the act with emotional significance. Rather than being a merely mechanical transfer, it was yet another opportunity for him to be of assistance to others. He was used to being concerned about their welfare, and as he was fond of saying, "sometimes little gestures mean as much [to people] as grand ones." To some of David's colleagues he seemed to lack perspective, for he often fretted as much about trivial interchanges as major ones. However, as his comment indicates, there was an underlying logic to his behavior. Whether the item or sum of money was large or small, it gave him a chance to let the recipient *see* that he cared. And that, every bit as much as the usefulness of the physical object changing hands, was the real issue in his mind.

Throughout the 1970s and especially 1980s, as physicians in the United States lost their bedside manner, it sometimes seemed as if every other white-collar professional adopted one. Lawyers, in particular, made good use of the apparent shift. Delivering the hand-holding services previously provided by doctors, they were able more convincingly to portray themselves as protectors of patients' rights against what David labeled as "mercenary and bungling quacks."

Gently handing someone keys or a can also gave David a chance to let the person change his or her mind. That would have seemed ridiculous to Bill, whose attitude typically was, "Look, either you want it or you don't." This seemingly arbitrary and authoritarian stance had its roots in Bill's action orientation. Clear-cut decisions were needed for an act to take place successfully. David's world, on the other hand, was one of thought more than action. It was perfectly reasonable to him that people might first decide upon one thing and, before putting the decision into effect, decide on another. The phrase "before putting the decision into effect" is necessary, because, like Bill, David expected people who made up their minds to do something to actually go ahead and do it. However, he permitted them—and himself—much more leeway prior to arriving at the final decision. That seemed to him not only more intelligent, but also more human.

Be that as it may, this attitude created a great deal more anxiety in David than would otherwise have been present. With so much room deliberately being left for uncertainty, the air was generally filled with tension. Individual choice was being given the maximum possible latitude, and that took its toll on David's nerves. Bill, by contrast, prided himself on his inflexibility. He was ever mindful of his father's insistence that "the little guy must stand his ground." Bill did so calmly and comfortably, and felt he had compromised himself, his family, and his friends when he publicly did an about-face. He didn't do so often.

David's uneasiness when handing someone keys or a can extended to intangibles, such as messages. If he called someone who was out and left word for the person, he was usually unsure about whether the message was received, and if so, how the person reacted to it. Since he hadn't personally been in touch, his continuing anxieties about contact maintenance moved to the fore. The opposite of Bill in this respect, David prided himself on his flexibility and was certain he could win the person over, but only if the two were in direct contact.

Even before he became an attorney, David continually tried to anticipate problems before they arose and typically made himself quite tense in the process. Bill considered this largely a waste of time and emotion. "If I do my job right, everything will work out," he said more than once. "And if it doesn't?" we asked him. His reply was, "If there's trouble, I'll handle it when it hits." The difference in the degree of anxiety generated by the two approaches was striking. Bill was intolerant of ambiguity; David had made it his profession.

HANDLING OTHER PEOPLE'S WEAK POINTS

Their respective approaches to two topics—secrets and insults—said as much about them as anything could. As we mentioned earlier, because Bill rarely saw the need for secrets in the first place, he respected few that he heard. Things he'd been told in confidence he repeated with an innocence that was genuine. So when someone chastised him for violating a trust, he would reply calmly, "I forgot." Rather than seeing himself as callous, he was firmly convinced that the other person was being too sensitive.

David, on the other hand, would have been appalled at the mere suggestion that he had done such a thing. If the feelings of others were involved, he knew that he must walk on eggs, if necessary, to avoid damaging them. That this guideline was one of his most central can be seen in the fact that, while Bill was often impolite to people he knew well, David was usually courteous to people he truly disliked. We have already commented on the amount of time he let them consume, but it went far beyond hours and minutes and instead could be measured in emotional exertion.

Bill made people come to him. He would sit back impassively and ask them, "What can I do for you?" When David asked the same question, it contained an unmistakable warmth. He always met people more than halfway, extending himself—even when it wasn't necessary—to make empathetic contact with others. Bill's attitude was, "I don't have to please you, you have to please me," while David's was a soft and sincere "How can I help?"

Where insults are concerned, Bill and David couldn't have been more opposite if they had tried. Ever since his teen years, Bill had inhabited a world in which one's flaws were held up to public ridicule by one's peer group. The children of both white- and blue-collar families do this at certain stages. The youngsters are indeed cruel at times, making fun mercilessly of their enemies and their friends. In Bill's case, the practice continued unabated right into his adult years.

For example, Rick, one of the members of Bill's circle of friends from the time both entered junior high school, was hit by a car at the age of sixteen when they were playing ball after school. Someone threw him a pass with a football. He chased it into the path of an oncoming car whose driver didn't see him until he bolted from between two parked cars to catch the ball on the fly. His right leg was operated on shortly after the accident and again a year later, but the knee was never the same. It bent only with difficulty and at times with pain, though it did bend. That caused Rick to favor his other leg, giving his walk a slight wobble. How did Bill and Rick's other close friends treat this injury? From the time Rick was back on his feet until the present, they have regularly referred to him as "the gimp." Phrases such as, "Hey, Gimp, get me a pack of butts, will ya?" were heard recently when the group went bowling and Rick was passing the cigarette machine on the way to the men's room. Similarly, another member of the group, who weighs 240 pounds and is only 5 foot 10 inches, is called "Slim" by the others, or "Tiny." The extra seventy or eighty pounds of fat he carries is overlooked by none.

David was extremely likely to ignore rather than publicly point to such infirmities and flaws. In fact, by the time he was in his twenties, he was used to doing this automatically. He would simply pretend that someone who was handicapped was actually intact completely. That may have been the polite thing to do, but Bill was undoubtedly right to insist that such "pretense is a real strain." On many an occasion the strain on David showed. For where another person's weak points were concerned, he told us repeatedly that he had to keep reminding himself to forget them: "It would be *rude* to do otherwise."

The self-imposed code of "remembering to forget" was applied by David both on the job and off. Not surprisingly, it was coupled with an attitude that called for him to find the bright side of any situation, no matter how bleak. Instead of tearing people down for the entertainment of others, he actively looked for something nice to say about each. In some cases that proved impossible, but even then he tried. Although David wasn't especially fond of his immediate superior, he had an upbeat reply ready when an attorney at another firm said to him, "Your boss seems very sharp. You can really learn a thing or two from him, can't you?" David's immediate response was, "Every day."

A fellow carpenter who had recently joined the crew made a similar remark to Bill about their boss's being very sharp. Bill's equally immediate reply was, "Boy, he really has you buffaloed, doesn't he? That jackass doesn't know whether to put his socks on first in the morning or his shoes." This was said behind the boss's back, but the point is that Bill would gladly have voiced the same words with the boss present. And on a subsequent occasion, he did exactly that.

While it would have struck David as bizarre, Bill was doing this precisely because he liked his boss—in fact liked him more than David liked his. That allowed Bill to openly poke fun at his superior, with a wink always hidden in the picture. That the words were said in jest was silently acknowledged by both. The harsh treatment each at times dished out to the other masked the affection and admiration they had for one another. As Bill put it once, and only once, "If I didn't think he was tops at what he does, I wouldn't be working for him. There are plenty of other jobs out there for me." However, that didn't stop him from thumbing his nose regularly at the boss, since this was one more way for Bill to publicly display his own independence.

It is essential to recognize that Bill and David are more than just people, they are polarities. Opposites in a variety of important respects, their attitudes toward friends and professions only begin to characterize their many differences. The key questions that need to be asked at this point are: Is it possible that the very approach that got each as far as he had gone professionally was also messing up his personal life in the process? And if so, how?

A closer look at their marital lives will enable us to see why millions of ambitious men have trouble keeping their quest for success on track.

·2·

IN-HOUSE EXPERT

The attitudes and habits David used daily to handle the world shaped his behavior with Susan. Not only did they become an integral part of his life long before she did, he thought of them as particularly appropriate in his relations with her. "She is a frail and beautiful flower," he said quietly, five months after they had gotten married. That she also could be hard as nails he well knew, having watched her negotiate a $14,000 sale of three pictures at the gallery. (She didn't know David was listening; he had come to pick her up at day's end, on the way to dinner with friends.) "The customer was shrewd," David recalled proudly, "but so was Susan."

David recognized during the early months of their marriage that Susan had little trouble disagreeing with him. "We like many of the same things," he said, after they had been married almost a year. "Of course, there are plenty of times when we *don't* see eye to eye." On most such occasions, David happily gave ground. He was used to doing this anyway, previously with friends and classmates, and he acted the same way with his wife, giving the matter little thought. "I love her," he said, "and I'm happy when she's happy." The honeymoon aura that surrounded the pair made David feel that if he was making too many concessions, it was only temporarily. Even if this became their permanent pattern, he was prepared to accept it since it brought them peace at what he felt was a small price.

David's day in the office gave him the measure of balance he needed to see himself as not always giving in. "Once he makes up his mind, he can be quite the mule," is how one of David's colleagues described him. Said another, "He doesn't shoot from the hip. He thinks about what the correct course of action is, and then he won't give an inch unless he hears a very good reason to." As the years went by, and similar assessments were voiced by a number of people who had been involved with him professionally, it became apparent that however flexible David was at home, he was usually the reverse at work.

"Sometimes I think of myself more as a judge than as a practicing lawyer," David stated carefully, in his third year with the firm. "I want whatever I do to withstand scrutiny in court." Some of his co-workers were convinced that he carried the process too far. "He's a stickler for detail," one of the marketing VPs said, "always dotting every *i* and crossing every *t*." Without any prodding from us, he then commented, "But I guess that's the nature of the job."

"And its holder," he might as well have added, for it came to characterize David more each year. As his experience grew, so did his confidence. If he annoyed his colleagues before by insisting that they follow his suggestions, he did so with greater frequency as he became more demanding on this score. "Lawyers kill deals, not help close them," one of the regional sales managers told us angrily, after a tentative agreement he had reached for a bulk sale was vetoed by David and another in-house attorney.

None of these comments should be taken to mean that David's co-workers didn't still recognize how responsive he was to their needs. The sales manager quoted above perhaps put it best when he said, during a subsequent interview, "David really does want to help. It's just that he wants to help you *his* way." In Bill's social circle it was quite common for members goodnaturedly to rib one another, saying things that outsiders would have considered offensive. Far less of this was done in David's circle, but when it did occur, it was even more revealing. One friend chided David gently for being too fussy. "You're so finicky," he said to David with a smile, "you remind me of Morris the Cat." (This was a humorous reference to a popular TV commercial in which a cat would eat only the sponsor's brand, naturally.)

David *was* fussy about food, and he was even more so about his clothes. He wanted the things he wore to look, as he put it, "just so." Making the right impression was very important to him. However, underlying each of these areas of finicky behavior was one central factor. David was flexible in so many ways that when he finally decided *not* to be, he could almost be counted upon to overdo it. Bill was the one who spoke often about how essential it was to "stand your ground," yet it was David who did this in a sufficiently conspicuous manner to cause many people to view it as his most noteworthy characteristic.

The point is that David usually did this in an area connected with his profession. Unlike Bill, who felt that standing one's ground was justified solely "on principle," David needed additional justification to do so. Work provided it. "Legal principles" were the authority which, he claimed, gave him the right to be uncompromising. Actually, it was something a bit more theatrical: a self-conscious picture of himself as a virtuous attorney.

Every profession has standards (that, in part, is what makes the field a respected profession), and they can be used publicly by members who need to shore up their determination not to budge. At times, that provides people with a gentle and impersonal way to say, "I can't do it." Meaning: "I've got nothing against *you*. It's just that it would be unethical for me to do what you're asking, so I won't." However, used in other situations— often subconsciously—the same stance allows members of the profession to be unyielding yet feel righteous rather than rigid. That isn't an easy combination to find, and it is hardly surprising that many who latch on to it never let go. Now, when anyone calls them brittle, they can say to themselves, "No, I'm ethical." And when they hear themselves labeled an egomaniac, they can say, "I am merely upholding my (field's) standards." Instead of feeling priggish, which is how others view them, they see themselves as being right and obviously above reproach.

There is an apparent contradiction here: unbending behavior in a man who generally tries so hard to please that he is willing to assume almost any shape in order to do so. However, there are limits to anyone's plasticity, even if they think of themselves as endlessly malleable. After they have compromised and subordinated their own ways and wishes to someone else's long enough, something in them balks. It isn't conscious, and it may even go unnoticed by the people doing it, but it causes them suddenly to take a surprisingly firm stand about what may be a trivial matter. Nevertheless, they feel the need to resist—something primitive and self-protective makes them marshal their strength and refuse, this time, to go along. We found that anger makes people feel stronger, so when they must resist (particularly if they aren't used to doing so), they may become angry in spite of themselves. The contrast with their ordinary, everyday style—and it strikes many as a contradiction—is glaringly apparent. Yet it provides a needed moment of balance, without which their personalities might well be overrun by that of others and collapse.

There are two crucial reasons for us to examine when and why people do this: first, it causes substantial harm to their personal relationships; second, it eventually limits their professional effectiveness.

OVERDOING THE ROLE OF EXPERT

That is a heavy price to pay for wanting to be more forceful and seizing upon the wrong device for being so. Nevertheless, millions of men besides David have fallen into this trap.

It happens slowly, and without their realizing it. The process begins with the satisfaction they find in being a force at the office. Instead of being based on personal strength—the power of their personalities—it is based on a knowledge of their field. That isn't a distinction they notice, much less care about. They want to be taken seriously; *how* that happens is a secondary matter to them. By presenting themselves as experts, they hope to gain the attention and respect of their listeners.

So they stop being "just like everybody else" and begin to elevate themselves, at least in their own minds. "I am much more knowledgeable about legal matters than the others here," David said cheerfully. "The salespeople in particular like to play amateur attorney, fielding customer questions about contracts and potential product-liability lawsuits, but they don't really have the answers." David did, and it made him feel special. That is par for the course for budding professionals in any field. The reason it proved so dangerous to David and the many others like him was that now, *whenever he wanted to be viewed as a man of substance, he would slip into the role of expert.*

Since law enters almost every dimension of life, directly or indirectly, David could don this cloak no matter where he was. At dinner with friends he objected strenuously when the wife of an old classmate said, "I bought a watch that was defective and they won't take it back or fix it. They just show me a sign on the wall—one that I didn't see when I bought the watch—that says NO REFUNDS, NO EXCHANGES, ALL SALES FINAL." David's sense of self soared. He knew that under the prevailing city ordinances the sign could not be valid. "They can't do that," he told her repeatedly. Long after she had gotten the message, David gleefully continued to lecture her about her legal rights in this matter.

Although there were many areas of law that David knew little about— for example, securities and matrimonial law—his growing fondness for the position of expert made him present himself (at least to lay people) as experienced in these areas too. The psychosocial benefits he derived were so great, he gladly offered rambling opinions that, once again, he was certain "would stand up in court." During lunch with a co-worker named Alan who had lost a stock certificate, David said, "There isn't a moment to lose. You have to send a certified—no, registered—letter to your stockbroker telling him what happened." David reacted so quickly to the story, Alan never got a chance to tell him that he had already called his broker and given him the number of the missing certificate. The broker was sending him a form to sign, to cancel the old certificate and obtain a new one. As Alan later put it, "Boy, David sure is eager to give people advice."

Finally, David started doing the same thing with Susan. During the first few years of their marriage, David would come home and listen more than he spoke. This was the "honeymoon phase" of their marriage. He found his own work satisfying yet somewhat routine and was thrilled to hear tales of what had gone on that day at the gallery. "It's so different there," he told us, almost as if describing a dream he had had. "You're dealing with the public, and that makes a big difference. I spend my day talking pretty much to professionals in my field. They pull tricks on you too, but the public contains many more real wackos." In a subsequent interview he stated openly what had been apparent all along: "I'm interested in what happens in galleries, but what really makes it interesting is that it is happening to Susan. If she were working—I don't know—at a bank, I guess I'd want to hear all about that too." By the second year of their marriage, and even more so by the third, the balance had begun to shift. Now David did more of the talking and was aware that he was doing so. When Susan would ask him a question, instead of answering it briefly and encouraging her to continue her tale, he would provide a more detailed reply. In fact, he no longer needed to have a query come his way for him to take the floor and hold it. Anything Susan said became sufficient cause for a lengthy comment from him.

The key point is that his remarks were rarely offered as mere opinion. Instead, they were *expert* opinion. That was how they were voiced and that, he hoped, was how they would be received. If the words themselves left any doubt as to his intentions, David's manner and tone made the ultimate goal obvious. Anyone who had watched him hold forth at work on a subject that was part of his profession would immediately have been aware that David was now doing the same at home, this time about subjects not connected with his profession but being made to appear an integral part of it.

In the beginning, at least, it succeeded. David had long been concerned about making a good impression, and there wasn't anyone he wanted to impress more during these years than Susan. It pleased him when his colleagues praised him, but, as he put it, "it really delights me when Susan thinks I've done something wonderful." He felt increasingly compelled to find ways to gain her admiration. Without realizing it, he took home the device for eliciting respect that he had perfected in the office: both on and off the job, David became an expert.

About everything. While he started giving lectures on legal matters to his friends and wife, he soon moved on to other topics that had nothing to do with law. He enjoyed the role of expert so much—both in the office and at home—that any script that allowed him to keep the role was seized upon. Fortunately, David knew enough about at least a few other subjects to use them for the purpose. For one thing, if there had been a classical music version of *Name That Tune*, David would have made a good contestant. After hearing only a few bars of a sonata, opera, or symphony, he was normally able to identify the piece. He hastily displayed this ability for anyone who happened to be around, and could usually find a pretext for doing so. Similarly, since he (and later he and Susan) often ate out, both for business lunches and leisure dinners, he had become familiar with quite a number of good places and, as he was quick to add, "real dives and overrated bistros." Supplementing his personal experiences with restaurant reviews in local newspapers and magazines made it possible for him to keep an updated mental file of suggestions for others, which he hastened to offer. Some of David and Susan's friends even referred to him as a connoisseur. Since that seemed an obvious synonym for "expert," he was elated.

THE QUARRELS OF TWO-CAREER COUPLES

Soon after the beginning of the fifth year of their marriage, David and Susan were sitting in the living room one weekday evening, talking. The telephone began to ring. Susan said, "I'll get it," and while she walked to the nearest phone, which was in the kitchen, David opened a magazine that was sitting on the coffee table. As he started thumbing through the pages, he heard Susan saying to a friend, "What are we doing? Nothing. David is pontificating again."

The words stunned him. In Bill's social circle such a comment would have been just another wisecrack, voiced in jest, but to David they were fighting words. "There was nothing at all amusing about the remark," he later said, visibly annoyed. It bothered David immensely to realize that the whole approach he had been using to elicit admiration from Susan wasn't producing anything of the kind. In fact, it chagrined and angered him to recognize that it was bringing him only ridicule. Not that he said anything to her. As he put it, "That would have been like begging her to respect me, when it was pretty obvious that she didn't." The event is worth exploring further since it represented a turning point in their marriage.

David was not a show-off. The pile of information he possessed was to be used to impress specific people, not just anyone. He was attuned to the audience's response and gave thoughtful answers to the questions people put to him.

Pontificating requires an insensitivity that made David unlikely to deserve the label. As opposed to some of the men he knew in college, who gathered a smattering of material—facts instead of wisdom—and repeated it tensely at their unwilling audience, David was not a "blowhard," or a "humorless nerd," titles that he pinned on such men. It was only his wife who used "pontificating" to describe his eagerness to impress. If it had been valid, others too would have used similar labels. As we've mentioned, David had been called fussy and even petty by people with whom he worked, but that was another matter, having more to do with the meticulous manner in which he handled important tasks. More to the point, during the third year of their marriage, and even more so during the fourth year, David and his wife began having a nearly nonstop tug-of-war about who deserved the floor. Interestingly, the same undercurrent of competition had been there the night they first met.

In an age of specialists, quarrels among experts are common. These fights attain particular ferocity when the parties involved either feel that their reputations are on the line, and may be tarnished if they lose the argument, or when they are trying to call attention to themselves in the first place. In that case they secretly welcome a public dispute, since it gives them one more arena in which to prove themselves.

What is so terrible about the logic of this situation is that the majority of white-collar professional couples we studied also used it at home and with their friends. It became the basis for the battles they had when the couple was alone and when company was present. Susan's attempts to shut David up by accusing him of "pontificating again" forced him to defend himself by pointing to her tendency to do the same. We found this to be a common quarrel among two-career couples; it is an even more fruitless fight than it first appears.

Friends really don't care whether husband or wife won the last tug-of-war. For they are well aware, even if the brawling couple isn't, that there are more battles yet to come. Nor is it particularly good entertainment when people find themselves caught in the role of spectator. The comment we heard most frequently from the members of David and Susan's social circle was, "When work is through, we want to relax, and watching those two bicker isn't very relaxing." To repeat: what David and Susan were fighting quietly about the night they first met, and much more loudly after they'd been married a few years, was a chance to demonstrate their own newly acquired professional expertise—to an audience that basically didn't care.

The emergence of a chronic tug-of-war between David and Susan would have been less lethal to the relationship had outsiders not been given a chance to witness it. "Some people like washing their dirty linen in public," David said, a few weeks after overhearing Susan's derogatory remark on the phone. "I don't."

While still living at home, David was repulsed when he watched his parents have a fight and then heard his mother giving her sister, his aunt Doris, a blow-by-blow account of the feud. "Why does Doris have to know so much about what goes on in this house?" he asked us rhetorically at the age of seventeen, his resentment visible. When we reminded him that he knew about the fights Doris was having with *her* husband, his immediate reply was, "Who wants to? That's not any of our business." David didn't have to swear to himself not to act the same way once he was married. His reactions over the years to this kind of behavior from his parents or couples his own age made his feelings about the matter quite apparent.

When Susan made her derogatory remark on the phone to a friend, something in David snapped. They continued to live together and do things as a couple; they even had sex that night before going to sleep. However, the relationship took a critical turn for the worse that evening. Less than a year later, they agreed to get a divorce.

It took us a number of years and the analysis of more than 270 similar cases to realize that David's reaction to Susan's comment was a common, not quirky, one based not only on unpleasant childhood memories. His peers were acting the same way. Like David, they usually didn't know they were, and if they did, they didn't know why. When a reaction is this widespread, especially among people whose formative experiences display major differences, it is always interesting to seek a common denominator, if one exists. In this cases, it certainly does.

PRIVACY IN MARRIAGE

The men in our sample typically had fewer siblings than either of their parents had had. We frequently heard them report that "My mother had three brothers and two sisters, and my father had two brothers and three sisters. I have only one [or none] of each." The family became less important from one generation to the next because there was simply less of it. Outsiders inevitably filled the gap. Sometimes the outsiders were friends, but—particularly when trouble developed—they were even more likely to be professional counselors.

Ironically, even though David was one of the professionals to whom people turned during trying times, he was resentful of anything that violated the privacy of his own personal relationships. For years, a large number of TV sitcoms and soap operas have been based on couples making their domestic quarrels public—everything from *I Love Lucy* in the 1950s to *Dallas* in the 1980s. However entertaining these programs may be when other people's troubles are at issue, white-collar professionals do not want a similar situation for themselves. Morever, we found this attitude increasing with every year during the decades under discussion. In that sense, afternoon soaps and prime-time TV series have often helped undermine marriages, since people mimic what they see. The shows not only do a poor job of reflecting the views of the most rapidly expanding and influential group in the United States—white-collar managers and professionals—they subtly encourage its members to act in quite a destructive manner.

To them, privacy isn't an optional part of their marriages, something they can take or leave. It is a large part of what they feel, subconsciously, makes themselves and their partners a pair. Once that privacy is shattered, in a substantial number of cases the marriage becomes much less likely to survive.

While David's reaction may seem excessive, it is shared by so many educated and upper-income men, we should look a bit more closely at it. When all is said and done, this hypersensitivity springs from the values they learn in—or which emanate from—large cities. To David, having other people aware of his marital ups and downs was a revolting reversion to small-town life. The picture he and his peers had of busybodies snooping endlessly in one another's affairs is indeed accurate, as our own studies confirm. Urban residents, on the other hand, are content not to know even their next-door neighbors in the apartment houses in which they live. David at times lamented the "coldness" and "self-centeredness" of the people he saw daily in the city. Yet their indifference was precisely what allowed him to feel free and independent enough to live as he pleased. Anonymity, the social essence of the city, formed the basis for the privacy he valued much more than he realized. When it was ruptured—even though his own wife was the one helping this to happen—the marriage was over.

DO FIGHTS CLEAR THE AIR?

Everyday events in Bill's life were paraded before friends and relatives with a nearly total indifference. The forthcoming chapters will make clear how central the subject of privacy is to the divorces *and* professional setbacks of white-collar men, yet it couldn't have played much of a role in the lives of couples such as Bill and Nancy. Everything about them already seemed to be "hanging out," spilling into public view for one and all to see. Needless to say, a great deal about each couple remained hidden, especially as their relationship began to deteriorate. The key point is that no single event—such as an abrupt puncturing of their marital privacy—took place that quietly marked the beginning of the end.

Changes in Bill's attitude toward Nancy were easy to see, but only over time. The comments they made to one another and the things they did together from one day to the next became similar. "I guess you could say that we have our own little routine now," Nancy remarked, fifteen months after they had gotten married. She was happy about it. It made her feel that her life had a sense of order and stability, even maturity. Nancy's parents, like Bill's, had fought a lot, and that made her determined to have a happier home of her own. "They would badger each other all the time," she said reflectively, nearly two years after her wedding. "About nothing."

The early years of Bill and Nancy's marriage were full of fun. They made love more often than David and Susan—every night instead of three times a week—and often frolicked like a pair of puppies. They also went out or had people over to the house more frequently than the other couple did. The two men had long been a study in contrasts, and their marriages became even more so. David and Susan married and, as a pair, went private. Each was involved primarily with his or her own career, and they spent most of their leisure time together. On the other hand, soon after Bill and Nancy got married, they seemed to throw open the front door and invite the whole world in. Neither had been particularly private before, but now that they had found what both called "my other half," they were rarely alone. No friend of David or Susan would have dared drop in without calling first, whereas at Bill and Nancy's, the event was commonplace. On many an occasion the unannounced visitors were even invited to stay for dinner, and did.

The good times waned as the routine set in. "Bill isn't as hungry [for me] as he used to be," Nancy told a friend during the third year of her marriage. "I can remember when he just couldn't get enough." Bill had his own version of what was happening. "She almost always has her mind on other things," he said, with a dismissive sweep of his hand. He wanted them to be important to one another, even vital. Yet in spite of the active approach he took in so many other areas of his life, where feelings were concerned, he was basically a fatalist. "Whatever will be, will be," he said more than once.

While the attitude seemed odd to us at first, it turned out to be one of the most widely shared characteristics of blue-collar men, particularly once they had been married a while. Tinkerers for the most part, adept at fixing light switches, small appliances and making household repairs, these men were strikingly reluctant to touch on the subject of feelings. Since they weren't willing to look dispassionately at the emotions that previously had brought them peace and happiness but now were increasingly causing trouble, they certainly weren't willing to take the next step and seek to modify those emotions. "What I feel is what I feel," Bill said with an air of finality a number of times during that third, eventful year.

Nancy wasn't willing to accept the situation, at least until she had done something to try to improve it. "I don't give up easily," she later told us, when discussing the distance she saw emerging. Their lovemaking had fallen to a frequency of twice a week, and that bothered her. She waited for, and found, the right moment in which to make her move. When Bill leaned over to give her a good-night peck on the cheek, intending to go to sleep that night again without the two having made love, she asked him for "a big kiss." As always, he responded to her evident interest (not her request) and was surprised to see how much of it there was. Once his lips were against hers, she reached up suddenly and held his head with her hands. They stayed that way for what seemed to him "an awfully long time," then he rolled over and simply said, "Sleep well."

He knew that Nancy was drowning but, in this area anyway, wasn't prepared to save her. The next night Bill would feel passionate enough to ask her to get to bed early, so the two could spend more time than usual making love. But, after saying, "Sleep well," to her that evening, he said to himself, "Not tonight, dear." The incident was repeated with increasing frequency in the next few years.

Bill's deeply held (but rarely expressed) attitude of "there are some things that you don't tamper with," may at first glance seem self-serving.

He often used it to get his way—or, more accurately, not give in to his wife's way. However, that is the smallest part of the story and clearly not the most crucial part. For his reaction wasn't in his control. To begin with, it is worth noting that feelings are internal and largely invisible, whereas Bill was wholly oriented toward dealing with externals or things (such as parts) that could be made visible by prying something open. By this measure alone, emotions were a topic from which he felt alienated.

What made matters worse was that since feelings weren't as tangible as bricks and boards, discussing them meant first converting them into— ugh—words. If they started out appearing troublesome to him before, now, in verbal form, they were downright repulsive. This was one quag- mire that Bill was dedicated to avoiding. His reaction was the reverse of David's and Susan's. David, in particular, was thrilled at any opportunity which allowed him to discuss his feelings in depth. Like so many edu- cated men and women, he viewed this as one of his strongest and most appealing suits. David had, as he put it, "a problem-solving approach" to emotional difficulties and frequently stated that "airing your feelings in a confidential setting can—indeed, *has to*—help."

Whether a hurdle he and Susan encountered together was sexual, romantic, social, or professional, the two were likely to produce many hours of conversation about it. (Only once did we hear David ask, half in jest, "I wonder what couples who have no problems find to talk about?") Verbalizing everything seemed to both him and his wife the intelligent and appropriate thing to do. Nevertheless, it is fair to say that, like most of their peers, they often overdid it and wound up talking the problem right into the ground. While Bill surrounded emotional conflicts with silence, David and Susan unwittingly made them vanish by converting them into a seemingly endless stream of sentences.

The verbal version of their differences that David and Susan were accidentally shaping while they talked had the added advantage of being ready for friends, should one of them ask for it. *Converting feelings into words served David's and Susan's many public as well as private purposes.* If they discussed their clashes with one another for hours on end, it was in part because they knew that ultimately someone would want a quick, even glib, explanation for what had happened. Rehearsing their tale by rehashing the event with the other party involved was ideal. As public figures, at least in their own minds, their marriage was one story about themselves they wanted waiting on the shelf.

Of all the things that made Bill wary about emotions, one was more critical than the rest. He wanted the feelings others around him expressed to be genuine, and he suspected that they weren't. That made him resolve repeatedly that, even if other people wouldn't play it straight, he would. He would voice the truth or say nothing at all. He would live by his true sentiments even if that made others, including his wife, wince. His unspoken motto was, "If your feelings aren't real, nothing about you is."

Bill's commitment to the principle was all the greater because he never stated it. David often made comments which he knew would lead to an argument. The prospect of a heated debate made him nervous even before he uttered the opening statement. Yet the anxiety about the up-coming battle was a small price to pay, given what he knew to be his undeniable verbal gifts. Once the battle began, he sensed that he would excel. "I would have made a good trial lawyer," David told us proudly at twenty-nine. "I think well when I'm on the spot"—and in people's living rooms, where these friendly but tense interchanges typically took place.

Bill would never have announced his motto to his friends, since, as far as he could see, there was nothing about it to discuss. It was a fact of life, like the blue color of the sky, and discussing it would only confuse the issue. Verbal battles weren't a way of "clearing the air," as David insisted. To Bill, they were a way of twisting the truth, of showing off, or, as he remarked on a number of occasions, of "pretending to be *doing* something when you're actually not."

Bill didn't have to put his motto into words. He had a version of it that, as one might have expected from him, said the same thing in more concise form and sounded more casual. When one of Nancy's longtime friends (trying to help what she could see was a deteriorating marriage) berated Bill for being cold, he retorted, "Did Nancy put you up to this or was it your own stupid idea?" Undaunted, the friend asked, "How can you turn your back on her? She needs you." His reply goes right to what he viewed as the core of this matter and most others. "I'm no salesman," he said with a sneer, and walked away.

By that he meant, "I'm not a fake." He didn't intend to display an interest that wasn't present. Bill took this unspoken guideline so literally that he couldn't allow feelings to build up *slowly* to the point at which they were indeed there. Instead, in light-switch fashion, he acted as though there were only two states, "on" and "off." Either he was feeling affectionate, or aroused—or he wasn't. Nancy's comment, "Make love to me gently, at first," might as well have been said to him in Chinese. Although the two came from similar backgrounds, he was unable to understand what she wanted. The more she reached out for him, the more he recoiled. Near the end she screamed, "You have *no* feelings. None!" He did have them but wasn't willing to reshape them to suit her—or anyone else's—mood of the moment.

Five and a half years after they were married, Bill moved out. A short time later, they were divorced. There was nothing in Bill's relationship with Nancy that wasn't also present in his relationships with friends and relatives. The bond to her, while it lasted, was more intense than it was with the rest. But the point is that there is no way to fully understand this marriage unless Bill's background and behavior with others is taken into account. There was a remarkable consistency in his attitudes and actions toward everyone he knew. That wasn't so with David, who was a different person with different people. Like his well-educated and upwardly mobile peers, he had a variety of faces and wasn't sure himself which one he would end up wearing in any given situation.

MARRIAGE AS A MIRROR

Sometimes there are few lessons to be learned from a divorce. Two people get married when they are young and eager to be adults, not yet knowing themselves well enough, and the relationship soon begins to deteriorate. It may take years for the two to call it quits, but outsiders often can sense how separate the duo have become. They are married only legally.

However, watching what happens over the years to a large number of marriages, interviewing both partners on a regular basis, certain patterns do appear. In the case of blue-collar men, the pattern consists of two stages. In the first stage the man is attracted to a woman he truly finds interesting as a companion and lover. As with white-collar men, some of the pairings are a mistake, but a much larger number seem undeniably appropriate. The two get along famously, at least for a while.

Nevertheless, it is typical for the harmony to end, most often after approximately twenty to twenty-four months of marriage. Cynics may say that it always disappears after the honeymoon anyway, and everything slides downhill steadily after that. (More than 60 percent of the wives of the blue-collar men in our sample eventually expressed this view.) However, there is more to the story. A blue-collar marriage generally doesn't deteriorate on its own. We found that it is given a helping hand in that direction by a change in attitude among both husbands and, to a lesser but still substantial extent, their wives. Why would they do such a thing? Because, however much they value intimacy, they prize self-reliance far more.

The problem is that they don't realize it. Having been raised with this as a central virtue—one born of necessity—it has become invisible to both. In criticizing his spouse, each man is convinced that he is finding only what is there, not something he is fabricating. He seems genuinely annoyed, yet there is good reason to doubt whether he understands what his desire to avoid being dependent on anyone, in any way, is doing to his behavior.

He likes women; it is wives he doesn't like. Especially his own. Marriage acts as a mirror in which he should be able to see how determined he is to avoid, at any cost, leaning on others. In the case of friends, he doesn't mind nearly as much, because the relationships are inevitably looser and more voluntary. His view of marriage during the second stage—when the pairing feels like a prison—causes him to hope that any needs of his own and his partner's that he overlooks will disappear.

His wife is a problem on three fronts: first, he has learned too well how to erase his own personality, in order to get along better at work with other men and not have the quirks of each interfere with the job to be done (though to some extent they always do). After a while, it becomes hard for him to abandon this self-suppressive orientation when he comes home, and he reacts to his wife's emotions by becoming even more suppressive of his own.

Second, her very presence pulls to the surface dependency needs that every human being has but a Bill-type wishes he didn't. They undermine a value that means more to him than any other—self-reliance—and pushing her away seems to him the only choice. However, it was revealing to see that Bill used the first problem—emotions (hers)—rather than the second—needs (his)—as the excuse for imposing distance.

Third, there is a time problem here. People with a backlog of dependency needs usually do one of two things: look pathetic or get mad. Most choose the latter, especially blue-collar men. Our study indicates that they are grumpy at home significantly more often than are white-collar husbands. How do we know that a striving for self-reliance is at the core of this irascibility, at least in the majority of cases? Because if, before they are married, we give men from *any* background a rating on a self-reliance scale [determined by the extent to which (1) they refuse help, even assistance that they need; and (2) they agree with the statement that they "don't want to depend on anyone, for anything"], then those with a high score are precisely the ones most likely to be chronically annoyed at and around their wives.

As it turns out, blue-collar men have no monopoly on the tendency to quietly subvert their own marriages so as to once again be free. Even highly educated men in our sample—doctors and lawyers—who our tests indicated prized self-reliance above all while they were still single (and knew it), were strongly inclined to keep prizing it after marriage (and be unaware that they were). They complained that "the strain of a two-career marriage" was the real source of their domestic troubles. We found that it was much more likely to be the result of each having selected a partner who was every bit as dedicated subconsciously to maintaining her independence as he himself was. With each pushing the other away—in order not to appear needy *and* to avoid reacting warmly to the other's needs—the relationship never really stood much of a chance.

They either got a divorce, or continued to live together but monitored their own and their partner's emotions guardedly. Blue-collar men in this situation unwittingly managed over the years to substitute *irritability* for a personality. By contrast, white-collar ones started carrying too much anxiety around daily instead, and were unable to pinpoint its source. They almost always assumed that it had something to do with work. Since it eventually interfered with their ability to be at their best day after day on the job, in an important sense they were quite right.

The polarities that Bill and David represent each radiate something undeniably appealing. In the next chapter we'll see a man who, starting from Bill's end of the spectrum, wants nothing more than to make his way toward David's more prestigious end. Then, in Chapter 4, we'll meet a man born with a silver spoon in his mouth who likes the idea of downward mobility—in fact, thinks it simplifies life to have money be of marginal importance—much to the chagrin of his educated wife, family, and friends. They are almost as puzzled by his behavior as he himself is. Like most men in his position, he has never really thought about the nature of the person he is trying hard to become. Small wonder that he is having so much trouble getting there.

CHAPTER
·3·

A SELF-MADE MAN

Most American parents want their children to do better than they have, and even when this isn't one of the parents' most important objectives, it often becomes the children's chief goal anyway. The desire of the young to elevate themselves in many cases turns into an obsession, one that becomes particularly apparent once school is through and they go to work full time. Money is always involved, though for many it isn't enough in and of itself. The profession, partner, and social circle each has, or would like to have, also play a pivotal role. As David put it on a number of occasions, "You are judged by the company you keep." In a large number of instances, including David's, that causes young adults quietly to shun their parents. Ironically, the very people who helped set the youngster on this road wind up being rejected as "not good enough," for they are capable of compromising the social ambitions of their own children. The quest therefore is typically much lonelier than it seems at first glance. The children can go home, if they wish, but they see it as a step backward, a reminder of where they have been. And all they can think about is where they want to be one day soon.

There are three things to keep in mind about ambitious men who seem interested above all in money. The first is that they are more *open* about their goal than men pursuing fame or those trying to be creative. Dreiser's principal character in *The Financier*, Frank Cowperwood, is dated in many ways—in his mode of dress and many of his expressions—but he is our contemporary in one important respect. He candidly states, both as a young man and when he is older, that money is what he is after most. Second, people whose main goal in life is to make a fortune are generally more *persistent* in their quest. The quantitative nature of their search makes it easy for them to keep score, and every dollar counts. By contrast, someone seeking fame (or as they always call it, recognition) is faced with an inherently more difficult situation, since there are negative as well as positive opinions about him. Do people who don't like him subtract from those who do? If so, he may at times feel he is in the minus column, not getting anywhere in spite of great effort.

Similar doubts plague those who attempt to be original, whether they are in the field of comedy, literature, business, or science. It was common for us to hear them ask rhetorically, "Does the world really need a new one-liner [Great American Novel, restaurant, or theory of the universe]?" Men who want money most voice far fewer such doubts. They want to be rich, that's all, and we found that they were much less likely to bring their own progress to a halt repeatedly by questioning everything from their motives to their current status.

Finally, and this third characteristic is in part a result of the first two, they are more *successful*. Any way it is measured, a larger percentage of those seeking primarily to become wealthy attain this goal than do those who want to be original or well known. While the stop-and-start nature of the pursuit of the latter two goals eventually takes its toll in time lost and energy squandered, men who are trying to make a fortune usually become *more* driven as they enter their thirties and forties. Because they know exactly where they stand—what their income and net worth is at any given moment—and they know exactly how much further they have to go to become a millionaire.

A psychological factor of enormous importance affects the outcome at this point. Call it "the motivational power of the light at the end of the tunnel." Once people can see the finish line in a lengthy race, most slow down and begin to coast, saying to themselves, "Well, I've made it, nothing to worry about from here on." However, we found that a small but important minority do the reverse; they try even harder. If nothing else, they want to finish with a flourish. The prospect of sprinting to the finish line, even if they wear themselves out doing so, doesn't worry them because they figure they can always rest and recuperate after the race. This "inspirational" factor isn't present nearly as often with other pursuits, since it is much more difficult for the people engaged in them to measure their own progress.

The three factors we've been discussing make men who are seeking to become rich remarkably indifferent to the emotional costs of their quest. Although many use a balance-sheet mentality in any event, and they are well aware that there will be some bumps and bruises suffered along the way, they don't care—they want what they want. One of their favorite remarks is, "There is no such thing as a free lunch." Moreover, they consider all the talk about the psychic costs of upward mobility to be phony. As one put it—and the majority agree—"Psychologists are people who make a lot of money for telling you that there is something wrong with trying to make a lot of money." Amateur psychologists—novelists and literary critics—are subject to even more scorn by these businessmen for being "self-righteous and envious."

We are therefore going to ignore the costs in what follows in this chapter and focus instead on what the men themselves care most about: who makes it, who doesn't, and why. Since the issue is more complex than it seems, and so much snappy but false advice has been offered, we will let the most representative self-made millionaire of this type in our sample tell as much of his own story as possible *as* it was happening.

PLAYING TO THE CROWD

Larry Maxwell, at fifteen, told us that what he wanted most in the future was to live in a mansion. The home in which he was being raised certainly wasn't one. A plain, three-bedroom house with aluminum siding and no grounds in a middle-class suburb, it was all Larry's parents could afford. That they kept it spotless was small consolation to Larry, who at the very least would have liked his own room. He shared it with his younger brother. His two sisters, one older than he, one younger, shared another bedroom. None of the other three seems to have minded it nearly as much. Larry's father, Ted, was an auto mechanic; his mother, Carla, was a full-time homemaker until the children were all in grade school. Then she worked part time in a local retail store. The two fought a lot.

Larry's father was nothing like Bill. While he too worked with his hands, he had none of Bill's public pride about being a skilled laborer. In fact, he would have considered many of Bill's mannerisms and comments tainted by theatrics. Then again, Ted was twenty-two years older than Bill and had lived through the Depression and World War II. In addition, Bill was subconsciously defending what he saw as a vanishing way of earning a living and the distinctive personality that accompanied it. Ted had a narrower though no less noble goal in mind each day: he wanted to do what was best for his family.

However, the means he had at his disposal were limited, and so were his ambitions. He was a frustrated man, who would argue with anyone, especially his chronically nervous wife ("with four kids, who wouldn't be," Carla once volunteered). The atmosphere in Larry's childhood home was rarely calm. "When they yell at one another," Larry told us at sixteen, "the whole neighborhood can hear." Just in case they didn't, either Larry's mother or father would tell them at the earliest opportunity. It was a kind of race: whoever broadcast the story initially got to think of him or herself as both the victim and the victor ("It's *me* they'll believe," Ted stated smugly, "because I got there first"). Larry didn't consciously adopt this way of handling a disagreement or calling attention to himself. He unwittingly absorbed the techniques involved and later made skillful use of them. He knew how to play to a crowd and manipulate it for his purposes. Onlookers were clay, to be molded according to his mood and motives of the moment.

Why Larry became the most ambitious of Ted's four children is hard to say with certainty. He was more restless than the others, and in the opinion of their teachers (all four had the same ones) he was the brightest. By the time he was a junior in high school, Larry was a muscular 5 foot 10 inches and weighed 170 pounds. His occupational interests hadn't yet crystallized but it was apparent that he wouldn't spend his adult days doing manual labor. He knew it wasn't likely to lead to the lavish life style for which he yearned.

Even during high school the forces pulling him in opposing directions—toward his past and his future—were evident in the girls to whom he was attracted. "Carol is classy," he said at seventeen, revealing an interest that was more social than sexual, "but Maryann is earthy." He dated both and was fully satisfied with neither. Since he was still finding his way in the world, it was only to be expected that he didn't yet know what he wanted in a woman. One thing was certain, he was at ease with his erotic impulses. There are sexually repressed men who divide the women they are interested in into two categories, "virgins" and "whores." Lusting after and having sex with the latter group is fine but is taboo where the former group is concerned. Larry was the only member of his group who never fell prey to this split and ended up sleeping with girls in both categories before graduating from high school.

The large state college he attended presented him with a wide variety of choices, few of which he was prepared to make. For one, he had to select a major yet found none appealing enough to do so happily. "I liked Economics 101 and figured that might make a good major," he said during his junior year. "But the courses got mathematical real fast. I sat in on a few graduate classes, and they might as well have been theoretical physics. It wasn't for me." Larry chose business administration instead because "the courses are no strain on my brain." He graduated with a B average, which was the same as the one he had had in high school. During the following winter he commented while at work, "College didn't do me a whole lot of good. I guess it didn't harm me any either."

To all appearances Larry was a directionless twenty-three-year-old, employed by a financial services company (a job he had gotten through a friend), who still hadn't decided what he wanted to be or do. But appearances can be deceiving, especially where men in their twenties are concerned. The clearest evidence we had that he dreamed of doing great things, even though he was presently doing little, was that he had managed to put $7,600 into a savings account. Someone tightfisted might have done the same, but that didn't accurately describe Larry. Living simply, denying himself many of the toys and treats recent college graduates usually set their sights on (everything from high-priced restaurants to sports cars), he was steadily increasing his bank balance.

It soon became obvious that, first, Larry was better than most of his peers at "delayed gratification." He could prevent himself with little difficulty from splurging on something appealing but expensive. "I don't really need—or want—it," he would say without any edge to his voice, and turn his attention elsewhere. Second, he was eventually going to be in his own business.

There are young men who become committed to a particular company's cause and do their best to associate themselves emotionally with its products, services, and outlook. Far from being mere altruists, they do this in the hope that their dedication will be rewarded and their future with the company bright. Larry tried but couldn't work up what he called "any gung-ho feeling at the office." Also, he wanted to make things happen quickly. "I'm getting older by the minute," he said at twenty-four, not hiding very well an abundance of underlying fear. Someone who didn't have great plans for himself wouldn't have turned white-knuckled regularly at the thought of running out of time before the plans were realized.

As with so many other ambitious men we studied, with his business life "on hold," so were his relations with women. Larry had curly brown hair, a small, "ski jump" nose, a quick smile, and a lively disposition. Rarely was he depressed, and when he was, it wasn't for long. "He was always able to make me smile," said Maryann, his first bedmate in high school, "even when I was annoyed or had my mind on something else." Carol, his second bedmate, commented that "Larry has a funny way of looking at the world—you know, a little kooky—and it makes everything sound kind of silly. He's very entertaining, without trying to be." What the comments don't convey is the basically driven nature of the man. While he was also entertaining in private settings, in public Larry aimed his witty remarks at everyone within earshot, using his current conversation partner as a prop, an excuse for unleashing his remarks to begin with. He badly wanted to be noticed.

A TWO-DAY HONEYMOON

When our study first began, we assumed that men or women of any age who were alienated from those with whom they had daily contact would show it in a particular way. They would remain socially aloof, with their remoteness visible to all. They would, we were sure, be loners. People who were acting in accordance with their true feelings, and hadn't found anyone to whom they felt close, would have no other choice.

We were wrong. The vast majority of alienated men and women we studied don't fit this Hollywoodized picture, in which their aloofness is projected so clearly that even an audience of popcorn-eating adolescents can't miss the message. In reality, the aloofness is emotional, not social. The people in question have dinners and sex with—and even marry— others from whom they feel estranged. That doesn't make them phonies. They often try to reach out to others, and are themselves amazed at times that the distance is there. Year after year, they go on thinking that it is only temporary.

As his first decade in the workplace slowly passed, it certainly didn't seem to Larry that his relations with women were on hold. They had much the same thing to say about him that Maryann and Carol had a decade earlier; "upbeat" and "amusing" were frequent characterizations. In his late twenties the word "intense" also began to be heard. However, the sheer number of women passing through his arms made us suspect that few—and perhaps none—meant very much to him, or else that he did care deeply for some, but only briefly.

It turned out to be the latter. Larry would become passionately involved with at least some of the women he met, hoping that the current relationship would be "the one." In the beginning, at least, he truly believed it was. "A beautiful blonde was directly ahead of me on the line at the passport office," he told us at twenty-seven. "It looked like we would be there a while. I asked her—her name was Ann—whether they would rent us cots as nighttime rolled around [it was three-thirty]." She replied, "I think some of us will need them *before* then. My feet are starting to give out."

The two talked for the hour it took before Ann was at the counter. Much to Larry's surprise and delight, she waited for him while he spent the few minutes required to answer questions and sign forms in the presence of the clerk. The two left together. "That Saturday and Sunday were like a fantasy," he later told us, "a dream come true." Although they did a number of different things together—jogged, ate, showered, and watched TV—each event blended into the next, thanks to the blanket of romance and eroticism that surrounded them wherever they went.

Instead of a fantasy, the weekend might better have been compared to a two-day honeymoon. Once it was over, reality returned. Ann was the same age as Larry, twenty-seven, and had consciously made up her mind that it was time to get married and have a family. While Larry appealed to her greatly from the moment she met him, the weekend they spent together gave her a chance to see that he wasn't ready, either financially or emotionally, for marriage. Like him, she wanted something to happen—and soon—but they wanted it to happen in different spheres. "I loved him—I *still* love him," Ann said ten months later, as she began dating the wealthy man she eventually married. Then, without a moment's hesitation, she added, "But he has a lot of growing up to do. I don't think he wants to settle down just now."

Ann knew something about Larry that he didn't, something that would have distressed him mightily had he heard it and realized it was true. Settling down to marriage and family was out of the question for him as long as his business dreams weren't yet fulfilled. Like most men, he believed he wanted to spend the remainder of his life with one woman, and sought out partners with whom he became deeply involved. Nevertheless, other women came to the same conclusion as had Ann: "As far as I can see, he may never get married." Some felt he was merely toying with them and walked away from the relationship hurt and angry, not realizing that *it is only during certain periods in the life of an ambitious man that he is truly available for a long-term relationship.*

One can't tell with great certainty beforehand when that period will start or end (we guessed wrong repeatedly, in the beginning), and it is different for men in different fields (historians and editors come into their own rather late, while mathematicians and athletes usually achieve distinction early or not at all). There is also a good deal of individual variation within any given field, with some men still boyish in middle age and others rather middle-aged though only in their twenties. We had hoped to arrive at a specific figure that fit the majority of cases—"If you want him as a husband, get to him at twenty-seven [say] or forget him, since after that he again becomes unavailable." But the data didn't fit this "peaked" picture. One man might not be ready till he was forty-one, while another might indeed be most receptive at twenty-seven. What we did find was that the periods of receptivity (as measured by the men's comments on the subject, together with their fantasied and actual partner choices) tended to last a median length of approximately two years and for there to be only two to three such periods during the working life of a typical ambitious man.

Not realizing this, most women took personally Larry's inaccessibility or the brief duration of the intimacy. Using their own experiences and emotions as a guide, the women believed that either "someone's ready to get married—and they remain ready for many, many years—or they're not, in which case it really doesn't matter *when* you meet them. I think Larry has just been kidding me, all along."

If that was so, he was kidding himself even more. During our study we were surprised to find that it was rare for men like Larry to knowingly mislead the women they were dating about the future of the relationship. Why did most avoid doing this? Given the men's verbal skills and ability to be persuasive, it would have been easy for them to concoct a new story any time one was needed. Like everyone else, they did indeed do this on occasion. However, it happened much less often than we had been led to believe, especially by the men's ex-partners. Ironically, the salesmanship and show-biz orientation makes people think these men are lying even when they aren't.

The main reason most are straightforward with the women they date has less to do with ethics or honesty and instead springs from the men's desire to see the world in an open-ended, "everything is possible" light. For each to tell a woman—or *himself*—that the relationship had no future would make it feel flat and even lifeless. He correctly senses that it will seem real to him only if anything can happen, and that "anything" has to include marriage. Limiting its possibilities beforehand by labeling it merely a fling would cause him to view it as unabsorbing and trivial.

Why, then, do the vast majority of these pairings fall apart? They certainly did in Larry's case. A number of them had the makings of an enduring relationship; the two seemed right for one another in every important respect. The consensus of Larry's ex-partners during his late twenties and early thirties was that Larry was a "workaholic." The explanation, like the word itself, is so superficial as to be useless. As we'll soon see, it masks rather than illuminates the feelings of the people being described.

A SPRINGBOARD TO WEALTH

At the age of twenty-nine, Larry went into business for himself and became an electronics wholesaler. The world of expensive stereo systems, color TVs, closed circuit cameras, VCRs, telephone answering equipment, and dictating machines had always fascinated him. Unlike Bill, Larry had never taken any of these units apart and lacked the patience to be a tinkerer. Using a more intellectual approach, he had instead learned enough from manuals and magazines to know which units had better "specs"—that is, technical specifications—than the others. These he recommended to co-workers and acquaintances.

This also led him to befriend the owner of a stereo store, who eventually offered Larry a job. "I leaped at the chance," he said with a smile, a few days after starting. Larry's enthusiasm and approach made him a better salesman than most technicians would have been, in spite of their superior training and hands-on experience. For they often overwhelmed or bored customers by spewing reams of irrelevant data, delivered without emotion. Larry's enthusiasm was infectious. That, together with his ability to compare various models knowledgeably, made shoppers respond. He became the store's star salesman.

It couldn't last. Larry was looking for bigger hills to climb and there was only so much he could accomplish on his feet, talking to customers one after another. Three weeks before he quit, he said, "I'm on commission—mostly—so if I don't sell anything, I don't make any money." Coming down with the flu, which put him out of work for nearly two weeks, and watching his income plummet had recently caused his thinking to switch dramatically.

When he worked for a salary, it was guaranteed but too small. When he worked on commission, his earnings could be high, but only if he was present every day and healthy as well. It occurred to him that in his own business, and only there, his earnings might be high even if he weren't at the office each day, because he happened to be ill or tired. Archimedes, the classical Greek scientist who shouted "Eureka" as he ran through the street to tell others of a discovery he had made, once said, "Give me a lever of the right length [and a place to put it] and I can move the world." Larry had a similar revelation at this time, and the intense feeling of expansiveness he experienced as a result is only hinted at in his remark, "I want other people working for me, instead of the other way around. I want that *leverage* going for me." With it, he believed that he too could move the world.

While he was working at the store, Larry noticed something interesting. When more stock was needed, particularly two or three units of a particular model, it wasn't ordered from the manufacturer. It was ordered from a distributor. "I guess everybody always knew that," he said, still surprised at the realization. "I didn't." This was the opening he had long been seeking. "I don't have enough capital to become a manufacturer—

not enough to open a fancy store, either—but I do have enough to become a distributor." Larry had nearly $36,000 saved up, and that would be sufficient seed money to start his own business *if* he became a distributor of inexpensive items.

That was what he did. Leasing a loft in a low-rent commercial district, he stocked it with electronic components—everything from cables and connectors to computer memory chips and transformers. Then, he went to dozens of stores that sold these products at retail and told them he had low prices, a large inventory, and would deliver "in an hour." It was rarely quite that fast, but it was quick enough to impress his customers, who steadily increased the volume of business they did with him. Larry worked long hours and loved doing so.

His bedmates during these years were even more likely than the ones he had had during his twenties to describe him as a "workaholic." What the word doesn't convey is that it wasn't the *work* Larry liked, it was the money and what it could buy him. This was hardly a labor he would have performed for free. "I'm on my way to making it big," he stated proudly at thirty-three, for the first time. "I'm going to be a winner." He had obviously believed it all along, yet his interests hadn't previously been sufficiently focused for us to ask, "At what?" While we too were convinced he would do well financially one day, it was only after he began to pour himself into the electronics business morning, noon and night, that we—and he—could finally see what his springboard to wealth would probably be.

THE CRUCIAL YEARS

Most of the men we studied had a number of false starts, in which they were excited about areas of activity that eventually proved barren for them. Each thought he was building something, including a reputation, only to be rudely awakened to the realization that he was on a dead-end road. "The sales field isn't taking me *anywhere*," Larry said, a few weeks before leaving the store to found his own firm. Selling, as a profession, had come to seem to him more a dead end than the golden opportunity he once considered it. His moods swung conspicuously as a consequence; excitement about where his job at the store was taking him (optimism that was usually the result of a large sale he had just made) was followed soon after by a slump (when he again reminded himself that the store wasn't his and he could be fired for any reason on any day).

Starting his own firm, and having it do better each month, made Larry open and accessible in a way that he had never been before. In some ways, he knew it. "I feel great," he said during the third year in his own business, "like I'm sending out some kind of high-frequency signal." He made a blaring sound, similar to the alarm on a submarine that is about to slip beneath the ocean surface. "I hope a gorgeous woman hears it. I'm not sure how long it will last."

Someone did. Larry met Gail Edwards six months after he rented the loft and became a distributor. Nearly the same height as Larry, lanky, with straight brown hair and a vampish look, she usually wore high heels, dark stockings, and too much eye makeup. The two were introduced by a friend. "I liked his energy," Gail, who worked for a travel agency, later remarked. "Larry is full of life." He could have used the same words about her. The two gave the impression of being an upwardly mobile pair with much in common. Perhaps too much. She was caught up in her own dreams of career success. While Gail hadn't been very interested in school, she did manage to get two years of business courses under her belt at a community college. In her mind, she felt sufficiently well prepared for a career in the business world and was proud to be "the right-hand" assistant to the owner of the travel agency. She knew that her long legs and attractive looks had helped her land the position, but compliments, whether for her brains or body, were all gratefully absorbed. "Just because a woman is in the business world, she doesn't have to look mousy," she frequently advised her friends. "Use whatever assets you've got." Instead of being companions, Larry and Gail fell in love, got married and quickly became antagonists.

Abilities and emotions that he hadn't previously mobilized because the setting wasn't right—wasn't *his*—had risen to the surface and made Larry feel exuberant. Unfortunately, the woman he chose was so bent on career success, she wanted to talk about little else. Every sentence he uttered about his work, she, in knee-jerk fashion, felt compelled to match with one of her own. She was mortified that their friends viewed him as the rising star of the pair. So much of this was occurring in every major American city in the 1970s and 1980s, it is small wonder that the two finally joined the more than 22,000 couples then getting divorced every week.

*   *   *

It is impossible to understand the lives of men like Larry without bringing "the competition factor" into the picture. People who work with such a man know how inflamed he can become when he is outdistanced by a rival. Rather than quitting because he has been handed a loss, he tries twice as hard to recoup. In fact, no one he knows can be allowed to upstage him, leaving him to look second best. To say that such man often carries to absurd extremes his attempt to catch up to and then surpass a competitor is an understatement. A defeat, even more than a victory, fires him up in the first place. At such moments he sounds much like "the great avenger," seeking to right a grievous wrong that was done, in this case, to him.

For some reason, colleagues and friends usually think this approach doesn't carry over into his personal life. Perhaps they don't realize what a major role it plays in his business life, so they remain unaware that it shapes his behavior even more decisively when he isn't working. People who see him trying to avenge a slight think of him as reacting to a *specific* situation in which he feels he was treated badly. No doubt that is true. However, when dozens of episodes in the personal life of such a man are examined, it becomes clear that one of his chief characteristics is that he is an all-out competitor, determined to keep up with the gains made by everyone else he knows—particularly the gains made at *his* expense. For instance, we found that where the sexual jealousy of self-made men is concerned, in most cases only competition is involved, not love.

"YOU'RE A NECESSARY EVIL, NOT A BLESSING"

Even before Larry's domestic situation began to deteriorate, his company began to expand. New customers were calling him, some of whom he had never heard of before. "That's a real switch," he commented gleefully. "I'm so used to chasing *them*, I was bowled over to pick up the phone and have one say, 'I've been trying all day to reach you,' and then have the SOB give me a big initial order."

While Larry may have been eager to have his business grow quickly, he realized that some of the customers who gave him orders would never pay him. "They'll be bankrupt by the time the bill is due," he remarked sarcastically. Particularly with so many new stores beginning to buy from him, he feared the problem would soon become a major one. To minimize his losses ("I know we'll have *some*, no matter what"), he hired Fred Ellis to be the company's chief financial officer and credit expert. "Fred is going to keep an eye on those creeps, aren't you, Freddie?" he said, sounding excited at the prospect. Looking at us, he continued: "If they can't pay, we don't ship 'em. Right, Fred?"

Anyone who wanted to know what Larry was "really like" merely had to watch him on the job. As Larry's thirties rolled by, his business continued to do increasingly well. More people had to be hired—Fred got one assistant, then another; Gary Walters, the shipping and receiving manager, eventually hired six more men to help him load and unload crates. The office staff had to be enlarged as well, with Wendy Peters and Cathy Ames handling the bulk of the correspondence, billing, and phone calls.

How did Larry treat these important additions to his staff? As Fred described it, "He's unpredictable—says one thing, means another—or says something and completely forgets that he said it." The observation was made without rancor; "He means well," Fred added. But the abrupt changes of mind, or forgetfulness (if that is what it was), were taking their toll on Fred's emotions. He related one story which was like two dozen others that had taken place at the firm.

"Larry asked me to check—*really* check—the credit of Franklin Electronics. 'I don't trust those bastards,' he said. So I did everything but put my hand in their pocket and count the greenbacks in their wallets. I called their bank, other suppliers they do business with—everybody. Then we boxed up $8,900 worth of stuff to send them—their first order—and he suddenly goes out on the shipping dock and nixes the deal. 'Unpack the stuff,' he tells the boys, without even telling me. I'm on the phone with their buyer saying 'The stuff is on its way,' and Larry is having the boys unpack it. I felt like a real jerk when I found out what he'd done."

It may sound as though Larry was just being cautious. Yet for every customer whose credit Fred approved and Larry refused to ship, there were ten that Fred considered questionable and Larry still shipped, often without telling him. "It gets me mad sometimes," Fred said, shaking his head. "It truly does. He's going to give me an ulcer."

Larry treated Wendy and Cathy the same way. After criticizing them gently for not having the files sufficiently current and neat, he would go searching for a file and make quite a mess of the order they had imposed on what had previously been fairly chaotic paperwork. "I did better," he once told Wendy offhandedly, "when I had everything in my head. Then it was *all* up to date. I could update it just by changing my mind." After working for Larry for three years, and getting substantial annual raises and bonuses, she commented, "Maybe he does these things—leaving folders everywhere—because he wants to see if we're on our toes."

Gary remarked that "Larry likes to throw his weight around," but there was more to his seemingly quixotic behavior. While he undoubtedly wanted to remind his staff that he was the boss, Larry's comments, taken collectively throughout his thirties, indicate that he was sending another, more critical message: "I don't need you—having you around hasn't improved my life at all. In fact, things were better before you arrived. You're only here because the business has gotten too big for me to handle alone. You're not a blessing, you're a necessary evil."

FEAR OF BEING IMMOBILIZED

Larry said little of this to his staff. And when he did hint at his true feelings he used charm, together with the prospect of an even bigger bonus this year than last, to soften the blow. His surface friendliness and money kept his employees placated.

However, his actions spoke volumes, and what they said in brief was, "I'm not prepared to delegate any authority to you." Other entrepreneurs we studied shared this attitude, not always consciously, but it meant that they had to do everything themselves. Larry couldn't; his company had grown too large. What he could instead do was undermine the professionalism of almost everyone who worked for him, discrediting them as candidates for real authority and responsibility. "I know more about this business than Fred ever will," he told us, early one morning before the staff arrived. "I was in it *before* he was." On another occasion, he said of Cathy, "So what that she's taken a word-processing and data-base course. I'm the only one who knows where everything is, not her." No one who worked for Larry could be perceived as having skills that were indispensable. "Everyone can be replaced," he said, and meant it. "Even me," he added, with mock humility.

Larry had to do it all himself in the beginning because, at the time, there wasn't anyone else. If he couldn't do something, it didn't get done ("I even designed my own letterheads and business cards"). He couldn't afford to hire assistants and no one was willing to help him for nothing. When there were finally people around him who sincerely wanted to be of assistance, he sneered. "They're here for the money," said Larry cynically. Then, switching to a more self-congratulatory tone: "And why shouldn't they be? I give all of them fat year-end bonuses and I stroke them real good when they need it." As far as he was concerned, they were merely "fair-weather friends," there because he paid them well and, in his view, didn't demand much.

Larry's willingness—or better still, need—to do as much as he could himself made him see everyone else's workload as being lighter than it actually was. After all, he was prepared on a moment's notice to do their job and his own as well. For that reason, he always did a little bit of everyone else's work. How could he do that? By using a very clever device.

His veto of a decision they had reached may have seemed like a merely headstrong assertion of power, yet it actually accomplished something more crucial: it did their work for them, and did it as it was supposed to have been done in the first place. When Larry dismissed Fred's conclusion about a customer's creditworthiness and decided to ship anyway, he was in essence saying to Fred, "I'm a more sophisticated judge of someone's credit than you are. You reached the wrong conclusion—and therefore wasted the money I'm paying you—but I fixed it. I did the job— *your* job—right." Similarly, he would rarely allow more than a month to go by without finding a customer file that Cathy had miscategorized. "These people are buying memory chips from us, remember? Maybe I should put some of those chips in your breakfast cereal. You need them." He would then go to her computer terminal and add their name to the list of stores that were to be notified when new shipments of computer supplies arrived. It took him only five minutes a month to stage these scenes with her or Wendy, yet it made him feel that he was basically doing his work and theirs—only better.

If we look at Larry in terms of applause, it would be accurate to characterize him as a *stage hog*. Looking at him in more private terms, he wanted to be in *control*. However, the most illuminating way to view his behavior is that he wanted these two things and, simultaneously, to be *free* and unencumbered. The biggest plus in Larry's life, the goal for which he was willing to strive day and night, was money. He was intent upon becoming rich, no matter what the cost. The biggest minus in his mind, the fear that exceeded all others in its degree of intensity, was being immobilized, trapped in one place. We know this because, over the years, when we asked him each time what his most recent nightmare had been, more than 70 percent of his thirty-seven replies had to do with being caught and held fast by some force or event. He didn't mind being fired or even going bankrupt; as long as he had his health and his mind intact; he knew he'd "start over again and make it all back."

Unlike Bill, who wanted above all to be self-reliant and therefore was reluctant to lean on anyone, even briefly, Larry leaned—in fact, leaned hard—only to push away his helpers when his claustrophobic anxieties once again closed in on him. Although it is easy to confuse the two, self-reliance wasn't his main goal, mobility was. He wanted to be self-contained so as to be ready to move elsewhere tomorrow, if need be.

How could he have done that if he formed deep attachments today, business connections to people without whom he couldn't function? The ambivalence he displayed toward his most important assistants was monumental. On the one hand, he wanted them to be good at what they did—"the *best*," he insisted—and he did indeed pay them well. On the other hand, they couldn't be allowed to matter, couldn't be deemed essential, lest his fear of being trapped transform him into a prisoner running his metal cup back and forth against the cell's bars, screaming, "Let me out! I have to get out!" Money was the driving force, but to this Bedouin in the business world, so was remaining mobile. He sensed that only by remaining free would he be able to seize the really important opportunities that came his way.

DEMANDING LOYALTY— AND PREPARING TO FLEE

"Larry never stops talking about loyalty," Gail had told us more than once, puzzled at his obsession with the subject. "He mentioned it on our first date and I still hear about it at least once or twice a week now."

There was no question in Larry's mind that his employees owed him their allegiance. "If I called any of them at 2 A.M. and said, 'Come in, there is work that has to be done now,' I'd expect them to do it." His words made it sound as though Larry was talking about his staff's dedication to the business; actually, without being aware of it, he meant something more personal—a dedication to him. If he could have done it without offending them, he would regularly have given each person who worked for him a loyalty test.

What about Larry's own behavior? How much loyalty did he display toward the people from whom he expected so much of the same in return? The answer is "none." When Larry wanted to charm a current or potential customer, he rarely hesitated to disown his co-workers and paint them in a negative light. He did this frequently even before starting his own company, while still working at the stereo store. It was always done in seemingly joking fashion. Jovially, Larry told us, "Gary is a good man, but only if you keep an eye on him. I have to do it night and day." About Fred: "He's smart as they come, but he can't see the forest for the trees."

People who hadn't been around Larry often enough to see how much of this he did were impressed by it. They truly believed that they had a "special relationship" with him, as some described it, and that of course was its intended effect. Larry had displayed the ability to shift alliances rapidly in high school and college. So had many of his classmates. However, at the time there was nothing unusual about it, since it is a standard part of the way in which adolescents orient themselves in an increasingly complex world. Larry never lost this skill (which he originally developed at home, watching how his parents fought). Instead, as an adult, he developed it into a highly useful sales tool.

For someone to use this technique daily and then insist on absolute loyalty from subordinates seemed to us a bit bizarre. When the same demand was seen in hundreds of other cases—more in some, less in others—it became clear that the underlying cause was the fear of being immobilized that we discussed moments ago. In fact, the more afraid a person is of being "boxed in," "cornered," "cooped up," or "locked in," to use some of their favorite phrases, the more likely he is to insist that those around him be loyal.

What exactly is the connection? Put simply, in Larry's life there was a carrot and a stick. The carrot was the fortune after which he chased; the stick wasn't poverty ("I'm not afraid of being poor—I've *been* poor"), it was an intense anxiety about the prospect of being trapped. To Larry, the ability to be mobile and active meant everything. Without it, he sensed that the riches for which he hungered would be irrelevant. Having money—real money—meant the freedom to move on a moment's notice. What his demand for loyalty was really saying therefore is, "If I have to move for any reason, you have to come with me, since you're *part* of me. I can let you into my life—and not panic—only if I know that you won't act as a nail, holding me here when I have to go."

It may appear at first glance that Larry was suffering from a form of "separation anxiety," a phrase popularized by the British psychiatrist John Bowlby. The trouble with the phrase, and the whole concept, is that it doesn't fit the facts here. To find an explanation that does, we have to go back to the "fight-or-flight mechanism" proposed by Harvard physiologist Walter B. Cannon in 1915 in *Bodily Changes in Pain, Hunger, Fear and Rage*.

The idea is simple enough: when faced with a threat, people are inclined either to attack or flee. One or the other. If this notion is to assist us to understand the business and personal behavior of ambitious men, it has to be modified: fight *and* flight, not the mutually exclusive "one or the other, but not both."

That makes sense even in a primitive setting, since, of a group of men menaced by a nearby saber-toothed tiger, it may well have been the one who was willing to approach closest to the tiger, throw a spear, and then run away as fast as he could, who was especially valuable in helping the group to survive. It is easy to imagine many other situations in which such fight-*and*-flight impulses were needed, against human foes as well. While we remain suspicious of all such "B.C." cartoons to help explain the motivation of moderns (after all, hundreds of thousands of years have passed since these alleged events took place), this one is a worthwhile analogy.

For what we found was that, paradoxically, the more aggressive a given man in our study had been over the years and the more he achieved (the two were correlated: hard work did indeed produce results eventually), the more likely he was subconsciously to want to be prepared to flee. The reason we don't think of this as the way men ordinarily behave is because of what we see in the movies. Faced with a threat, Clint Eastwood, Charles Bronson, and John Wayne don't run. They stay and fight. However, this cinematic depiction is probably appealing because it is *not* the way the vast majority of men are inclined to react, though, especially in the United States, they think they should. Nevertheless, it is safer in most cases for the individual and group to flee, and to do so in the ninety-nine times when it is unnecessary than in the one time in a hundred when it is essential and their lives are lost because they don't. In the movies, men who stand their ground and fight are rewarded; those who run are branded cowards.

In reality, and particularly in business, it turns out that ambitious men do both. Their drive is visible; their preparation for flight is less so. One may label their demand for loyalty as egotistical or authoritarian, but such labels are merely insulting and, worse, they close our eyes rather than open them to the powerful underlying forces in operation here. If we are truly determined to understand these financially successful but troubled individuals—a difficult task in a country that feels little sympathy for wealthy people with problems—a different approach is needed. Aggression *can* coexist with fear; someone may strive unceasingly to achieve a goal, yet be afraid that what *he* sees as his most important asset, his mobility, may vanish along the way.

This isn't Fear of Success, one of pop psychology's most hilarious recent concoctions. Rather, it is the realistic recognition that as one's business grows, an increasing number of people become integral and important parts of it. Many have minds—and directions—of their own. It is hardly surprising that entrepreneurs and, as we'll see later, top executives worry about each new addition to their staff who occupies a pivotal position.

"THE GOOD ONES QUIT, THE BAD ONES I FIRE"

A wife is, in many ways, the most worrisome addition. Although a personal, not a business matter (since it is assumed that she doesn't actually join the firm), we found their marital relationships to be affected by the same forces that plagued the men's work-related behavior.

To be specific, two factors that would seem to involve only the office produced trouble for such men both at work and at home: *the failure to delegate authority and the demand for loyalty led to a significant increase in employee defections,* the very thing these executives feared. *It also led their wives to have, on average, a greater number of extramarital affairs and the marriages to end significantly more often in divorce.* We found that this applies every bit as much to managers as to entrepreneurs.

The usual explanation for all this turmoil simply isn't accurate. "The men worked too hard," we are told, "gave everything to their businesses, and had nothing left emotionally for their wives and children." Yet, as we'll see, there were men in our sample who worked as many hours as Larry did, and then some, but who remained happily married. The difference was that, first, they didn't squander their prodigious energies putting out brush fires they themselves unwittingly kept starting. Instead, they devoted themselves to the most critical tasks that needed doing and let others look after the rest. Second, they were able to do this because they truly welcomed the assistance they eventually received, rather than subconsciously resenting it as Larry did since, in his view, it compromised his all-important ability to flee on a moment's notice.

We hear some phrases so often we don't give them the thought they deserve; "failure to delegate authority" means much more than it says. For when one examines the daily behavior of people who are failing to do the delegating, they aren't acting in nearly as passive or reluctant a manner as the phrase seems to signify. Rather, they actively discredit subordinates to whom essential tasks would otherwise be given. This is a necessary step because, after all, the subordinates are being *paid* to render assistance. Presumably, they are willing as well, since they took the job voluntarily. They must therefore be made to seem unfit for the position.

A brief look at Larry's treatment of Donald Layton, whom he hired as a salesman, reveals how this is typically done. Don was a history major in college, became enamored of his field, and after graduation landed a job with a major publisher as an editorial assistant. As he described his three-year stay there: "The pay was inadequate, the work was dull, and moving up looked like it would take forever." The sales field offered the prospect of a higher income, and he considered becoming a stockbroker. An ad in the Sunday paper placed by a "rapidly growing electronics-supply company" caught his eye, especially the line, "No experience necessary." The line was Larry's idea, since he himself hadn't had any in the beginning, and he was more convinced than ever that persistence "and the right-priced products" were all that anyone required for success.

Yet he ridiculed Don behind his back from the day he hired him. "Why would *anyone* major in history?" he asked us, scrunching up his face. Don was asking himself the same question at the time, but he still retained some of the lofty cultural aspirations he had absorbed with his major and was letting go of them only slowly. In his sales case, which was the size of an overnight valise, he usually carried a classic or quality contemporary work, hidden from view. It afforded him solace, a measure of security during a stressful period of transition when he had one foot in each camp.

Under the guise of looking for a particular component, Larry opened the bag one day when Don was at lunch and found a copy of Charles Beard's *Economic Interpretation of the U.S. Constitution*. When Don returned from lunch, Larry cackled, "You still working for a publisher or for me? The only constitutions I want you interpreting are the customers'. Figure out how to sell them *more*." Don didn't reply. "I knew I'd say the wrong thing," he later told us.

He had been with the firm nearly a year and a half at the time and, much to his surprise, was doing better each month. Larry only noticed what Don *hadn't* done right that month and became especially critical of the young man after Gary, who knew the sales figures and liked Don, said, "You know, he might become as good a peddler one day as you are." With Larry complaining bitterly of late about what a chore it was to call on customers, one might have expected a warm response to the budding talent he had on his staff. The reverse occurred, with Larry chiding and poking fun at him, primarily in his absence. Two and a half years later, Don quit. (He is now the sales manager of a major electronics firm, earning well in excess of $100,000 a year.) Three weeks after he left, Larry said resentfully, "He really disappointed me. I had high hopes for him. With me, he could have gone places."

Other key employees also defected. While this happens at any firm, the turnover at Larry's firm was excessive by any measure. No one stayed for long, and when they left, they later reported they were glad to be elsewhere. Gary, Cathy, and Wendy quit; some of the others, including Fred, were abruptly fired. It was unusual for anyone to stay with Larry more than three to four years—which, by no coincidence, was the length of time his marriage lasted.

So many employees quit or were fired over the years that Larry—and most of the other ambitious men like him in our sample—developed an extraordinary attitude toward those who stayed. Rather than thinking of defectors as his enemies, now that they had openly displayed their disloyalty and gone to another firm, his feelings about them suddenly turned neutral or positive. Since they were no longer a threat to his need for instant mobility, he could afford to be generous: "They had potential—

that's why I hired them—but it never blossomed because they didn't stick with me." As far as Larry was concerned, his past and present employees fell into one of three categories: "The good ones quit, thinking they can do better elsewhere; the incompetent ones I fire. So what am I left with? Mediocrity."

BEING SEEN WITH THE RIGHT WOMAN

Larry's divorce put him back on the party circuit, where he paired up with a variety of women who liked his free-spending ways. "I like beautiful women," he told us at thirty-four, "and they like being with me." For the first time in his life he could be seen regularly in expensive or fashionable restaurants and was usually among the loudest patrons in the place, especially when he laughed. Larry wanted to be the center of attention, a desire that grew as his wealth did.

By going "wherever the action was," he hoped to be included in any magazine pieces written about the resort or restaurant. "If you're in the right place at the right time," he said, straightening his tie, on the way out for the evening, "you never know who'll be there. Click, just like that, a photographer snaps your picture and everybody in town sees it the next day in the papers. You've got to look your best."

That made it mandatory, in his view, to be seen with the right woman. But what was "right" for Larry at this point? His partners during this period all appeared to be stamped from the same mold. They were, on average, six to ten years his junior, and, as he put it, "sexy, free, and fun-loving." Larry didn't mention that they liked his money, but *they* did. When we asked Marie, a tall, blonde receptionist who wore plunging V-neck sweaters, what she found most appealing about him, she replied, "He takes me to such nice places." Fortunately, Larry didn't hear the remark. The relationship lasted for two months, after which he could be seen squiring around a stewardess he had met on a brief trip to an electronics show in Dallas.

The rate at which he traded in old partners for new ones nearly matched the turnover at his firm—and the underlying reason was the same in both areas: his powerful desire to maintain his mobility. With a revolving-door personnel policy, he sometimes seemed determined to give everyone in his field a chance to work for him—but not for very long. His business continued to do well, "because I work hard and play hard," is how Larry explained it. He also had a good eye for picking people who, at least for a while, anyway, would involve themselves in the business with the same intensity Larry devoted to it. They did this because they were copying him, wanted to learn from him, and, most of all, wanted to emulate his success. "Boy, I'd like to be in a position one day to throw money around the way he does," said a new salesman, who was staring, as if hypnotized, at a $56,000 maroon Mercedes that Larry had just bought to replace his two-year-old one.

Some of the women who met and fell for Larry were baffled and dismayed that they weren't able to land him. "He seems so *eligible*," one complained, "a real catch. But he breaks lots of dates. Calls at the last minute and says he can't make it. Maybe he's already married—to his business." The label had been pasted on Larry before, and it fit even less well now than it had previously.

For one thing, his standards had shifted. In the past he had selected partners based primarily on their erotic appeal. He also wanted each to be attractive, "so that I don't have to apologize for her to my friends when we go out." As so often happens, once he became financially successful, his tastes in women changed. Larry still used the same vocabulary to describe the ones he found desirable—"Wow, she's a real turn-on" and "That one gives me goose bumps"—but there was a world of difference between his past and present preferences. Formerly, he wanted his partners to be visibly sexy; currently, he was drawn to women who were visibly classy.

Some of Larry's business associates, seeing him out on the town during these years, each time with yet another new partner, claimed that he had "returned to adolescence" and was "trying to sleep with every foxy young chick in the city." However, by the time they were making such statements, Larry had already slept with dozens and was finding each episode less exciting than the one before. "It's not as 'wild and crazy' as it used to be," he remarked, doing a good Steve Martin imitation.

Still, it must have been at least moderately satisfying because Larry continued his "searchin' and screwin,' " as he described his leisure time. One thing that obviously affected his partner choices was the amount of money the woman was making. When he met Sharon Kellner, who had also started her own (realty rental and sales) company, became successful, and at thirty-four—the same age as Larry—was looking for a husband, he shunned her. "She isn't anything special," he said, dismissing her obvious interest in him. "Kind of plain." Larry's comments, voiced after she had asked him to dinner a second time, made it seem as though Sharon's principal drawback was that she wasn't sufficiently photogenic and newsworthy. Since a brief story about her success had already appeared in a business magazine, he clearly meant that she wasn't suitable for the society page, his new focus of interest.

It gave him more of a boost than he realized when one of the women he was dating complimented him on his financial achievements. This, above all, was the measure he had been using of how far he had come. However, it had the unintended effect of limiting his choice of partners to those who didn't have as much money as he did and who, in addition, were impressed by anyone who had more.

LIVING ONE'S FUTURE SELF, NOW

All the subterranean pressures broke to the surface when Larry met Stephanie Phillips at a restaurant opening to which he had been invited by the owner, François. (He had been a frequent patron at François's other place.) Larry arrived with a date but ditched her fast ("You stay busy—circulate—I have to talk to some people") as soon as he was introduced to Stephanie, who had arrived alone.

"I flipped when I caught sight of her," Larry said later. "She was the most perfect human being I've ever seen." She was also very different from any he had been attracted to until then. Larry had always liked women who were a little buxom and had round hips; Stephanie was flat-chested and had no hips. Larry had long liked women who were carefree and openly erotic; Stephanie was austere, and projected, without effort, an image that can best be described as sexless. Social she was, and at this stage of his life that was apparently what Larry lusted for more than another roll in the hay.

Stephanie's long, straight brown hair was held away from her head by a barrette she always wore at the back. From there, her hair spread out and was draped neatly on her shoulders like a mantle. It accentuated a high forehead, straight nose, and clear skin. Instead of a haughty manner, she used a silent stare to accomplish the same thing. While some people who knew her were put off by her lack of responsiveness, Larry's passions were inflamed. "This one," he told us proudly, "has got what it takes. She could go anywhere. Do anything."

Larry got her a drink, some hors d'oeuvres and acted as if he, not François, were the host. Given the amount Larry had already spent at François's old restaurant, and seemed even more likely to spend in the new place, François didn't object. "You must know him very well," Stephanie remarked casually. "It's no exaggeration to say," Larry replied with affected humility, "that I helped make him what he is today." When the two-hour gala was drawing to a close, Larry asked Stephanie out. "Well, I don't know," she answered. Interrupting her before she could give him a definite no, a sales technique he had practiced for so many years that it emerged automatically when needed, he said, "Join me for dinner *here*. It is the very least we can do for poor François." She agreed.

"I left there walking on air," he told us with a smile. As Larry correctly anticipated, their first date was friendly and pleasant. Both talked non-stop, yet the topics revealed not only the size of the gap between them, but also Stephanie's uneasiness about it. The pattern of conversation was a back-and-forth in which, in essence, she would ask, "You don't do that, do you?" and he would reply, "Who, me? No, I don't do any of those mean and nasty things." Instead of using these particular words, what she actually did was tell him on the way to the restaurant about how rude a sales clerk had been to her that day. While they were eating, she continued, "There are an *amazing* number of people who just bang into you in the street. They don't even look where they're going. They are *so* impolite." Larry, reacting as he was supposed to, replied, "Yes, I've noticed that too."

No doubt he had. Often in a hurry, he was "a human bowling ball" at such times, as he described himself, and all the passersby mere pins. "Out of my way, bozo," he would exclaim, as a pedestrain and even more so behind the wheel. Be that as it may, Larry was comfortably able to respond to each of her tales with "It's really appalling, isn't it, that so many people lack common human decency?"

Stephanie's stories of abuse were intended to convey the impression that she was much more refined than anyone she knew, perhaps even her listener. By accepting her message ("It's true, so true"), he could give her the stamp of approval she apparently needed and pin a badge of refinement on himself as well. By dessert, they had tacitly reached the conclusion that they were perhaps the only two truly civilized beings on the planet. Naturally, they agreed to get together again soon. Larry drove home so carefully, "it made me feel like I was part of a funeral procession," he chuckled. "I'm not used to driving that way."

Larry could easily have felt hemmed in by the severe restraints Stephanie imposed on her own behavior and therefore of necessity on his, if he was to be around her for any length of time. Instead, he felt free. In his mind, he had finally arrived. The realist in him might have made him see his own actions as fraudulent, and in some ways he wasn't far from this conclusion. For instance, when describing their first date to us, he commented, "Imagine that! Some son-of-a-bitch banged into her on the sidewalk." Pausing for a moment, he said, "I hope it wasn't anyone *I* know." What he really meant was "Gee, I'm glad I wasn't the guy."

The reason Larry didn't feel like a fake was that he was doing what most ambitious men in his position do: living his "future self" in the present. He was well aware that there was a sizable difference between the persona he was presenting to Stephanie and the person he currently was. However, he had come so far financially—with no one's help—that it was simply inconceivable to him that he couldn't make similar headway socially, especially if he teamed up with an appropriate partner.

Events that he knew nothing about made Stephanie an especially good candidate for the role. While she seemed more straightforward than most, not nearly as devious and dishonest as Larry was at times inclined to be, her past was more complex than she led people to believe. It contained many things she had good reason to hide.

THE "SHABBY GENTILITY" CHARADE

While it was true that Stephanie had gone to a private school and then a good college in New England, the picture of inherited wealth that she continually hinted at rather than boasted about was false.

Stephanie was the oldest of the Phillipses' two children. Friends remembered how snobbish both her parents were. "They were always name-dropping," said one. "You'd have thought they were intimate with the world's royal families." The analogy is a useful one. Henry and Ginny, as everyone called her, might as well have been part of a government in exile. Impoverished aristocrats, with not enough cash to prop up their pretensions, often become parasites who are fed by nouveau-riche climbers wanting to associate with "the real thing." Stephanie's parents tried to adopt a similar role for themselves; but as Stephanie was well aware, the depiction was fragile.

By the time Stephanie and Larry met, her attitudes about work and money were as well formed as if they had been carved in stone. Her "station in life," a phrase she used only once, *entitled* her to a variety of things she didn't yet have. "A cultured woman shouldn't have to work," Stephanie told him near the end of their second date. "It turns her into a groveler, she becomes a slave to her job—even if she is her own boss." Employed at an antique store, Stephanie was surrounded by wealthy people yet had none of their leisure or luxuries. Larry decided that it was up to him to give them to her.

Their third date ended in bed, and as Larry put it, "I nearly climaxed before I entered her." That surprised him because he'd never had a problem in this area before. "She—well, she just lay there. 'I'm not very demonstrative,' she said." From any other lover Larry would have found the sentence totally unacceptable. Once he and a woman were naked, he would do anything and everything to make the session more exciting. By then, he felt, it was time to shelve restraint and concentrate on pleasure. If his partner wanted to be "talked dirty" to or watch a rented porno-graphic videotape with him on his VCR before—or while—they made love, that was fine with him. One bedmate, a waitress, had wanted another woman in bed with them; a second, a nurse, had wanted another man. In both cases he happily obliged. "You can always find the right 'extras,' " he chortled, "if you want them." He didn't simply ask his partners what they wanted. Rather, he attempted to guess, and, during lovemaking, would sometimes suggest things. If he noticed a hint of interest, he followed up on it. Attempting to heighten the intensity of their coupling, until both collapsed after a frenzied climax, was some-thing he did automatically.

Not with Stephanie. Her aversion to exercise ("All those people getting so *sweaty*") and obvious lack of interest in sex, even while it was occur-ring, made his approach more muted. Under ordinary circumstances, that would have left him frustrated. In this case it didn't because he was receiving the bulk of his satisfaction on other occasions, when the two were dressed. The pace of their dating quickened, and they began getting together for dinners during the week. "We go to some pretty fancy joints," Larry said proudly. "I like being with her." What he really meant was that he liked being *seen* with her, for he wasted no time introducing her to any friends they met, something he hadn't done with any previous partner. Sometimes he would take her hand and walk clear across a restaurant to say to business associates, "I'd like you to meet—" Other times, he dragged them to his table to meet her.

While Stephanie was cordial to her family, she deliberately remained aloof from them and had done so for years. On more than one occasion relatives openly labeled her "icy" and "distant." As Stephanie's younger sister Hillary (mischievous, talkative, and six years her junior) later explained to us, "I think she's just sick and tired of their 'shabby gentility' charade." Stephanie had good reason to be. "I'm having trouble paying my rent," she had recently told Hillary. Unable to turn to her parents for financial assistance, and unwilling to spend decades working for the high income, position, and prestige she felt entitled to *now*, Stephanie was forced to fend for herself. Larry in some ways was a godsend, making substantial sums annually and tossing it around, in his own words, "like a drunken sailor."

Still, Stephanie was more than a little concerned about what her friends might say. "He *is* a little different," she told Hillary. "A diamond in the rough, you might say." Hillary, who considered her older sister "a gas bag," replied, "Come off it, he's a hunk." That wasn't particularly important to Stephanie, and the two sisters frequently looked at one man but described what sounded like two different ones. She was torn. A choice had to be made, and soon: get rid of her old friends or find a new boyfriend. Stephanie was prepared to do neither.

The two did get together that Saturday night as previously planned, mainly because Larry wasn't willing to be refused—not unless she explicitly told him to "go away," and perhaps not even then. Persistence had brought him everything he had attained thus far in life and it was nearly inevitable that he'd keep trying, at least for a while. Men who didn't, who instead resented the disdainful treatment they were receiving, rarely ended up marrying women like Stephanie. On the other hand, men like Larry relished the chance it gave them to "*prove* that I'm good enough," as he defiantly described the task he faced. Paradoxically, he considered the challenge elevating rather than demeaning. But then again he was looking beyond the insults to a time when he would emerge victorious, as a full-fledged member of the social elite.

Stephanie's resistance crumbled as her bills mounted. However, even if she had been debt-free and loved working, her desire to live in the elegant style which she felt befitted her would have made Larry's undeniable drive and success appealing. At thirty-one, having waited eight years for Mr. Right, she told Hillary that she was ready to settle for Mr. Rich. Hillary snapped, "You could do worse, fathead. If you get tired of Larry, tell him he can put his shoes under my bed anytime."

PASSING THE POINT OF NO RETURN

Eleven months after they met at François's new restaurant, Larry and Stephanie got married. Always social, Stephanie grew still more so. A much greater number of calls, cards, and visits was exchanged with friends during the next two years than during the previous two. "When I was single," she commented, "get-togethers were catch-as-catch-can, depending on who was around. It's becoming organized. 'Our fifty closest friends,' and all that. They're the regulars." By "fifty" Stephanie actually meant six—three couples that she had liked before but was seeing with greater frequency now.

Larry, on the other hand, grew more sedentary. Always active physically, often frenetically so, he slowed down somewhat and was visibly more at ease. No one was as shocked by this as his old acquaintances and business associates. "I didn't think he'd ever do it," one said, the implication being, "I didn't think he *could*." Earlier in Larry's life, this assessment may have been correct. However, he had consciously set his sights on becoming a millionaire, and with a current net worth of approximately $1.3 million, he was one. Also, he had subconsciously aspired to move up socially, and by marrying Stephanie, he felt he had done so. This double achievement made him noticeably more relaxed.

The pair settled in in a variety of respects, including the manner in which they began to needle one another. Larry happily gave Stephanie plenty of money to spend, to supplement the modest amount she still earned from her job. Nevertheless, he found plenty to criticize about the *way* in which she spent it. An inveterate shopper, Stephanie would indeed buy things on occasion just because she had devoted a number of hours to shopping. If "time is money," a comment she often made flippantly, then she was determined to get something for her time—even if that required her to part with some money. Aware of the underlying irony, she once admitted with a half-hearted grin, "It bothers me to come home empty-handed."

Little purchases, rather than major ones (on which Larry usually accompanied her), precipitated their first fight. When Stephanie came home with a parasol that cost $140, Larry took one look at it and asked, "What do you need *this* for? You have five umbrellas already—and this one is made for sunny days, not rainy ones." Stephanie replied, "I know, but it's cute and nicely decorated, don't you think?" Larry countered with, "You'll never use it, and it's only worth twenty dollars." He would have said the same thing to her even if she had used her own savings to buy it. The purchase seemed merely frivolous to him. Where money was concerned, he was used to speaking his mind.

Where manners were concerned, she was used to doing the same. So instead of answering him just then, when he was holding the parasol as if it were a dead mackerel, she waited. On a cold day that weekend, when they ran into another couple and stopped to chat for a few minutes, Stephanie found the opportunity she was seeking. It was a chilly day, and she and Larry were both wearing gloves. Their noses began to run after they'd been outdoors for a brief period. While the four were standing and talking, Stephanie noticed that Larry casually ran his gloved index finger under his nose, to wipe it. Then, as his hand fell back to his side, he deliberately brushed it against the designer jeans he was wearing.

Once the conversation ended and the couples again went their separate ways, Stephanie lit into him: "Why do you have to embarrass me like that?" Larry was certain that his behavior had been exemplary. "Everything was fine," he responded. "What are you talking about?" She glared at him and said haughtily, "You have a snot stain on the finger of your glove—and *they* saw you put it there." He had made the motion in question so many times before when the weather was cold, the stain was merely widened slightly by what he had done a few minutes ago. Brushing off her angry remark, he said cheerfully, "Well, I think it gives them character. You don't want gloves—or attaché cases—to look like you're wearing them for the first time." Stephanie made a few more comments about his "lack of polish," something she hadn't previously done to his face, but he apparently felt little need to defend himself. In his view, he had done nothing that he hadn't done dozens of times before when she was present; yet, for some reason, she chose this moment to criticize him. He suspected an ulterior motive but didn't know what it was.

Their subsequent quarrels fit nicely into the pattern established by this two-part fight, with round one fought on one day and round two on another. Larry felt on firm ground in money matters and could say with a genuine smile, "You're a financial idiot—beautiful and charming, but a monetary moron." She would counterpunch effectively by using what she considered her strong suit: "You're a slob sometimes, you really are. You have some very boorish ways about you." Since a rejoinder was usually hours or days in coming—and when it did, was about a very different subject—neither was aware of the close connection between their respective thrusts. Even had they been aware, both soon lost sight of *which* insult they were avenging and who it was that had fired the first shot. During the second year of their marriage the two passed the point of no return.

THE PRICE OF BLUE BLOOD

Larry and Stephanie began to comment publicly on one another's weaknesses. The three-step deterioration in their relationship was the same as that seen in most other unhappy marriages we studied.

In stage one: each notices the partner's most glaring weakness but says nothing about it.

In stage two: each says something to the partner about it, in private.

In stage three: each says something to friends about it, usually with the partner present.

Larry and Stephanie got to stage three by the end of their second year of marriage. As we mentioned, most other unhappy couples also do, though it typically takes them a little longer (four years is average for duos with Larry's and Stephanie's background). While the transition from stage one to stage two generally takes years, the movement from stage two to stage three takes place more quickly and can usually be measured in months. The point here is that the pairs may be discontented to begin with—that is what makes them start ridiculing or sniping at their partners in public—but stage-two and, especially, stage-three sniping accelerates the rate of deterioration. It, in and of itself, becomes a corrosive force.

What made Larry and Stephanie's union so fragile? Why should they have been making a special effort *not* to insult so central a characteristic of their spouse, particularly in front of others?

The initial goal of men like Larry may seem strictly financial. "I'm interested in only one thing," such men say emphatically. "Money." Once they've made a fair amount of it, however, their interests change; they want to elevate themselves socially. This was obviously one of their primary goals all along, but until they had become financially secure they considered it premature and perhaps ludicrous to do much about it.

Even before their net worth becomes substantial, there is usually evidence of the men's hidden social ambitions. Adopting a slightly arrogant manner or more "upper-class" (that is, British-sounding) way of speaking doesn't cost anything, except possibly a few friendships. Those who are willing to spend money to project the right image may buy a Cadillac, Porsche, Mercedes, or Rolls. Once they make their fortunes, some men even buy themselves a mansion or luxurious apartment. Then they are shocked to discover that this accomplishes much less than they thought it would. Money alone—no matter how much of it they have—doesn't bring ambitious men the elevated social status to which they also aspire. To the chagrin of some and the delight of others, they learn that they need a wife to make the picture complete.

Larry was startled to see that an unmarried friend of his who had bought a multimillion-dollar triplex co-op and lived there alone was viewed as eccentric, not aristocratic, by the people he wanted most to impress. "Wealthy folks are kind of conservative," Larry concluded after hearing their comments about his friend. He didn't like the conclusion, and it would have bothered him much more had it not been that he intended to get married as soon as he too was wealthy.

His thoughts on the related subjects of money and women weren't nearly as conscious as we've made them sound. For one thing, he didn't have a long-term plan in mind, other than to become rich. Nevertheless, examining a wide variety of cases similar to Larry's allowed us to see how close a connection there was between the men's net worth and their choice of partners. As long as Larry didn't think he had succeeded financially, he paired up with women primarily for sexual purposes. Everyone who knew him figured erotic satisfaction was what he wanted most in life in any event. It soon became clear that *the main reason ambitious men like Larry who are in their thirties and forties have so many bedmates is that they haven't found—or aren't yet ready for—the one woman who they feel is sufficiently elegant.*

Some self-made men do not view themselves as candidates for exalted social position, regardless of how much money they have. The men may feel themselves excluded permanently because of something physical (for instance, they are too short), facial (they are, in their own view, unattractive), or linguistic ("I sound like a gangster," a mode of speech they may have previously cultivated to help them appear more aggressive in business). These men may end up using their money to "wallow in debauchery," as some of them gleefully described it to us, each feeling that if he can't join his social superiors, he will make the riotous best of what *is* available to him.

As long as such a man (Larry included) hasn't yet encountered a woman he considers blue-blooded enough, it is nearly inevitable that he will keep trading in old bedmates for new ones. He wants badly to move up, but, unable to find the woman who makes him feel that he has, he keeps dumping the ones he meets. He seems sexually dissatisfied with the women he knows but is actually dissatisfied with his own social status.

When does the transition occur—that is, how much money does a man typically have to make before his focus shifts from good sex to good breeding?* Our repeated surveys indicate that the answer depends on the city in which he lives: half a million dollars makes men in Boston, Miami, Seattle, Phoenix, Dallas, Denver, Toronto, and Chicago feel wealthy, but it takes a million to produce the same feeling in New York, Washington, D.C., and Los Angeles. It isn't just a matter of numbers; education also plays an important role, affecting how the men view their net worth. We found that those with only a high-school education feel *more* money is necessary before the shift in focus is appropriate, while those with a college degree think *less* is. Men in our sample who have graduated from Harvard, Yale, or Princeton often think *none* is. They feel eligible, even with a zero bank balance, to marry a stylish woman with inherited wealth.

Oddly, obtaining a graduate professional degree in law, medicine, or business administration made the men's outlook more like that of high-

* The shift was easy to spot, since every year we asked each member of our sample first, how much he was earning and his current net worth; second, how did those amounts make him feel; third, which male and/or female companions he would like to be seen with. The men, unprompted, often volunteered information about the third, indicating that the thought was on the minds of many. We avoided asking the three questions in the order presented here, and instead inserted them among other inquiries, to prevent the respondent from thinking that the answers might be linked.

school dropouts: suddenly, a larger sum was unwittingly (little of this was conscious) seen as essential before class could replace cash as their primary goal. Apparently these professions saddle their members with a quite high—and visible—standard of success (expensive office, homes, and cars). This made Ivy League graduates in their twenties and thirties who had also gotten a graduate degree in law, medicine, or business administration among the most confused men we studied: in their minds they were all right "as is" with their college degree alone, yet they still had to make a substantial sum once they had an M.B.A., J.D. (LL.B.), or M.D., lest they be viewed by their peers as professional failures.

Interestingly, our most recent surveys show that the shift toward concern about social status and good breeding is occurring earlier and earlier among young urban professionals. In 1966 the median age of men making the shift was forty-two; in 1976 it was thirty-nine; by 1986 it had dropped to thirty-four. Where picking partners is concerned (and in dozens of other, more obvious respects, such as choosing restaurants, snack foods, and recreations), professionals in each decade are "acting richer" than their peers in the one that preceded it.

Should the figure drop to the late twenties, as it will in the late 1990s if the present rates of decline continue, the emotional strain may well prove sufficient to cause a mass reaction against the trend. After all, at this tender age very few people have the financial wherewithal to prop up the image of social status they are being asked to project, so they may reject it altogether rather than feel like failures. In that case, another "leveling" decade like the 1960s may occur, when people with money aren't supposed to show it, and their children play "poor little rich kid" so as not to embarrass their less affluent friends. Sex, a younger person's game, in which almost anyone, regardless of his or her material assets can participate freely, will return to center stage. Then, with everyone back to square one—and the median age for the shift from the erotic to the social having once again returned to the more manageable, higher-income years of one's early forties—the process of one-upping the past can start over again.

A PEDESTAL FOR THE ELITE

From the start of our study the question we wanted most to answer was: which ambitious men would become successful and still remain happily married? After a while it became clear that there was a public dimension to this question that we hadn't foreseen, particularly where men like Larry were concerned. It wasn't enough that *he* liked a woman, he wanted others—in fact, almost everyone—to feel the same way.

Sad to say, most ambitious Larry-types do what he did. In their early adult years they concentrate on making money, moving up (if they work for someone else), and locating sexually uninhibited bedmates. Then, once they have done well financially, the men subconsciously switch and attempt to find a socially elite woman. Men who make their fortunes early (say, by thirty-one) make the switch early; those who take till their late forties to do well generally make the switch later. However, the vast majority do indeed make the switch. Then, like Larry, they can look back on a time in their lives when they were young and carefree, versus the present period, in which they have shouldered the social obligations that come with the woman of their choice.

Unfortunately, it is precisely this split that causes their marriages to collapse eventually, even if the pair never gets a divorce. The men have painted themselves into a corner. They can't go back to the rollicking good times they had while single—or worse, *wanted* to have but never got a chance to—because they have established a very different life for themselves as a result of their marriage. On the other hand, they can't fully become part of the social elite, regardless of their burning desire to do so, because their wives are the sole judges of which candidates gain admission or are refused.

Who gave the woman this powerful position? Her husband. Far more than he realizes, he has granted her the authority to determine who (including himself) has class and who doesn't. This is no act of charity or generosity on his part. It is essential for him to believe that she can make such a judgment accurately—as a result of her own inner elegance—or else she'd not have been an appropriate choice of partner, given his newly revealed social aspirations.

Some women intuitively recognize how fundamental to the marriage this aspect of the relationship is and therefore each attacks any and every other woman who appears to have as much class as she. That makes her seem quite competitive, and perhaps in many cases she is. However, it is also true that if her husband comes to consider someone else more aristocratic, he may demote his wife as not being "the real thing" and seek to tie up with the other woman.

The frequency with which such tensions arise should come as no surprise. Relationships like Larry and Stephanie's aren't based on love and companionship so much as they represent mutual social climbing. In a private ceremony that is even more important than the actual wedding, each man puts his prospective bride on a pedestal and then insists that she boost him as well. "I'll accept your snooty stance," he in essence says to her, "but only if you'll allow me to look down your nose with you, as an equal."

Stephanie would never have allowed that. Neither did *any* of the more than four hundred women in her position that we studied. They couldn't begin to challenge their husbands on the money-making front and wanted very much to believe the regal picture of themselves they were trying hard to project. So, without exception, they wound up putting down their husbands (not always verbally) as uncouth. That left each man in a terrible bind. *Forced to accept his wife's pretensions in order to validate his own, he also felt compelled to attack her snobbery because it was regularly aimed at him.*

Festive get-togethers with friends often turned into merely another opportunity for the couple to compete quietly in public. For instance, Stephanie had a smile that had taken her years to perfect, one that was deliberately drained of energy and spontaneity. Her rationale for this self-suppression was simple: "Only hyenas laugh loudly and country bumpkins guffaw," she said to Larry, as if lecturing a child. The comment was made without reference to her own smile, but it was apparent that she had no intention of being dethroned as a result of a hearty laugh that slipped from her throat. While she couldn't use Queen Victoria's famous "We are not amused" line and get away with it, she could grin a bit and convey a different version of the same message: "We are only mildly amused." True aristocrats, she felt, had no animal urges.

When a friend of Larry's at whose house they were having dinner told a funny joke, everyone laughed except Stephanie. She merely smiled wanly, to let everyone know that the burdens of royalty prevented her from taking things lightly, though commoners of course could cackle. Wanting her to join in, Larry said, "Admit it, honey, that's a scream."

Then he added, "We all know *you're* human too." Stephanie said nothing, but she was furious. To her the word "human" in this context was little more than an apology for their vulgarity, not an indication of their sensitivity. As Larry later commented, "You'd have thought I'd asked her to drop her pants." That must have coincided with Stephanie's view of the interchange, for after waiting a few minutes she pasted him with, "Well, how would Larry know? He's so lacking in taste." That stung him, since he was well aware that her favorite euphemism for "class," a word she rarely used, was "taste."

Anyone who spent some time with these two from the end of their second year on would have had trouble avoiding the conclusion that the basic emotion they felt for one another was hostility. The attitude conveyed by their words to—and even more so, their remarks about—each other, was contempt. She openly criticized his "crassness," while he began to sound increasingly like her younger sister Hillary, ultimately calling her everything but "gas bag."

"SHE LOOKS LIKE ROYALTY AND MAKES LOVE LIKE A SAVAGE"

During their fifth year of marriage Larry had a fling. The very thing that Stephanie hoped would never happen, did. He met Meredith Weaver, who worked for an ad agency, at a party given by Stephanie's boss, the owner of the antique shop, and, as Larry put it, "fell head over heels in love—this one reeks with chic." He spent as much time talking to her as he could without having Stephanie become openly jealous. What amazed him most about Meredith was that she was more beautiful than Stephanie, and yet she had a sense of humor. Even raucous laughter, the kind Larry liked, didn't seem to her primitive or disgusting. Near the end of the evening he said to her, as if thinking out loud, "I'd love to have my arms around you." Looking at her drink, she replied quietly, "That sounds very nice." Excited at the positive response, Larry said, "But you're married." Looking right at him this time, she replied, "And so, my dear sir, are you." They made plans to meet soon.

He talked to her every day that week on the phone at the office, with Meredith doing most of the calling. Their first lovemaking session took place the following week at the apartment of an unmarried friend of hers.

"She's away for a while and I promised to water her plants," Meredith explained as they entered. "It was *wonderful*," Larry later told us. "She looks like royalty, and makes love like a savage. It's been six years—six years!—since I cut loose like that." Three days later, they met for the second time at the friend's apartment and Larry got the shock of his life.

"We had just finished making love—it was great, again—and suddenly Merry jumped up and said, 'I have to make a phone call.' It was to [an advertising agency client]. I was still in a sensual haze and thought she was too. But she had *business* on her mind. It didn't really matter, I guess. We were already done."

Larry liked the idea that there were women in the business world. He enjoyed seeing and dealing with them. However, he didn't want to be *married* to any who were serious about it. His reason could hardly have been more straightforward. Before she and Larry were legally wed, Stephanie tried to prevent him from meeting any of her friends, fearing that she would be embarrassed. That bothered him much less than we thought it would because, in his words, "I noticed that I was doing the same thing. I didn't want her to see me at work—and never invited her to my office—because I didn't want to end up embarrassed." He explained, at the time, that, "If she thinks I'm uncivilized when her friends are around, she ought to see me when my customers are. We yell, sometimes, and I curse—something she *never* does. And they curse me back. She couldn't stand it."

It turned out that although he would argue with Stephanie when she said at dinner parties that devotion to their professions had demeaned her women friends, making them "grovel and growl to get more money and a promotion," he accepted her basic point of view. "Having a baby without a husband may seem radical and new to my old classmates," Stephanie stated, "but slum mothers have been doing it for decades. It doesn't seem so terrific to me. It's a step *backward* for civilization."

When all is said and done, Larry's view was—and still is—that while business looks glamorous as presented in the glossy pages of a business magazine, it is in fact dirty, endlessly competitive, brings out the worst in people, and causes the majority to feel like failures, even though in many cases they have given it their all year in and year out. He was prepared to do this kind of work—"I was born in the trenches"—but he *also* wanted very much to move up socially. As long as he was the one "shoveling dung all day," in his words, he couldn't be "ritzy," even when the day was over. His wife, therefore, would have to be. He would raise her status financially, and she in return would elevate him socially. "If *she's* working hard too, engrossed in her career," he said, "she becomes more low grade every year, whether she knows it or not." The second sexual encounter was the last for Larry and Meredith.

A SENSE OF UPWARD MOMENTUM

While Larry didn't consciously realize that he was never going to become a member of the social elite, he reacted to his troubled marital life in the same manner as the majority of men in his position do. Unable to make additional forward progress, he resentfully started moving backward and became openly more crass. He had spent decades wanting and trying in essence to be like David, debonair and able to make light chatter endlessly. But when that proved impossible, he became more like David's opposite, Bill. Each year he has found himself sliding a little further toward that end of the spectrum.

There was only one way Larry could have fulfilled most of his social ambitions: to pair up with a woman like Sharon, the real-estate broker, or Meredith, the ad-agency executive. Both had started where he had, were pulling themselves up by their bootstraps, knew how difficult it was, and harbored the same social aspirations as he. They would have understood him, and he, in turn, would have had no trouble seeing who they were and what they really wanted. Companionship, love, and affection could finally have found a central place in Larry's life.

He couldn't have been less interested, and if we are to understand why his personal life turned sour—a distress that continues because Larry and Stephanie have no intention of getting a divorce—we should first look at his business attitudes. As far as he is concerned, the world is divided into winners and losers, those who are destined for stardom and those who will never be "up there." When he hired a talented young salesman (for instance, Don), his unspoken belief was, "I don't have to help you—if you've really got what it takes to make it, you will." Even though he was a father (he and Stephanie had a boy and a girl in the first few years of marriage), there was no picture in Larry's mind of growth and transition—abilities slowly developing and relationships taking time to gel. "Look, either something works or it doesn't," he told us more than once.

The words expressed the impatience of youth, but they were being voiced by a man in his thirties and forties.

It is small wonder that although his company grew, thanks to unceasing effort on Larry's part, it never thrived. "Why can't I make this a *big* business?" he asked, pained at the departure of yet another key employee. The whole idea of *gradually* giving people increasing responsibility at the office, of bringing them along year after year until they came into their own, was out of the question. In his view, either people were fit to run the company *today*, in spite of their inexperience, or they were eliminated forever as candidates for the position.

This pivotal work-related attitude spilled over and poisoned his personal life as well. As we've said before, there are sexually repressed men who see women as falling into two categories, virgins and whores: a woman in the first is all right to marry, while one in the second is acceptable for lusty sex. As was clear from his choice of high-school and college girlfriends, Larry wasn't afflicted by this split.

He suffered instead from a worse one—women fell into polarized social, not sexual, categories: classy and vulgar. Larry felt he could tell in an instant the category in which any woman he met belonged. Short or fat women, for instance, were permanently excluded from being considered elegant and quickly became objects of ridicule. "Now *there's* a class act—her royal obeseness," he would say sarcastically, sometimes loud enough for her to hear. Other women, like Stephanie, struck him as being aristocratic. It didn't once occur to him that this was what she wanted to *become*, not what she already was. However, there was no such thing as a middle category for Larry, so the minute he realized that Sharon and Meredith belonged in neither category, they slipped between the cracks and vanished. Thereafter, they might as well have been vulgar and unacceptable.

There is a towering irony here: marrying a woman he felt was "already there" eventually thwarted Larry's powerful desire to move up socially (since she was boosting herself endlessly at his expense), and ultimately forced him back in the direction from which he had come.

Although Larry started with little and worked his way up in the world, he considered this a highly unusual event. Seeing everyone around him as occupying a static position in a social hierarchy served to increase his sense of upward momentum. It made him feel he was moving so fast, others might as well be a picket fence that turned into a blur as he passed it. His static world view of everyone else also permitted him to believe that he had done the impossible: jumped unaided an abyss as wide as the Grand Canyon. Exaggerating the distance between where he started and where he wound up allowed him to conclude that his achievement was superhuman. No other man or woman could have accomplished the feat, much less done it together with him, arm in arm. In fact, only one person he had known in his entire life could—and did—make this leap: he himself.

BEYOND THE FINISH LINE, ANOTHER

A few statistics may help shine a revealing light on how other men like Larry have handled the same opportunities and setbacks that he faced. Studying more than fourteen hundred Larry-types long term allowed us to see that what at first seems a quirk in one person's makeup is actually a widely shared characteristic of these men. To begin with, the Larrys of the world have the highest divorce rate (64 percent of such men in our sample have been divorced at least once; 21 percent at least twice). They are also the ones most likely to become wealthy (approximately 5 percent—one in twenty—of such men in our sample became millionaires). Are these two events linked? The main reason we've taken such a close look at the life of a representative Larry is to see what the connection might be. As it turns out, instead of one event causing the other, they both spring from the same source. The restless search for instant riches may be what other people notice most about these men, but they themselves have a "hidden agenda," and that is what motivates the restless search in the first place.

Whereas other men, who are equally talented, make a certain amount of money and then slack off or become more cautious and conservative in their financial dealings, these men don't. If wealth were their ultimate goal, they too would probably rest a bit on their laurels once their monetary goals were attained. But that isn't what they do. The interpretation usually offered by such a man's friends and associates—"His greed knows no bounds, and that's the reason he keeps striving to make more, even though he already has plenty"—is flatly contradicted by the evidence we have accumulated.

These men have no real interest in money, only in what it will buy.

Unlike some tightfisted types, who hoard every last dime and would keep it all on display in a giant goldfish bowl in the bedroom if that were safe and didn't seem gauche, the Larrys of the world spend it almost as fast as it comes in. They are in a hurry to become rich, but in their minds money-making isn't the main event. It is merely a preliminary race, one they must win in order to be able to enter the finals in this all-important Olympic games: a race for respect. Unless each survives the "elimination heats," with accumulated wealth as the score, he knows he will be excluded from participating in the main event.

However, since there is no well-defined finish line ("you have a million dollars now, so you can stop running"), he keeps right on going at full speed—always with an eye on the Big Race yet to come. Why, then, do such men become wealthy disproportionately often? Not because they are interested in money, but because they sense that they need a lot of it to be a serious contender in the competition that means most to them. The key conclusion that emerges from our study of such men is that, ironically, the man who pursues money as his number-one goal in life is likely to make less than one who sees wealth as a means to a different goal altogether—a dramatic increase in social status. Although he apparently doesn't realize it, for him no amount of money will be enough, so he never allows himself to stop running.

This is a man who only understands "trading up"—not just where possessions are concerned, but partners as well. Thus the exceptionally high divorce rate.

CHAPTER
•4•

THE CREATIVE
LONER

Men like Larry are easy to study. They talk openly about what happens to them, and since so much that is crucial to them involves other people—who are also willing to talk openly—a complete picture can eventually be obtained. Their action orientation makes the principal events in their lives visible. Finally, they embody the American dream: the passage from rags to riches thanks to courage, cleverness, and hard work.

There are millions of such men, many successful and a much greater number who aren't. They appear larger than life because they know how to call attention to themselves; indeed, they feel compelled to do so. Yet for every Larry-type in our sample, spending his life consciously trying to move from Bill's end of the spectrum to David's, there were two who were heading in the opposite direction—and not consciously aware of it. (Bill and David weren't moving; they were relatively happy right where they were.) That is an extraordinary amount of traffic, and what is more surprising, it is traveling in a direction Americans believe no one would want to go. They have a strong sense of upward and downward, and this seems to them clearly downward.

Those making the journey don't agree. Upward mobility sits at the core of the American dream, but for many people in so affluent a society the dream has already become a reality. They don't have to spend their lives striving to climb into an upper-middle or upper-class stratum. Their parents have already done it for them. Raised in comfortable suburbs; healthy, well fed, and well educated; able to fulfill almost all their material desires (even whimsical ones) at an early age, these youngsters grow up with a different set of goals from the ones Larry yearned to achieve. They are no less ambitious than he and often more so, even though parents, teachers, and acquaintances may think of them as lethargic and unfocused. They themselves may not realize how driven they are.

Everything about them is less obvious and more subtle, as is only to be expected given the white-collar families in which they spend their formative years. What makes these men still more difficult to know is that their work isn't manual, it is mental. Much of what is important to them and occupies the bulk of their day isn't visible to an outsider. There is little to be seen; the real action is internal. Our portrait of them is inevitably more psychological, and frequent comparison of their behavior with that of other men, especially Larry's, makes the unique texture of their experiences more vivid. The main tool people like Steven Cooper, whom we'll meet in a moment, use to get what they want most in life is very different from that employed by the three men we've examined thus far. Bill used his muscles; David, his mouth; Larry, his money; Steven, on the other hand, used his mind.

As a Horatio Alger type, Larry had aspirations that echo widely shared hopes that have been present for decades and even centuries in the United States. Nevertheless, we feel that Steven's life has an importance that is only beginning to be recognized. Stories similar to his are likely to receive greater prominence soon, since people like him will play a pivotal role in determining what kind of economic future, if any, this country has. With an increasing proportion of our manufacturing being moved "offshore"—that is, to foreign, low-wage countries—invention and innovation become more critical each year in the United States. While there will be room for many others to duplicate Larry's success, he was among the first to point out to us the limited base on which it was built.

Watching a stack of boxes being unloaded on his dock, he said, "I'm a distributor—a warehouse—for *other* people's brainstorms."

That wouldn't have been a very satisfying career for Steve. People like him secretly want to be on the firing line, forced to come up with something new and different merely to be taken seriously. And that was where he wound up. For him, as we'll see, it was create or go under financially. As a computer programmer who had founded his own rapidly growing software firm, he knew that as soon as he rested on his laurels he would risk bankruptcy. "I *have* to run scared," he told us at age thirty-six. "Everything moves so fast in this field." Allowing himself to be pleased with a prior accomplishment would, he felt, cause him to slow down. Steve was comfortable with the idea of taking a risk, but this was one chance he didn't intend to take.

Does this kind of pressure (which is only partly self-imposed) affect such men's personal as well as professional lives? Does it make a difference whether the man is an entrepreneur or employee, in a technical field or a novelist or playwright? The answer to the latter question turns out to be no. We found Steven's experiences to be characteristic of the large majority of men with his socioeconomic background who live day to day with the need to come up with something new—on their own— for next season.

RESTLESSNESS AND RICHES

Steven Cooper was raised in the kind of upper-middle-class setting that Larry excitedly looked forward to having for himself one day. However, what other men longed for, Steve took for granted. He watched his parents play, in his words, "Monkey see, monkey do" with their neighbors and found it offensive. "When do people stop trying to keep up with the Joneses?" he said with disgust during his junior year in high school. "They're supposed to be grownups. They sure don't act it." If a neighbor had gone to a fashionable resort, eaten in a fancy restaurant, or bought the latest in consumer electronics, Steve's parents quietly rushed to do the same.

Steve's stance didn't start out being as articulate as it later became. In his preteen years it was based instead on emotion. A bright and temperamental youngster, Steve resented having to sit through long dinners with his parents' "nouveau riche" friends, as they on occasion even described themselves. (That the phrase was self-deprecatory was apparently offset in their minds by the opportunity it gave them to brag about their financial achievements and to say something, with flair, in French.) Steve's restlessness made it nearly impossible for him to "just *sit* there," a phrase his parents repeated endlessly, especially when company was present. However, it wasn't until he was fourteen that Steve began to develop the vocabulary needed to defend his actions openly. "They're all fakes," he would say to his parents. "You don't like them and, you know something, I think they don't like you either," he told his mother, shortly after his sixteenth birthday. She became furious, and replied, "You're looking for trouble, and, boy, you're going to get it." Then, as an afterthought, she added, "Your brother doesn't act this way."

The argument was unlikely to work, since by this time Steve was able to see for himself that his parents and the neighbors were, in his words, "only putting on a show for each other." That his older brother, three years his senior, went along silently with his parents' social aspirations didn't bother Steve one way or the other. "I can't hate him," he said at seventeen. "He's just their pawn." Steve didn't intend to be the same.

The majority of adults (neighbors, teachers, and relatives) who came to know Steve during his teen years echoed his mother's sentiments that he was heading for trouble. It was particularly hard for his mother and father to avoid this conclusion. To begin with, parents often act in a self-consciously well-behaved manner at home in the hope that their children will "do as I say, not as I do," and will copy the best of what the parents present, not the worst. "Not in front of the children," is the message one parent most often sends the other, as a reminder of their "onstage" position when the youngsters are watching. Steve, who wouldn't have liked it even in milder amounts, was therefore reacting to what in this case was a deliberately exaggerated display of good manners, being staged by well-intentioned parents.

Second, their own status goals, and the visible signs of success that come with achieving them, made Steve's parents feel they had a right to be heard. Since they had done so well for themselves materially, they were convinced that their way was the right way for those who wanted to "make it." Any other route seemed to them a detour, and perhaps a dead end.

Most American parents truly want their children to do better than they themselves have done, or do at least as well but with less difficulty and fewer setbacks along the way. To his parents, Steve seemed likely to reverse this trend. The social aspirations they had for themselves were sizable, and, as Steve well knew, the realization of those aspirations depended to some extent on his adopting them as his own. Instead, he kept calling the loud, drinking, and smoking crowd that gathered in the living room on many a Saturday night, before or after going out together, "pretentious."

Steve might have felt more alone than he did had it not been for his uncle Mike. Steve's mother began lecturing him once in front of his relatives at the dinner table about which hand to use for holding his knife and which to use for his fork. "How many times have I told you?" she asked him, although she was looking at the others and shaking her head. "Why don't you leave me alone and let me just eat?" Steve, then fifteen, replied. "You always complain when I *don't* eat." When his mother got up to help his aunt, at whose house they were having dinner, Mike, his aunt's husband, just rolled his eyes skyward and made a conspiratorial grimace. No one else saw him do it. Steve was stunned. Until then, he had always thought of Mike as "one of *them*." Mike was indeed an integral part of their social circle and went along with whatever they did. Yet later, in the living room, Steve's new view of his uncle was confirmed when Mike said, "Your mother is a pain in the neck sometimes." As Steve put it, smiling, nearly three weeks later, "I didn't feel so alone after that."

He felt even less alone once he started dating. Less shy than most of his classmates, because he wasn't as concerned with what others thought of him, Steve had little trouble in high school meeting girls or, when a situation involving one he knew presented itself, in capitalizing on it. "I heard she liked me, so I asked her out," he told us in response to our inquiry about how he started dating a girl named Jane. He had wanted to get closer to her anyway, and as soon as he got word that the interest was mutual, he acted on it.

As his final year in high school began, there was no doubt in his mind that for the first time in his life he was falling in love. It was with Karen, who sat next to him in most of his classes. "I don't know why I never noticed her before," he said a few weeks into his senior year. "Maybe she changed. Maybe I did. It doesn't matter." Six weeks later they made love for the first time. It became approximately a thrice weekly feature of their lives after that, as they started spending afternoons and weekends together. "He wasn't very interested in extracurricular activities," Karen later told us, "except sex." For Steve, alienated from his parents and brother, girlfriends were in fact the only real intimates he had. He looked to them for the kind of companionship he—unlike Larry—wasn't interested in getting from male buddies.

Despite his lack of involvement in high-school athletics, Steve was well liked in school. Former classmates mentioned his wacky sense of humor, an ability to see comedy in quite ordinary situations and an overall good nature. That made him fun to be around and he had plenty of friends, few of them serious athletes. Neither thin nor muscular, his 5 foot 11 inch body was unremarkable in most ways, and he dressed neatly except for an occasional prank. "I loved the looks on their faces," he grinned when telling us at seventeen about the VIVA CASTRO T-shirt he had worn while walking through the living room one evening a few weeks previously, when his parents were entertaining business associates. The girls he dated in high school and, especially, college found him to be an excellent dancer, a talent that netted him as many bedmates as his blue eyes, straight brown hair, and ready smile.

"YOU WON'T MAKE A DIME"

The gap between Steve and his parents widened further when he went to college and subsequently chose English as a major. Steve's father, a manufacturer of office furniture and a self-made millionaire with a personality profile similar to Larry's, considered the choice "moronic" and said so. "You won't make a dime," he told Steve. "You're on your way to the poorhouse. Don't look to me for handouts." The warning was unnecessary. "I'd rather starve," Steve said flatly, "than ask them for *anything.*"

Majoring in English may not have enhanced his future chances of making money, but it gave him an opportunity to do something he wanted even more at this point: to argue. "Literary critics aren't gentle types who just read novels all day," he said in amazement during his junior year. "They're vicious—they attack each other constantly. They may be mousy, but they're *mean*. Cruel." That they were waging war with words, instead of with bullets, pleased him, for it allowed him to throw himself into such frays without hesitation. Afraid of being hurt, Steve had always avoided fist fights in junior high and high school. Here, he wasn't hampered by similar fears. He knew he had at least as much venom as his adversaries, and since all were limited to words ("No one's going to shoot me for what I write about their novel"), he was convinced that he would land far more blows than he received. Steve had found the safe outlet he had unwittingly been seeking for what he called his "spleen."

The blistering reviews of the works he had to write about for term papers might well have gotten him shot. The authors who were his subject all were dead, and hence no threat, and they had attained a stature that wasn't likely to be diminished by the literary assaults of a malicious adolescent, no matter how insightful his papers on Poe, Melville, and Mann.

As much as Steve enjoyed venting his spleen in this way, he eventually got tired of it. Together with a friend, he took a course in computer programming. He found it easy and enjoyable, and, much to his surprise, it made visions of dollar signs dance in his mind. That was an unexpected development because, until his senior year in college, Steve hadn't given so much as a moment's thought to how he would make a living. "Money doesn't matter," he had told us at eighteen, twenty, and twenty-one. "You have to do something you *like*." Others his age in our sample said the same thing in the 1960s but didn't mean it. He did. Fortunately, Steve not only liked programming, he came to love it. And he did so just at the time his appetite for the jugular of novelists and literary critics was decreasing. As we know from studying a variety of similar cases, this was no accident. Steve had found an alternative outlet for his abundant energies and it allowed him to wean himself away from what he was later to label his "rabid-dog days."

Steve sank his teeth into programming problems with the same ferocity he had previously reserved for distinguished figures from the literary world. Here, however, the energy was being used more productively and seemed much more likely to bring him distinction of his own. We say that because, without realizing it, Steve was passing an important test during these years, one that we found usually separates men who go on to be successful from those who continue decade after decade to do poorly.

Steve had long had a problem with restlessness, and the literary attacks he launched while in college only seemed to magnify his impatience rather than relieve it. When he read something with which he disagreed, he would react in an immediate and fiery manner. Rushing to his type-writer, he would dash off a response as quickly as he could. No thought, no period in which he reflected upon what he had read was allowed to intervene, and for good reason. Steve was worried that his written reply would lose its spontaneity and its "bite," as he characterized it; also, in his words, "I am afraid I'll forget what I want to say."

That was a telling admission. Steve was using emotion as his guide (when there was none, he felt directionless), and the intensity of his feelings as a public calling card. If he restrained his assessments, he was concerned that "they would sound just like everybody else's [in the field of literary criticism]." People who try to stand out in this manner rarely do; or else they shine briefly and fade. They may think their hostile diatribes are worth reading, if for no other reason than, as Steve re-marked, "What I write is *alive*." Yet the thoughts he put down on paper rarely had enough depth to warrant serious consideration by anyone other than the teacher who had to mark his paper. "He rambled a lot in his essays," an English professor (who liked him) later told us, "and he was frequently repetitious."

By contrast, when Steve was solving programming problems, he stayed in his chair in front of the computer for lengthy periods that would have been unthinkable for him in the past and would have struck his parents as unbelievable. He was absorbed and didn't notice time passing. Of course, the absorption was more important than merely sitting for hours, since for the first time as an adult he was dwelling on the same problems for days and even weeks on end. They accompanied him wherever he went. In fact, he did some of his best thinking while walking. The fidgeting that had been prominent for many years soon vanished as Steve, in his early twenties, settled into his newfound field. Taking a tranquil-izer might have produced the same effect temporarily, but this was dif-ferent—at last he knew how he wanted to spend the rest of his professional life. Less than 30 percent of the men his age in our sample attained a similarly high degree of occupational self-knowledge.

"YOU'RE NOT WHAT YOU SEEM"

Steve's first job was with a small software-development company. He hated it. "I thought I'd be working alone," he said, visibly irritated, "but they don't want you to do anything here on your own. I'm surprised I don't have to ask permission to blow my nose." Seventeen months after joining the firm, he quit.

His second job was even more frustrating. This time it was dissatisfaction with his boss rather than with the company's team-oriented style that irked him. "There is nothing worse than working for a know-it-all," he told us, more resigned than angry. "When I try to tell him something he should be aware of, he just answers, 'I know.' He *always* says, 'I know.' If I made up a lie and told it to him, I'm sure he'd say, 'I know.' "

Steve finally decided to go into business for himself, and although he would probably have argued the point, he had learned something valuable during the more than six years he spent working for others. The bad taste these periods as an employee had left in his mouth made him inclined to overlook the knowledge he had acquired vicariously about various dimensions of the business—for instance, sales, billing, bookkeeping, and customer relations. Nevertheless, it soon became clear that he was better equipped to deal with such problems in his own company because he had seen how other, profitable firms he had worked for handled them.

Steve had been out of school for five years and dating different women regularly when he first met Carol Jenkins, the woman he ultimately married. They were neighbors, and although the two had never spoken, each had caught the other's eye. Neither had to make the first move, for almost as if it had been arranged in advance, one day when they passed on the street, both said hello simultaneously. "It made me feel good," Carol later told us, smiling. "Steve seemed to me a little standoffish." The next encounter took place that weekend, a hot summer day. "I ran into Steve on my way to the supermarket on Saturday. The sweat was running down our brows. We laughed about it for a few minutes and then went to [a local café] for a cold drink."

Carol was in for a number of surprises with Steve, the first of which hit her when she realized he was anything but standoffish. "You're not what you seem," she finally said to him, once they had cooled off and chatted a while. Steve asked, "Is that good or bad?" Carol unhesitatingly replied, "Oh, it's very good. I thought you were the cold silent type."

As the years passed, it was easy to see why this would have bothered Carol greatly. There sometimes seemed no limit to the number of hours each day she would happily have spent talking with friends—"about anything," she was quick to add, when the subject once arose. She liked her work at a real-estate management company but didn't consider it a career. "This is a job," she said, "a good job. I've had better—and I'm sure I'll have worse." Although the position paid well and she had been promoted a few times, she never viewed it as the most important thing in her life.

Other interests gave her more of an emotional lift, even when she merely thought about them. Her favorite sport was tennis, an activity for which her body appeared designed. There was a sturdiness to her 5 foot 4 inch build, a strength to her stride. Friends at times teased Carol for her purposefulness but were drawn to her directness and open warmth. Her clothes were functional and no-nonsense, as was her haircut—chin length, straight, and shiny. "Brown eyes, brown hair—how plain can you get?" she once groaned, yet most people found her very attractive. They liked her optimistic approach to life as much as the tilt of the brown eyes and the healthy glow in her cheeks.

If opposites attract, the two were a good match. The nearly monomaniacal manner in which Steve pursued the things that interested him stood in stark contrast to Carol's more relaxed style. Her professionalism was a result of experience and intelligence; his was based, above all, on the relentless and determined way he handled tasks. "If I do something at all, I want to do it well," he said, in a disarmingly candid manner. As we'll soon see, others said the same words to cover up what turned out to be a generally procrastinating or slipshod approach to their work. It was a sales pitch, or smokescreen, not an accurate description of their on-the-job performance. Steve, on the other hand, meant it.

Perhaps not surprisingly, it was this profound difference between them that caused the couple's first serious fight. In Carol's apartment house lived a woman named Sandy, who, like Carol, was single and twenty-seven at the time. Sandy was seeing a fellow named Bob, who was essentially her live-in lover. The apartment was hers, but he was there at least five days a week.

Steve and Carol were coming home one Saturday, after having gone to a nearby museum, and they ran into Bob and Sandy who were leaving the building. Carol and Sandy exchanged a few brief pleasantries and then, since neither pair was in a hurry to go anywhere, the four found themselves making small talk. Steve had seen Bob and Sandy but hadn't previously been introduced to them.

Somehow the word "computer" was mentioned and that made Bob launch into a self-congratulatory and long-winded tale about how many such machines there were in his office (a large financial-services firm) and how comfortable he had become with them. Steve could tell that the words were false. Already well on his way to becoming a recognized programming expert, he could gauge how much someone knew about hardware and software simply by listening to the person talk about the subject for ten minutes. Here, he got twenty. Later, to Carol, he commented, "I nearly laughed out loud when Bob the Blowhard said, 'I'm about to become computerized myself.' " (Meaning, he was going to buy a personal computer for his apartment.)

Carol defended them. "They're harmless," she remarked, casually dismissing the encounter. "They're stupid," Steve shot back, unable to let the matter drop. "This guy is a real bullshit artist." That wasn't news to Carol. She didn't think much of Bob either, or of Sandy, for that matter. However, she wanted friends—dozens of them—and that meant having to overlook their flaws. It wasn't a decision she had reached consciously and she had apparently been doing it for years. So, when Steve began scrutinizing Bob and Sandy, Carol found herself almost automatically taking their side.

Steve was puzzled and offended. The woman he thought special, and whom until then he had thought of as bright, suddenly seemed to him a dunce. "How can Carol not see what that blimp bastard is?" he asked us rhetorically. What offended him was that Bob was so caught up in his own self-aggrandizing tale, he hadn't even bothered to ask Steve what he did for a living. "He talks only about himself," Steve later said. "He thinks only about himself." That was doubly offensive in this case because it resulted in Bob making a fool of himself, without realizing it. Steve wanted him to know it; in fact, wanted to "rub his face in it."

A PRISONER OF HIS OWN POLITENESS

The fight was soon forgotten. Months passed; Steve and Carol became inseparable and finally got married. However, since similar arguments could easily recur about anyone else they knew, Carol became a bit tense whenever the mere prospect of a social encounter arose. Four months after their wedding, she offered an interesting explanation for her tension. "Steve sees through people," she said, trying to sound casual. "He's very sharp." Almost as an afterthought, she commented, "He can't help seeing them for what they really are." She viewed herself simply as "more tolerant than Steve—*and* my friends," she added diplomatically. "I'm more forgiving."

No doubt that was so. However, the very braininess of Steve which she had found so appealing at first was now emerging as a threat to the vigorous social life that Carol also wanted. In essence, she had a snarling Doberman on a leash and wasn't sure she could hold on to it if the wrong person crossed their path. The key point here is that *her tendency to side with acquaintances, in order to preserve her social life, served mainly to magnify Steve's tendency to snarl.* He felt abandoned and alone, and, as odd man out, stated his case even more strongly than he had moments before. Ironically, the slightest hint that she agreed with him—and she did—would have quieted his criticism. As things stood, he felt compelled to open her eyes. Arguing and explaining, sometimes for hours, he tried hard to do just that.

The two loved each other deeply, and that allowed them to spend long periods together without the company of other couples to entertain or distract them. Steve's "X-ray vision," as Carol called it, therefore only rarely forced her to see acquaintances "for what they really were." Once she had, though, she was no longer able to socialize happily with them. For better or worse, she sensed subconsciously that her blissful and self-imposed ignorance needed to be left intact where neighbors, co-workers, and "old friends" were concerned.

When Carol wanted additional company—for instance, "to hear the latest dirt"—she would make lunch dates with girlfriends. That was safe, for them. (Steve worked on the other side of town.) To further safeguard them, she usually neglected to mention the get-togethers to Steve that evening at home. If she did, their importance was downplayed ("Oh, it's just someone to kill time with while I'm stuffing my face," or "You can't get served at lunch in midtown restaurants by yourself"). In an equally subconscious manner, Steve was doing his part to keep peace between them. He made few remarks to Carol about any of her friends or co-workers whom they encountered by chance. "It upsets her when I do," he said, shrugging his shoulders, "so I don't." In the first two years of their marriage the change in him was dramatic; Steve would now remain silent and smile a little even with people he held in pretty low regard. "It doesn't matter," he said in an uncharacteristically philosophical manner. "They're her friends, not mine. I don't have to live with them."

The comment seemed to indicate a growing social maturity, but it had larger implications: Steve was learning to be more tolerant of the weaknesses of others. As we'll see, this is an important topic when analyzing the reasons for the successes and failures of ambitious men.

Steve is of special interest to us not only because there are so many men like him, but also because, as we mentioned at the beginning of the chapter, he was heading in a direction opposite to Larry's. While Steve was raised in an affluent and social setting, thanks to his indifference toward money, he had lived in modest circumstances as an adult. It didn't bother him very much ("I have all the material comforts I need"). He was in many ways the middle-class son of upper-middle-class parents. Larry, on the other hand, got many things that his parents denied themselves. They couldn't afford much, but what they could, they wanted their children to have and enjoy. He was in essence the middle-class son of lower-middle-class parents.

The difference between the two men didn't stop there. Psychological as well as socioeconomic contrasts were readily visible. Larry was the more outgoing of the two, a characteristic that became increasingly prominent as the years passed. We can better understand what happened to Larry and Steve's respective business and private lives by looking closely at how they handled simple events, such as a phone call with someone else present. This is a trickier situation than it seems and, sad to say, many people handle it poorly. They don't know which person should receive priority: the one physically present or the one there in voice only.

Larry never felt it necessary to make such a choice. If he was talking to us or anyone else in his office or home and the phone rang, he would merely reach for it and start talking. Then, to show that he hadn't switched his attention from us to the caller, he would make gestures intended to make us feel included. For instance, he would say something about himself to the caller, such as "You *know* how I am about stuff like that," and then wink conspicuously at us. At such moments he might as well have been an actor who, in the midst of a scene, suddenly turns to the audience and gives it a blatant sign that *he* knows they are there, even if the others on stage didn't.

Larry loved situations such as these because they made him the center of attention. They also enabled him to be in control of both conversations simultaneously, since he alone could determine which listener was to be the recipient of his next sentence. So easily and often did he switch from the person present to the one on the phone that he could regularly be heard to say, "No, no, not you; I was talking to Jack, here."

It was equally revealing to see what happened when the shoe was on the other foot, and the people Larry was talking to in *their* offices or homes received a phone call. After listening to a few sentences, he would attempt to guess the name of the caller and the nature of the call. Whether he had or not, he would then blithely barge in by asking the person present, "Is that so-and-so on the phone?" If it was someone he knew even vaguely, he would leapfrog the person present and address a remark to the caller. He might say, laughingly, "Tell him I think he's all wet." The words seemed to be addressed to the person in the room with him, yet they were always said loudly enough so that the caller could hear them too. Larry considered his behavior "natural and friendly," though many viewed it as boorish and intrusive.

By contrast, when a visitor was in Steve's office and a phone call came, he would try to shut out the person present by looking down, putting his hand to his forehead and using it as a visor. That made Steve appear to be addressing the blotter on his desk. Forcing himself to forget the visitor made Steve's comments to the caller come out with a nearly exaggerated intensity. Humor was out. Larry reveled in the idea of putting on a show for his guest and caller simultaneously. Steve bent over backward to focus on one or the other, but not both at the same time.

He would apologize to the people present before taking the call, and would do so again after hanging up. It would never have occurred to Larry to do the same. He didn't feel there was anything to apologize for, since he hadn't excluded anyone. In his view, he always generously included in his telephone discussions anyone and everyone who happened to be there when a call arrived, even going so far as to use them as topics of conversation as though they weren't present. The more people who were within earshot, the more ebullient Larry—and the more serious Steve—became when talking on the phone.

If we had any doubts about how Steve was inclined to react, they were erased when we saw how he behaved in someone else's office when the person received a call. It made Steve visibly uncomfortable. He didn't want to be there at that moment, and usually asked, almost in a whisper, "Should I leave?" Since the person typically replied no, Steve was stuck, an immobilized victim of his own politeness. On one occasion he had to go to the bathroom but dutifully waited more than ten minutes till the call was through to blurt out, "I've got to take a leak. Is there a men's room nearby?"

AMBITIOUS BUT EASILY THWARTED

These differences were part of a larger pattern that had a profound effect on Steve's and Larry's lives. Their business styles were as different as their behavior on the phone. Larry manufactured nothing, whereas Steve spent morning, noon, and night trying to come up with something new—and commercial. "All crackerjack young programmers think they can improve on someone else's word-processing or spreadsheet [financial planning] program," he said thoughtfully. "Maybe they can. The big question is: can they do it in a way that makes customers pant for the product? In this field, marketing alone won't do it. It really has to be a *better* mousetrap."

While both men gave the appearance of merely being dragged along by the pressing needs of their respective occupations, they had fashioned for themselves the setting they each inhabited. Neither could have traded places with the other. Larry's business was based primarily on sales and marketing—or "hustle and hype," as he often called it—while Steve's was based primarily on creativity.

On a day-to-day level that made Steve's life a lonelier one than Larry's. Although both were married, it was much easier for Larry to discuss with others what he had done, say, that afternoon. People who dropped in could even watch him signing for and receiving boxes of merchandise, moving them around, unwrapping samples to show to current and prospective customers, all the while talking nonstop to any onlookers present. Steve's day was almost silent by comparison. The things he was moving around were in the computer's memory and his own. He could show them to others, but not many. They would have needed to know as much about programming as he, and even then the explanation would have been lengthy. He spent his time solitarily solving problems and finally came to terms with the fact that that is how things would have to be—at least for the time being—if he was to come up with something truly original.

Even more striking than the differences between Steve's and Larry's typical day was their respective behavior as bosses. Larry was visibly in charge and didn't mind telling someone to "do this, do that." Even when he was at his most dictatorial, the people who worked for him seemed not to mind. They knew that much of it was playacting. Oddly, Larry's openly acknowledged willingness to say anything to close a sale made his employees realize that he was merely trying to sound impressive when he barked an order. His basic insincerity made his bossiness more bearable.

Steve, on the other hand, treated everyone as an individual. That sounds good, and many top managers attempt to live by this ideal. However, an executive who takes this guideline too literally—as Steve did— becomes nearly incapacitated. He felt compelled on a Monday to ask his bookkeeper, Beatrice, how her family was and how her weekend had been before requesting that she send a customer a bill or record a payment. Since something had always gone wrong at Bea's home ("Dennis has a toothache," she said, "and the paint on the ceiling of the garage is peeling and falling on my car"), it could take fifteen minutes for him to complete a task that Larry got done in fifteen seconds. Sometimes Steve never got around to making his request at all.

At first glance that made him seem similar to David, who often found himself in such situations. Nevertheless, the two were a study in subtle but important contrasts. Unlike David, Steve listened, yet didn't really want to hear *or* help. He always had a purpose in mind in talking to someone—no idle chatter for him—and if the person's problems prevented Steve from accomplishing his goal just then, he would wait. Nodding his head, going through the motions of empathizing with the person's plight, he would walk away at the earliest opportunity and try again soon to accomplish his original aim. It was a strange combination, one we were surprised to encounter so frequently in bright, ambitious men: Steve was a driven individual who was easily thwarted.

This is less of a contradiction than it appears since his driven state acted in a long-term and general manner, whereas his ability to be thwarted operated on a more immediate, minute-to-minute plane. In fact, each minor setback merely increased his determination to get where he ultimately wanted to go. Other people in our sample who ran into similar roadblocks often became furious, subconsciously sensing that if they didn't hurdle the obstacle right then and there they might not be sufficiently motivated later to launch another attempt. Although Steve seemed in some ways like an "executive wimp," as a subordinate labeled him, he could afford to give in to such minor hindrances more readily than most precisely because he knew he *would* try again, and again, if need be, until his initial goal was attained.

This approach meshed neatly with another attitude that set Larry and Steve decisively apart: the all-important question of loyalty, a topic that had a major effect on the men's businesses and marriages. Larry never hesitated to make someone an ally—or enemy—if that suited his purposes at the moment. A few minutes later, especially if the goal had already been achieved, he might quickly reclassify the person as the opposite.

Steve never did this, and in fact had considerable difficulty merely switching his attention from one person's needs to another's. The demands a customer or co-worker made upon him—just by standing there—consumed him. Bouncing back and forth between two people's problems, a situation Larry loved, was a real strain for Steve.

JUSTIFYING A SPLURGE

Shopping was one of the many daily activities on which our researchers accompanied the men they were interviewing. In analyzing their comments, we found the details to contain some very revealing information about the four men. Describing their shopping styles provides us with a magnifying glass, an ability to focus on more than the surface visible at a casual glance. If one substitutes the sales staff and their relationship with the four men for the world at large, a clear picture emerges of the men's central drives.

When Bill entered a store, he would go straight to the merchandise that interested him. If he couldn't find it, he would wander around and, as a last resort, ask a clerk for help. What was distinctive in his case was that, as far as he was concerned, the sales staff might as well have been a bunch of wooden Indians standing around with signs pointing customers in the right direction. His response to them emotionally wouldn't have been less if they had actually been inanimate. There were rare exceptions (he met his future wife when he went to buy some shirts), but his general attitude was, as he once put it, "I'm not there to entertain them. I go about my business."

David was the reverse. From the moment he entered a store until the time he left, what he responded to most was the salespeople, not the merchandise. A careful shopper, at least in his own mind, David was certain that he was devoting his energies to scrutinizing the shop's wares. His reactions, however, told another story. The salespeople might as well have been muggers waiting in hiding. For David tensed up when he saw them and grappled emotionally with each one once the person began asking him questions. To say that he was "trying to gain their approval" doesn't do justice to the situation.

Nervously, and using his fine sense of humor to break with banter the tension in the air, David would visualize his every move from *their* perspective. He assumed they were watching him even when they weren't. Like a jet approaching an airport for a landing, he was highly alert to any messages they might be sending his way so that he might better guide himself and avoid a catastrophe.

Larry, too, responded emotionally to the sales staff and was aware of their presence, even if he spoke to none of its members while in the store. However, he was able more calmly to focus on the goods being displayed; not as much as Bill could but substantially more than David did. While Larry too may be said to have been seeking the approval of the salespeople when he shopped, it would be more accurate to say that he wanted to *impress*—whereas David wanted to *please*—its members. (We will return later to this important distinction.)

Finally, Steve fit somewhere in between Bill and Larry. He was certainly more aware of the salespeople than Bill was yet had less trouble focusing clearheadedly on the merchandise when a salesperson was present than Larry did. Nevertheless, it is fair to say that Steve was inclined neither to impress nor please the sales staff. He wanted to be left alone to do his shopping as he saw fit. His basic reaction toward salespeople while in the store was resentment. Steve didn't want their assistance, aware that it might color his judgment inappropriately. If he did need it, he became very much on guard while a salesperson was addressing him.

As the four described their attitudes in casual conversation (that is, without our explicitly asking them how they generally responded to salespeople), Bill's was, "I don't care what they think." David said, "I want them to like me." Larry: "I like to leave them wowed." And Steve: "I want to make up my *own* mind."

The financial consequences of these attitudes were readily and regularly to be seen. Bill wasn't bothered in the least when he took up a salesperson's time and bought nothing. He purchased only what he needed. The same can't be said of David or Larry; they bought more than they really wanted to—in Larry's case, much more (though he shopped less often than David). Steve, on the other hand, usually bought less than he had planned to. On a number of occasions he deliberately walked out of a store without buying anything, just to assure himself that he wasn't being pushed. When walking, he would often wonder when he was going to allow himself to "splurge" and buy some of the things he needed; Larry and, especially, David spent a similar amount of time—trying to justify to themselves the items on which they had already splurged.

Summing up, Bill wanted to live a private and quiet life unless he was with his friends, which made him switch to a much more raucous and fun-loving mentality. David wanted his years to be social and outgoing, pleasant and civilized, and for the most part they were. Larry was trying to make the transition from Bill's end of the spectrum to David's, because he wanted the world to show him "the respect" he felt he had earned for boosting himself by his bootstraps. More than anything, he expected his money to buy him "class." Steve was heading in the reverse direction and clearly didn't realize it. Bright as he was, it never occurred to Steve that his most pressing long-term goal was to become secure enough professionally to be able to tell the world to "go to hell."

WORDS AS WEAPONS

Steve isn't the only ambitious man who secretly harbors this hope—and is doing himself great harm in the process. The maverick is present in every society, but nowhere is he more respected than in the United States. Whether his actions are antisocial or for the public good doesn't even make a difference in most cases. The audience admires him for taking a stand against that of the crowd, and for distinguishing himself in the process. What is truly remarkable is that most Americans believe they too are doing so daily, and are therefore unique. Put ten Stevens in a room and they will all proudly state that they are the lone contrarian: theirs is the only opinion that is the reverse of what "all the others think." Many Americans want to know what the consensus view is so that they can take a diametrically opposite position in public.

Steve did this without even thinking about it. Adolescence never ended for him; in fact, it couldn't. His line of work had institutionalized it. By demanding that he come up with something new, it made him continually try to reject the old. We doubt that this was truly the best way for him to come up with something original, but it was indeed the way he was inclined to react—both on the job and at home.

Even with all the subtle encouragement given to creative people in the United States to act in such a manner—be they artists, musicians, writers, scientists, or designers—there must be more to this approach to life than meets the eye. For it soon comes to dominate the person's every important action and reaction. Steve would often recoil from a comment someone else had made as if the words were a spear, capable of wounding him fatally. Anthropologists tell us that primitives were afraid of curses their neighbors hurled at them, and that that was one of the main reasons they turned to magic—namely, to help ward off the possibility of a "voodoo death" as a consequence of someone else's words of anger aimed at them.

Paradoxically, our study indicates that people have become *more* frightened of such an outcome, not less, as the United States has become an increasingly services-oriented instead of goods-producing economy. Embedded more each year in a sea of words and images, people see these as possessing all the power they ever did—and then some. The advance of civilization has heightened each person's vulnerability to damage from intangibles, since, in a world of services, reputation counts as much as physical strength used to when producing products occupied most people's days. Apparently, that was easier on them psychologically in some ways, though harder physically, because at least they knew where they stood. They could see with their own eyes how productive they had been. They had an undeniable physical measure of their own output, one that didn't require someone else's interpretation to validate.

Another factor making people jumpy besides their dependence on something as fragile as a reputation is the market-oriented world in which they live. Inundated by advertisements, moderns are continually being sold one thing or another. Whatever else television is, it represents one of the most effective marketing mediums ever invented. Newspapers, too, bombard readers with messages to buy. It has always struck us as extraordinary that so many TV viewers and newspaper readers in our sample claim to be able to "look past" the ads that take up more space on the page than the news and almost as much time as the TV program itself. We don't believe their claim, for we found that even if one particular ad doesn't propel them to their nearest dealer for a product, the sheer weight of repetition does indeed make itself felt in a variety of subtle ways.

In short, a consumer society eventually converts most of its bright and educated members into silent resisters, people who know how to dig in their heels and not respond to the seductive ads that surround them. This stance brings them much closer to that held by creative artists and scientists than has previously been recognized. Instead of hastily cheering this seemingly uplifting overlap between the views of innovators and ordinary people, let us look at it more closely.

Someone like Steve, who decides to devote his life to coming up with something new, starts his career with a heightened inclination to resist his environment. This is the legacy he brings to his creative efforts, even if he never succeeds in creating anything. Without realizing it, he awakens each morning with a chronically high level of cynicism about most of what he will hear in the next sixteen hours. If he is also to be an innovator, he feels compelled to take the next step. The result is that he ends up dismissing instantly just about everything he hears others say.

In surveying the men in our sample more than 26 percent felt that creativity was their "true inner self" and was highly vulnerable to intrusion from a "coarse and superficial" outside world, one that could easily sever the tie with their "spring of truth." Only by concentrating in solitude could they continue to mine this precious vein and keep it from being soiled by someone else's ideas. For the Steves of the world, using other people's concepts meant becoming a "hack," a word many used to describe anyone who compromised too much.

Where, then, is the danger? In overreacting. *The creative man often becomes afraid of every strong image he sees and sound he hears. After all, they might influence him, and he badly wants to come up with something on his own.* Soon he is spending more time running than working, fending off the world's many intrusions.

Or, should we say, trying to. It isn't as easy as it sounds. Even as a teenager, Steve was essentially a raw nerve; his choice of profession made that state a permanent one, rather than a condition that would slowly decrease as he became better over the years at insulating himself. He reacted emotionally to his parents' efforts to sell him on a particular way of life and then, after leaving their home, found himself exposed to the full force of the commercial messages and pop stereotypes aimed at him each day by the world.

To some extent he knew that he had a battle on his hands that wasn't even connected with his work, though it might—and eventually did— harm it. "How did people ever watch TV *before* these gadgets were invented?" he asked jovially, holding up a remote-control unit with a "mute" button. "I don't know what *any* of these commercials sound like. I turn them off the minute they start."

CREATIVITY AND OUTSIDE INFLUENCES

Would he be able to do the same with the people who worked for him? Larry, we knew, was alienating his own employees by giving them an enormous abyss to hurdle. Since none could, he felt perfectly justified in taking potshots at them—"for letting me down"—whenever he was in the mood. Steve was unwittingly creating a similar bed of nails for himself for a different reason. The people around him might as well have been itching powder. He wanted them there because he needed them, yet their very presence irritated him, since he couldn't help but take them seriously.

To prevent himself from doing so, he gunned them down verbally (mostly in his own mind), as if he were still doing a term paper in college. Unlike Larry, who did this jovially, since he felt so distant from them to begin with, Steve did it with real ferocity. They became a part of him just by being there—and remained that way long after they had left. Expelling them from his emotions and trying again to focus calmly on his work consumed an inordinate amount of his time. Whereas Larry's wrestling matches were out in the open, visible to others, Steve's were internal civil wars, fought in his inner depths. For that reason they sometimes went on for weeks without the people involved even knowing about the battle.

What *did* come out was tension and a visible desire on Steve's part to be in control. People who worked for him called Steve "meticulous" and "demanding," but they also recognized that there was something boyish and innocent about his approach to things. Each time he did something, it might as well have been his first. The enthusiasm was still there, and so was a hint of uncertainty. Not everyone was thrilled by the inherent looseness of this approach. "He talks a lot about getting it exactly right," a co-worker told us about a project he and Steve were working on. "But *he's* the only one who knows what that means. Steve isn't a 'procedures man,' someone who sets rules that he and his staff can live by. He's always *inventing* the rules—and then expects everyone to follow them, until he issues the next batch."

Presented with such opinions, Steve would have argued that there was no other way for him to be productive. "I have to stay flexible," he remarked more than once, "since I never know what I'll run across." That sounds fine, yet Steve's fear that his work would be "just like everybody else's" if he allowed himself to relax, a comment he had also voiced in college, was making him lash out at the views of others instead of sifting through them for any useful nuggets they might contain.

At the core of Steve's problem is the belief that true creativity springs from a deep inner source, influenced by nothing and no one. Unless an idea is solely his, it is contaminated and worthless. He aims a barrage of criticism at potential rivals and external sources of influence, no matter how remote, using an argument that couldn't be simpler: they aren't as pure and full of integrity as he.

As we'll later see, this view naturally spills over and has a major impact on the personal lives of men like Steve. Since each envisions creating as a solitary task, one that must at all times be done alone, he cannot allow his wife or friends to intrude. Vague answers, given reluctantly, are all that is permissible in response to any questions they ask him about his work, since even a casual remark might be responsible for triggering an important thought.

What is profoundly disturbing about these beliefs and the hostile habits they generate is that they produce failure on both fronts, on the job and off. The fact remains that creativity can and does coexist with numerous outside influences, not all of them consciously noticed. Because Steve was concentrating so intently on being "pure," each aspect of his work was taking longer to complete, was exhausting him repeatedly, and often failed even to meet the needs of the customer—who, naturally, had also been excluded.

DIRTYING ONE'S HANDS FOR A GOOD CAUSE

Steve didn't invent this set of beliefs. He couldn't have; it was shared by many other people in our sample, not all of whom were doing creative work for a living. Where, then, did it originate and why is it clung to with such tenacity, in spite of the obvious damage it does its more active proponents?

Two seemingly plain words that men like Steve use in defending their approach—"purity" and "contamination"—are at the heart of the matter. As we've seen, Larry divided people into those who were "vulgar" and those with "class." A similar split was plaguing Steve's life. This time, instead of being social, the split was financial. People who handled money were "vulgar"—the same word Larry used but with a different meaning here—and people who concerned themselves above all with creativity were "pure." In prior eras they might have been called "spiritual" or "artists." Whatever they were called, Steve had no doubt which category he wanted to belong in.

Instead of turning the clock back many centuries and attempting to find the first glimmerings of this view, let us look at the past quarter of a century. During this period people themselves have been telling us, starting in many cases from the time they were teenagers, how it came to occupy so pivotal a place in their lives.

In the 1950s and especially in the 1960s it was commonly assumed that it was best to shield creative types from the rigors of the financial world. They should be free to labor away, blissfully indifferent to the economic pressures to which others were subject. "Their imaginations and insights should be their only goal, not commercial considerations," was a view with which nearly 53 percent of the 1,000 executives we surveyed in 1958–1959 agreed. By 1963, 67 percent of a comparable group felt the same way, and by 1968 more than 74 percent of the top managers surveyed held this view. What was the basis for their position? The argument offered by the majority was that "being concerned about money

is too constricting if you're trying to come up with something original."
Who, we asked, would worry about the needs of the end-user, the people
who were supposed to enthusiastically embrace the product once it was
available? The answer, in essence, was "protectors"—individuals who
were by definition dirty, for they dealt with money and the marketplace.

This was a neat arrangement for both sides, a division of labor in each
firm that the business world found believable and effective. Creative types
could envision themselves as pure, while viewing purveyors of their products as irretrievably crass. Those doing the purveying didn't mind such
descriptions (which they rarely got to hear), since they too had a highly
self-complimentary picture of themselves. While someone watching them
at work might say they were involved merely in selecting, shaping, marketing, packaging, and promoting the works of the creative—crucial parts
of the process, to be sure—they had a more flattering way of interpreting
their own daily activities. They were guardians of the innocent, captains
of commerce, and benefactors of mankind, thanks to what they knew to
be the spiritual purity of the products they were selling. If they were
dirtying their hands, at least it was for a good cause.

Between 1969 and 1987 this arrangement quietly collapsed. In field
after field, one profession after another, the division of labor stopped
being workable. An era of soaring inflation, expenses that weren't being
recouped, growing competition at all levels (local, national, and inter-
national), and the high and rapidly increasing cost involved in launching
a new product nationally all undermined it. Unaware of the radical
transformation that was taking place, each side unwittingly took steps that
only accelerated its pace. The centuries-old compact, filled with hostility
though it had been, caused each side to complain openly throughout the
1970s and 1980s that the other no longer understood its needs.

Scientists and engineers, artists and architects, writers and designers
were slowly engulfed by the developing trend, yet remained unaware of
its scope. Most clung to the old view, believing that their detested sponsor
was merely experiencing a temporary shortage of funds and that, once the
economy rebounded, things would revert to the way they had been during the 1950s and 1960s.

However, it wasn't only balance sheets that changed; so did attitudes.
Although there were periods of prosperity during these eighteen years, the
jarring recessions of 1970–1971, 1973–1975, 1980, and 1982 were chill-
ing reminders that change was needed. Even during good times, man-

agers didn't revert to their former approach. The main reason workers everywhere were prevented from realizing what was happening to them was that different industries were affected at different times. For instance, physicists and engineers were affected early in the eighteen-year period, architects in the middle, and writers, apparel and graphic designers closer to the end, with the years 1980–1983 a time of brutal awakening. The old way was a conspicuous failure. Mass firings in 1986, this time of middle managers (frequently as a result of a merger or acquisition), accelerated the trend.

The best index of the trend's progress could be seen in an area that at first glance doesn't appear related: the number and also the kind of malpractice suits filed against physicians. Nevertheless, the very same pressures were at work here. Instead of taking Larry's view of the matter (that doctors were losing their social status), it is more illuminating to use Steve's perspective on the world. When all is said and done, medicine has always been an art form as well as a science. The audience for this group of artists—namely, patients—were supposed to see its practitioners as spiritual and not particularly interested in money. (It worked; that doctors often became wealthy was widely considered a serendipitous byproduct of membership in the profession.) As the split between the sacred and the profane generally disappeared during the 1970s and 1980s, the public stopped seeing doctors as sacred and themselves as profane.

Many patients told us they were filing suit mainly because "I can make a bundle if I win." For the first time, the majority of people in our sample commonly spoke about "the *business* of medicine." The public's mood had become more aggressive and even punitive toward this previously protected group, with seven-figure damage claims being filed regularly.

In short, the sweetly simplistic historical division of labor into the innocent and the corrupt, depending upon who handles the money, has crumbled. The insulation has been stripped away, exposing creative types to the same cost-consciousness the purveyors of their products must live with daily. A key finding emerged from our study: those who came to terms with the new reality—and, like Steve, learned how to express their individuality in spite of it—were significantly more likely to become successful innovators. On the other hand, those who have taken an uncompromising stand, and feel that their artistic ideals allow no concessions to the world of commerce, have fared poorly. Where have they gone? Sometimes into business for themselves. There, they can have the

prestige of saying, "I own my own company now," without having anyone know that, in most cases, they are booking very little business. As a
result, there has been an explosion of entrepreneurial activity in the
United States, with more than 600,000 new firms founded annually in
recent years. While in many instances that is indeed something to cheer
about, the glowing publicity is serving to mask the unhappy reality experienced by millions of idealistic men.

The toll in chronic frustration and lost earnings has been huge, for
although the business setting in which they labor has changed, their
views—shaped during adolescence—have not. The irony is that they
were convinced that becoming self-employed would free them forever
from their mercenary colleagues, especially those in marketing and sales.
"I'm no one's pawn anymore," said Andrew, a friend of Steve's who left
the same time he did, also to go into his own business. "Now I can create
anything I please."

That he can, but more than ever the crucial question becomes: "Can
he sell it?" If he can't, it is unlikely that anyone else will. Whether he
recognizes it or not, ridding himself of the firm's sales force has forced
him to become his own. Instead of liberating him to do as he pleases
creatively, his time must now be divided between creation and sales—
with a growing emphasis on the latter. For, like most creative people, he
feels less inspired when he is unable to move the sizable backlog he has
already created.

RUNNING OUT OF TIME

Although Steve handled the problem better than most men with his
aspirations, it still consumed him. While Larry happily sold anything—
including himself—Steve resented doing so. He did it anyway, mainly
because he believed so strongly in the quality of his own work. It didn't
happen often in the beginning, but others eventually found his enthusiasm contagious. "Leave me a copy of your program," one data-processing
manager at an aerospace company told him, "and we'll see if it flies."
Steve did so reluctantly. He didn't mind giving potential customers a
demonstration of what his programs could accomplish. However, the
idea of leaving his work in someone else's hands made him uneasy for
days afterward. Afflicted by the mild paranoia that is apparently a part of

every creative person's makeup, he asked his wife, Carol, repeatedly, "What happens if they steal my stuff, make a copy for themselves, and then say, 'Thanks, we don't want it.' How would I even know they *did* that?" Carol humored him, confident that the deception would eventually come to light ("probably when they need his help," she said with a smile) or that another customer would be more receptive.

Steve's worst fears never materialized. The aerospace company happily bought his program and then hired his firm to do a substantial body of custom work for them. A few weeks later, two days before Steve's thirty-seventh birthday, another company also responded positively to an offer Steve had made to do some work they needed done in a hurry. "It has to do with a LAN [local area network] they are installing," he said cheerfully. "The kind of stuff I like to do best."

The sizable contracts Steve suddenly landed had the same effect on him as any undeniable success does on the majority of people his age trying to come up with something new: they made him *less* unyielding, more willing to meet the world halfway. When we offhandedly asked Steve's former customers why they hadn't renewed their consulting contracts with him, their replies spoke volumes. Said one, "He stubbornly resisted making *any* of the major modifications we needed. Finally, we told him, 'Let's call it quits.' " Said a second, "He's a very pigheaded guy—wants everything done as he sees fit."

There are adolescent adults who haven't yet been in their fields long enough to have a preferred way to handle most work-related matters. So they wait till someone else takes a stand, and then, to help make a name for themselves, they take the opposite position. That wasn't what Steve was doing. Instead of contradicting others automatically, he insisted adamantly that his way was best. "It ought to be," he told us irritably, "I've been polishing and refining it for years." It is one of the most important paradoxes of his life that, when a major customer ultimately agreed with his view, he melted.

Ever since college Steve had wanted to become outstanding by doing things "my own way." He clung to this goal so tenaciously—and was aware of it so continually—it nearly prevented him from becoming a success. As some of his old customers correctly stated, "He has something to prove." What they didn't know was to whom. It was, in fact, his father. "See, I made it anyway," Steve secretly longed to say, "without help from you, Dad, *or* anyone else." In this case, as in so many others, decades of intransigence evaporated when clients at last began telling him they truly liked his approach.

The point is that this stroke of luck didn't happen a moment too soon. Steve's recalcitrant stance had scuttled his chances for success on so many previous occasions, he was running out of time. He and Carol were fighting more frequently, since he had to go home year after year with yet another report of a setback. That caused them to quarrel, though they weren't even certain what they were arguing about in most instances. Steven was simply unhappy, and so was his wife. "I like my job—and am doing well—but I want to have a baby," she told us glumly one Sunday. "I can't do that at fifty, which, from the way it looks, is the earliest that Steve is going to make any real money."

That isn't what the evidence we've accumulated shows. Rather, the longer Steve insisted on doing things "my way or not at all," the less likely he was to land a contract large enough to cause his stand to soften. Failure usually produced more of the same, as the position of the would-be creator went from resistant to brittle. There were two reasons why Steve was able to break out of this downward spiral, damaging on the job and off. As we've said, unlike many equally talented and dedicated men, he found himself in demand professionally for the first time in his life *before* he entered his forties. After his mid-forties, with twenty years of striving unsuccessfully to be a self-employed innovator behind him, he would have become more like a block of petrified wood, unable to bend even a little. "My *standards* don't allow me to give so much as an inch," said Steve's increasingly arrogant old friend, Andrew, who was also in the computer-software field but was "going nowhere fast," as those who worked with him characterized his progress.

Steve's personal life also played a role in his professional progress. In what way? For one thing, he was married to a woman he loved. Men who scrapped their relationships early (typically in their late twenties) and lived alone thereafter were significantly less likely to have a "stroke of luck" of the kind we referred to above—a business windfall—come their way. Obviously, it isn't just luck. That Steve stayed with his wife despite the obvious stress both were experiencing heightened the odds that he would eventually emerge *and remain* a success. The give-and-take involved in living closely with anyone, much less someone he loved, helped keep him more open-minded than he realized. "I'm as bullheaded as I ever was," he told us proudly at thirty-six, eight months before he landed his first major contract. Fortunately for him, that wasn't so. Revealingly, once he landed the contract, he never again repeated this purist's pledge of allegiance.

(It is noteworthy that men who didn't love their wives, as judged either by their own remarks or other measures we'll look at later, reaped none of the benefits seen in Steve's case. In fact, in more than three out of five marriages that were considered unhappy by both spouses, the men evidenced even more inflexibility than their unmarried peers—and paid the price in stunted entrepreneurial efforts. The arguments the pair were having apparently served only to make any positions the men took still more rigid, at home and at work. Divorce actually helped make these men succeed in some cases, by allowing them a degree of inner latitude so much greater than they had previously had that they could physically feel it.)

SUCCESS: THE BEST SOFTENER

As Steve's business became more successful, he stopped finding fault with all of Carol's friends and most of his own. It isn't a change he made consciously, and he still was every bit as good at spotting their flaws. However, he felt much less of a need to call them to Carol's attention. This seemingly minor shift in his attitude had a dramatic, healing effect on their marriage. For it prevented *her* from leaping to the defense of the person being attacked.

Steve was astonished to notice that she slowly began to do the reverse: Carol herself started criticizing friends and co-workers, something she had previously been loath to do in front of Steve. Also aware of their shortcomings, she still wanted to hold on to them at least as occasional companions. The blistering comments Steve had used to describe them made that difficult. In Carol's words, "Once he takes them apart, I can't always get them back together again." Yet if she was the one doing the dismantling, there was no problem. For she could reassemble—that is, tolerate or forgive—them if and when it suited her needs, which it often did.

Steve viewed this new feature of Carol's behavior as a bit odd. "She tears them to shreds while we're having dinner," he said, shrugging his shoulders, "and then is full of giggles and gossip on the phone when they call an hour later." In the past, such inconsistencies from Carol or anyone else would have caused him to call the person a hypocrite. He stopped doing so. Steve recognized that something fundamental had shifted in their relationship; how and why was of little concern to him. His income was growing but that, in and of itself, as we know from other cases, would not have led to such an improvement. "I'm not one to look a gift horse in the mouth," he told us, at thirty-nine. "All I know is that we have *real* conversations now."

They had been having them all along but, of necessity, frequently avoided using words. For these two bright and opinionated people, discussions could easily lead to debates that became acrimonious. That was an outcome which pained both, so they often said nothing and merely held hands while walking or watching TV. Their daily body rhythms were different, Carol being an early riser and Steve a night owl. "My mind is clearest on some days only in the evening, after nine," he remarked, not pleased at the thought. Wanting to be close, the pair over the years found a way to make an asset of this difference. On many an evening, with both sitting on the living-room couch, Carol would fall asleep by ten-thirty with her head on Steve's lap. Continuing his reading, he would stroke her head tenderly from time to time. "Seeing her there is better than watching glowing coals in a fireplace," he said, almost to himself.

By contrast, Larry never did this with Stephanie unless someone was watching. Steve and Carol knew a few couples like Larry and Stephanie, and, as Carol insightfully described it, "They have a *deal*, not a marriage." Larry and Stephanie, on the other hand, knew pairs like Steve and Carol, and always characterized such relationships as "boring." What bothered both Larry and Stephanie—in fact, puzzled them considerably—was that two people could keep each other company for so long. "If I have to put up with Stephanie for more than twenty minutes by myself," Larry quipped, "I'm ready to pull out whatever is left of my hair." She felt the same way. Only a month before, she had told us bluntly, "If it weren't for all the dinner guests we have, we'd have been divorced ages ago."

Not until Steve relaxed and Carol opened up more did we see how revolted she was by this kind of relationship. "It's what my parents had," she said, uneasily. She found their "endless trench warfare" totally unacceptable. "I don't know how they did it all those years—how they both stood the needling. I couldn't have." Carol had always wanted to have a family ("a *real* one") yet was prepared to have none rather than endure what she'd seen at home. The attitudes that prevailed in the 1970s made it easy for her to postpone and even forget her desire. However, the psychological changes in Steve that occurred as a result of his success—not the success itself—made her start looking at children's clothes in stores, wanting to put them on a baby of her own. Less than a year later they had a boy, whom they named Eric.

Steve's rigid stances in the workplace had sorely needed modification. Success, it turns out, is the best softener, but it isn't the only one. The number of men who could solve their personal problems by first solving their work-related problems would increase substantially if they realized the idealistic source of their difficulties and recognized that each year they delay only makes matters worse. As we've said, the changes in Steve's life took place just in the nick of time.

There is typically a limit to how long a dedicated and creative entrepreneur can continue striving fruitlessly, and Steve was reaching that limit. The many people in our sample who exceeded it became increasingly quirky loners. Chronically hostile and moody now, they could find no satisfactory outlet for the abundance of frustration they were accumulating. Andrew, for instance, could not achieve the dream he and Steve had once shared—namely, to be able to tell the world one day to "go to hell." He wasn't able to tell it to potential customers either, since they wouldn't even return his phone calls. So, like the majority of men in his position, he has wound up over the years telling it to his wives. All three of them.

·PART·
TWO

CHAPTER
·5·

MANAGERS, MONEY, AND MARRIAGE

While it is important to know that a particular man more closely resembles, say, a David than a Bill, the real question is: what kinds of problems can each man expect to encounter if he is ambitious?

All men are not alike; the problems they confront are as different as the men. The four we have met thus far are typical and give us a vocabulary to describe the rest. However, after establishing which category someone belongs in, we have to see how he handles himself in his business or profession. Highly motivated men face difficulties daily that the lazy or indifferent rarely experience. For example, delays in the completion of a project frustrate and even irritate people who care, while a more relaxed—and less taxing—attitude characterizes those who don't. Someone who wants to do well may be pitched into depression by rejection from a customer or disapproval from a superior, while someone who isn't trying (perhaps because he doesn't really expect to rise in the company) may consider the work a joke—and hence despair about its quality as absurd.

Generally, the more ambitious the man, the faster he wants to move, which causes him to hit any potholes on his particular road more jarringly.

DOING OLD THINGS NEW WAYS

We want to focus on *the* most pivotal problem encountered by men who go into business for themselves. As might be expected, it has something to do with deeply embedded attitudes about money—their own and their company's. But before the problem can surface, the fledgling firm has to get on its feet. Making the company survive its first four years in operation is certainly a major hurdle, one that at least three out of five firms don't surmount. Nevertheless, that still leaves plenty of survivors—a net addition of well over a hundred thousand companies per year (out of the more than 600,000 new business formations annually). Some of the startups go on to do quite well, while others languish. What separates the winners from the also-rans?

The usual explanation is that a man who is a good entrepreneur makes a lousy manager. When the company is young, its founder's entrepreneurial skills are needed most—a willingness to take risks, change directions, do old things in new ways. But once the firm is on its feet, an ability to manage the company's everyday operations is presumed to matter more. The founder is generally viewed as being unable to make the switch. The talents he possesses that helped get the company going initially are precisely those that prevent it from growing beyond a certain limited size. Veteran business analysts voice this view and so do amateur observers.

Be that as it may, these statements are not only incorrect, they are also insulting and harmful. While there are indeed instances where someone who has started a company is later seen to be clearly lacking the ability and interest to run it now that it is many times its original size, the fact remains that the majority of entrepreneurs make the transition to the role of manager quite well.

One thing that facilitates the transition is that the founder grows older as the firm grows bigger. That allows him to develop a different view of himself and his activities. Headstrong at the start, determined to do things his own way, he typically becomes more compromising and receptive to suggestions once he ages a little and the company is a going concern. "I *have* to be more open-minded," many told us. "I simply can't do everything myself anymore."

These largely uneventful transitions receive little or no publicity, the business press preferring instead to dwell on the vastly smaller proportion of instances where the man eventually becomes his own worst enemy on the job. A reflection of popular prejudices, these cases crackle with drama and even have a touch of classical Greek tragedy in modern dress about them. "He wanted to build an empire," is a common comment one hears from contemporary businessmen, "but, as fate would have it, he couldn't get out of his own way."

What sits at the core of this envy-laden view is a belief that the gap between originality and innovation, on the one hand, and production and management, on the other, is enormous. Creativity has become so thickly surrounded by myths it can barely be glimpsed. Far from being a recent phenomenon, we can trace these distortions all the way back to the Bible. God created the world in six days, we are told, and rested on the seventh. Too bad the Old Testament didn't go on to state, "After that, He managed the world with great joy and insight for tens of thousands of years." In short, creativity is divine and is also evidence of genius; management is pedestrian and is obviously the province of dullards.

This powerfully held belief leads to the paradox of millions of ambitious Americans who perceive themselves as secular in orientation, rather than religious, yet who become entrepreneurs in part because they (secretly) hope to be seen as divinely inspired creative geniuses. They like the money they hope to make, but they also want a reputation for being highly original. As one put it candidly, "I want to be thought of as having the imaginative mind of an artist rather than the sterile one of someone who oversees an assembly line."

In many cases that makes the individual so full of himself and his self-proclaimed godlike role on earth that he can produce only sermons, not miracles. Writing his biography long before he has produced any of the startling advances that would justify our reading it, he becomes a legend, as they say, only in his own mind.

The public unwittingly fosters this kind of megalomaniacal thinking in ambitious men. By insisting that creative people "are what they are"— always have been and always will be—it reduces them to stereotypes. Imprisoned in a simplistic picture of themselves, people who are viewed as creative eventually accept the limitations of the stereotype and at least consider themselves exciting. Managers, by contrast, are considered boring; they are mere caretakers.

However, the distinction is much more artificial than it seems at first glance, and, as we've said, it is flatly contradicted by the facts: most men can and do make this change out of sheer necessity. Quietly scrapping the distinction, they slowly switch from entrepreneur to the role of manager. It is fascinating to see what happens, then, if the company continues to grow for a while but ultimately runs into trouble. The public's strongly biased view makes itself felt at this point. Without even knowing the details of the company's setback, they leap to the conclusion that the entrepreneur tried to become a manager, and couldn't. The leopard attempted to make his dots into stripes and himself into a tiger. The effort was doomed from the start.

What makes this widely offered instant analysis so revealing is that (1) it is never mentioned as long as the company is doing well, and (2) it isn't uttered if *exactly the same problems* befall a company that is perceived as having a manager, rather than an entrepreneur, at its helm. In that case, "market forces," "changes in technology or public taste," or "foreign competition" are more likely to be viewed as probable sources of the company's troubles. Even management "mistakes" may be mentioned, but not "inherent inability to run the company well, because the guy is too creative in his orientation."

RESPONDING TO A FINANCIAL SQUEEZE

Larry's business *did* experience serious difficulties. As it grew, it seemed to his associates that he fit quite well the stereotype of the inspired entrepreneur who was ill suited, by temperament, to look after the everyday affairs of his own company. They commented frequently on his inability to delegate authority. In fact, this is the major criticism that entrepreneurs of all varieties face as their companies begin to expand rapidly. "He is used to doing everything himself," said one, about a man much like Larry but in the financial-services field. "And now that he can't, he still doesn't want to hand over to anyone else even a little bit of control."

There is no question that people who operate in this manner seriously limit the growth of their companies.

Nonetheless, before we condemn people for having a personality that prevents them from being effective managers, we should see if other factors are also present. As it turns out, in the majority of cases—including Larry's—the underlying source of the trouble afflicting the firm is as much financial as emotional.

Larry wanted to live well, not just earn well. "Money is for spending," he commented more than once, usually with a smile. Marrying Stephanie made a lavish lifestyle not only desirable but mandatory. The high-priced setting they established for themselves as a couple was an essential part of what kept them together. As Stephanie remarked, two years after their wedding, "I got tired of living like a welfare recipient." Larry, too, had been eager to move up on the socioeconomic scale. And although he spent freely on himself while still single, primarily for cars, clothes, and travel, it wasn't until he met and married Stephanie that his annual expenses really climbed.

The point is that this type of spending can't easily be reduced when a financial squeeze develops. "What am I supposed to do?" Larry asked, during a slow period when sales were soft. "Lay off my kid?" Since the lavish life style he and Stephanie enjoyed couldn't be cut back without disrupting (and perhaps terminating) their marriage, Larry had to make cuts elsewhere.

He made them at the office—without realizing the dramatic consequences of his actions. Although he spoke repeatedly and proudly about hiring "nothing but the best people" to staff his company, he had no illusions about how expensive such top-notch professionals were. What he was forced to hire instead were talented younger workers, typically dedicated ones, who nevertheless lacked the years of experience needed to make them seasoned pros.

It shouldn't be surprising that he—and millions of other entrepreneurs who have found themselves in a similar situation—then resisted delegating authority to such untried lieutenants. He was wary of these untested key employees and voiced his doubts about them openly. "If I died suddenly," he asked us rhetorically, "would the people I have working for me be able to carry on, and make this outfit grow? I don't think so."

What Larry never realized was that he had unwittingly created a destructive situation that was feeding on itself. Contrary to his many protestations about the subject, he was *not* hiring the best people, because he couldn't afford them. He needed to stay financially flexible somewhere, and, by default, it was at the office. There, he was ready and willing to fire any or all of the people who worked for him. Bringing costs into line with revenues and net profits in this arena was easy.

In short, the single greatest cause of failure among men who start their own business—and experience success initially—is to be found in their personal lives. What our data shows is that 54 percent of the men who were doing well financially at first, yet subsequently failed, raided the company's treasury repeatedly, long before it could support such sizable and continuing withdrawals. The main reason they did so was to support themselves and their wives, as the men usually put it, "in the style to which we both want to become accustomed." Some feared their marriages wouldn't endure if they *didn't* do this.

SETTING OFF A CORPORATE STAMPEDE

Nothing we say is intended to blame the women involved for the stunted growth—or, in some cases, collapse—of what previously had been fast-growing firms. Larry wanted to live in a grand manner even more than his wife did. On many an occasion *she* was the one to say, "We don't need another $150 dinner tonight at a fancy restaurant. Let's just fix a salad at home." In this respect the two were typical. For every couple in our sample in which the wife was pushing her husband to earn more, so they could live better, there were four other couples in which the men were pushing themselves to achieve the same goal for the pair. In more than 40 percent of the cases, the men didn't even have a girlfriend at the time, much less a spouse, yet they squandered the company's profits—and even assets—in a remarkably careless manner.

Nevertheless, it became possible as the years passed to predict *which* men would succeed in their own start-up companies. A large part of the answer came from assessing the degree to which the men and their wives already were—or sorely wanted to be—living high on the hog. Early purchases of a mansion and a Rolls-Royce, together with a free-spending social whirl calculated to impress friends and neighbors, were associated with a flattened growth curve for the firm and, in many cases, one that soon turned downward.

That outcome may puzzle some readers as much as it did the entrepreneurs we are discussing, so a few words of explanation may be worthwhile. The connection isn't as direct as it seems. Until someone proves
that a particular route can be made profitable, other executives may be
reluctant to travel on it. But once its profitability has been amply demonstrated, a corporate stampede may ensue. This confuses owners like
Larry, who look forward to living lavishly, because their view is that,
"Above all, I have to battle customer indifference. That is the number-
one obstacle to riches." The attitude of these entrepreneurs is that the
public is set in its ways (which is largely true), and that a change in
established habits of consumption will probably have to take place for a
new product or service to do really well.

The attitude is fine as far as it goes, but it doesn't go nearly far enough.
Larry was as good as anyone we studied at "getting his foot in the door,"
introducing himself and his product line, and then persuading potential
customers to at least consider doing business with him instead of with
their traditional suppliers.

However, it is important to spell out what Larry overlooked; namely,
that once other business executives see that a new way of operating (for
instance, Larry's aggressive marketing approach) works better than theirs,
or that a new idea of operations (for instance, becoming a distributor) can
be lucrative, then and only then does the level of competition increase
dramatically, even if it was low before. Competitors are attracted by (1)
the money, and (2) visible evidence that the public is adopting a different
style. The latter is especially important to someone contemplating a
start-up in the field because it means that there is clearly decreasing
public resistance to the specific new product or service.

The reason these considerations are so crucial to the business lives of
men like Larry is that he started living more extravagantly precisely at the
time that larger competitors were moving in on him. He didn't notice
them. Celebrating the increased acceptance he and his company were
experiencing, confident that it would ensure his success, he concluded,
"Now it's time for me and Stephanie to start living more elegantly." An
understandable desire, it nevertheless was implemented at what turned
out to be a dangerous moment.

This happened in a startling proportion of the cases we studied. Nearly
60 percent—539 out of 906—of the initially successful entrepreneurs in
our sample began spending more liberally in their leisure hours just

when, unknown to them, rivals were gearing up to move in on their company's turf. The typical justification given by Larry and proprietors like him was that "My customer base is expanding—the money is pouring in—so why not live it up a little?"

If he had lived it up only "a little," all would have been well. However, as with the majority of other entrepreneurs who made the decision to increase their personal spending, the phrase "a little" was obviously a mere euphemism for "a lot." Proof that their wives generally were not instrumental in this poorly timed decision (as some men later claimed) can be found in an analysis of the spending patterns of single entrepreneurs. Unmarried proprietors not only acted the same way, they tended to spend in larger clumps and did so more often. Wiping out their companies and themselves usually took less effort than even they thought it would. A representative remark from one who went from a net worth of $1.1 million to zero in less than three months, when the bank foreclosed, was, "To tell you the truth, I thought I could afford as many planes as United Airlines has. [He had bought three, as well as a Maserati and a Porsche.] I thought the money would never run out."

Which couples handled the pressures best? Recent South Korean immigrants. The sixty-one proprietors of fruit and vegetable stores we studied* (all of which were located in major urban areas) worked long and hard, often keeping their stores open twenty-four hours a day. Husband and wife both worked in the store. Sometimes three generations from the same family did. Living simply, they put much of the profit they made back into the business. The result was a constantly expanding variety of products. Starting with only a few basic items, the stores were soon offering everything from salad bars to, in some instances, over twenty different kinds of coffee and tea.

Most Americans in our sample, even those who viewed themselves as ambitious, stated that they were unwilling to put in such long hours, especially in so unglamorous a job. "That type of life was for my parents'—or maybe my grandparents'—generation," said a twenty-year-old from Westport, Connecticut, majoring in business administration at a state college.

Korean proprietors faced the same reactions to their success that was

---

* In conjunction with Korean graduate students in the social sciences, for a national business publication.

seen in other fields we examined. Financially stronger rivals eventually appeared once they realized that there was money to be made. Nearby supermarkets, which had been around for decades, suddenly got the bright idea that they too should have salad bars. Koreans drew many customers from dingy "convenience stores" by staying open longer hours and then adding the personal touch of homemade foods and gourmet snacks for a busy, upscale clientele. Supermarkets tried to do the same, but their long lines, higher rents and labor costs—and the absence of even a "hello" when customers arrived—nearly guaranteed continued profits for Korean grocers who remained dedicated to their business.

FAST BECOMING AN EXPERT

Leaving hardworking recent Asian immigrants aside for the moment, let us ask another question: which native Americans not only became successful initially but were also able to continue adding to their success, instead of later losing most of what they had achieved? Roger Davis is typical of the majority who did the right rather than the wrong things, and to this day are prospering as a result.

An aimless and fidgety young man with no close friends when we first began interviewing him, Roger didn't seem the type ever to go into business for himself. "I'm basically lazy," he told us at age twenty-two, and he was a bit overweight as well. The physical flabbiness seemed to reflect the "total absence of self-discipline," to which he repeatedly referred between puffs on a cigarette. A bright but indifferent student, nothing appeared exciting enough to Roger to get him to pursue it day in and day out for years on end. That remained the case for most of his twenties, when we and his co-workers often labeled him as "coasting." Nevertheless, like Larry, Roger wanted to be "classy."

He was acutely aware of the cars other people drove, the restaurants they went to, and the places in which they lived and vacationed. Making sizable sums of money seemed to him the only way to move up in the world and attain "respect." He believed this every bit as much as Larry did, as his comments and the dreams he described made quite clear. Since the two men had similar personality profiles and came from similar backgrounds, and since each made so many remarks the other could have voiced, the two should have experienced comparable difficulties in attempting to become wealthy and content. They didn't. One had a significantly easier time of it than the other, and it is revealing to see why.

A business administration major, Roger chose a large conglomerate to work for once he was out of school because, as he said, "I'm interested in what happens in manufacturing—economies of scale, and that sort of thing." With the Japanese becoming the least-cost producer of so many products, thanks to their manufacturing efficiencies, this was destined to be a "hot area," as Roger correctly labeled it in the early 1970s. However, his interests had already switched slowly during the prior decade to home improvement.

"People spend a bundle fixing up their houses and apartments," he said more animatedly than was typical for him. Unlike so many other topics, which had captured his fancy temporarily, only to be forgotten by the next time we interviewed him, this subject was obviously of enduring interest. He and his wife, Sharon, who worked as a manager at an office temporaries agency, had spent nearly $8,000 remodeling the kitchen and bathrooms of a well-built older house they had bought in a nearby suburb. Until then, it hadn't occurred to him that many other people each year did the same. "This is a *big* business," he told us with obvious enthusiasm, soon after his twenty-eighth birthday. It wasn't only the industry's total dollar volume that enticed him, but also the variety of products available, a good portion of which he knew would appeal to the area's young but upscale consumers.

"This town doesn't have a 'home improvement center' that's *serious*," he commented, almost as if thinking aloud. "I mean, there are a few hardware stores that stock venetian blinds and wood trim, but that's not the same." With a $30,000 loan from his parents, together with $25,000 that he and Sharon had saved, he opened a store. "This is my first career change," he said, smiling, just before turning twenty-nine.

Customers came, just as he expected, but they bought more than he expected. Interviewing nearly a dozen, we found that they liked Roger's confident manner and knowledgeable suggestions. He was fast becoming an expert. Maintaining contact with a growing number of builders and carpenters, who received quantity discounts (and hot coffee and doughnuts whenever they stopped by), helped. Reading about the field in his spare time, keeping up with new products and trends through trade magazines and a flood of brochures from manufacturers, was also useful. Soon Roger expanded, taking over the store next door.

A few years later he opened a second, much larger center in a more populated city nearly twenty miles away ("I don't want it too close to this place"), and it also did extremely well. Most people didn't know he owned the new store, since he advertised its wares separately. A series of events occurred in the next few years that produced major changes in Roger's life. The first was an offer from a public company to buy him out. "When the guy came to the store and asked to see me," Roger told us, "I thought he was a salesman. He sure looked like one—blue suit, carrying an attaché case." Instead, he had been sent by his company to "feel me out," as Roger described it, "to get my reaction to joining them for some combination of cash and stock."

Roger had no intention of selling ("I don't want anyone telling me what to do"), but he had a burning curiosity to see how much his business was worth to an actual buyer. A million dollars had always seemed to him so far out of reach as to be almost unattainable, yet it was a vivid dividing line ("there are people who have that much money—and most who never will"). When the blue-suited buyer stated flatly during a second visit that his company was willing to pay in excess of a million, Roger was ecstatic. "I wasn't a millionaire by thirty," he told us, "but I made it by the time I was forty. Not bad, huh?"

Living well seemed to him the best revenge for the decade-long delay, so we anticipated that he would soon be having many of the same problems Larry experienced. In particular, we expected him to start raiding his company's coffers in order to buy a larger home, not to mention a second vacation home in the mountains. Sharon wanted badly to do both, and in fact was applying more pressure to him to spend freely at last than Stephanie had to Larry.

Nevertheless, Roger didn't. On the contrary, he suddenly seemed more content with his financial and, more important, social status than he had at any time during the previous two decades. That was odd because, throughout the period, he had repeatedly stated that, "without money, you're a nobody." Now that he had a fair amount of it, we expected it to be spent freely to make certain that people viewed him as a "somebody."

That wasn't what happened. The mere realization that he could cash in his assets for a seven-figure fortune gave him peace of mind not only privately, but also in public. Paradoxically, he began to take real satisfaction in being able to say to himself when someone treated him shabbily, "I could buy and sell you, you creep. If you only knew how much I was worth, you wouldn't act this way."

He never did sell his company, which would have given him plenty of cash to play with, and he now found it much easier to resist Sharon's arguments that they "live it up while we're still young." Calmly but firmly he told her, "We're doing just fine, and we'll do even better. But we're going to increase our spending *slowly*—without splurging and having nothing left later."

Instead of spraying money in every direction in an attempt to wring respect from others, he found that "my secret weapon," as he referred to his million-dollar net worth, was giving him self-respect. As in Larry's case, it had previously been there only for brief periods, before vanishing again without a trace, and that above all was what had made each man so intent upon getting people to constantly acknowledge his importance.

INNER STRENGTH

There is an illuminating way to look at what Roger was doing, which helps explain why he subsequently did so well both professionally and personally. During this period Roger was unwittingly reshaping his personality, making it more like Steve's and less like Larry's. The reader may be asking (as we did), "How could he do that?" Unlike Steve, he had no technical training to which his reclusive tendencies, if any, could latch on to.

Much to our surprise, it turns out that money in a man's pocket—if there is enough of it—can serve many of the same psychological purposes as technical knowledge in his brain: both provide their respective owners with a sense of security and self-worth. Larry never kept the money in his pocket (bank account, actually) long enough to have this happen, but even if he had, it wouldn't have produced any changes in him. There is nothing inevitable about the process. He was what he was, as he was fond of saying, and saw no need to change. Roger did. He didn't like the idea of "buying friends and admirers," as he once remarked contemptuously about someone who he felt was doing so. But if he couldn't get them any other way, he had long made use of this route (for instance, Roger was a chronic "check grabber," picking up the tab for a group dinner even when he was almost broke). Once he became wealthy, however, "respect" stopped seeming like the single most important goal in life. He had located a source of "inner strength."

Some may object that this was largely a delusion on his part, since his money could be lost or, through inflation, reduced in value. That is true, but obsolescence could take a similar toll on the technical knowledge in Steve's brain. While not obvious at first, the parallels on both the downside and upside were striking: each man had to make an effort to maintain the value of the impersonal possession (Roger his money, Steve his creativity) that did the most to make him feel good.

The point—and it is a crucial one—is that previously in Roger's case there hadn't been any such thing. Like Larry, he was scrambling ("hustling," he always labeled it), certain that money in sufficient quantity would solve all his current problems and any that might arise in the future. Yet what really allowed him to do well over the years, both on the job and at home, was that he eventually became an amalgam of Larry and Steve, able to draw on the strengths of both, as needed.

The changes were subtle, and not immediately apparent to his employees. For instance, he certainly didn't become more inclined to delegate authority, not did he modify any of the other egoistic or abrasive qualities that made him and Larry difficult to work for. But the moderate measure of inner peace ("strength," he'd have insisted on calling it) Roger had recently found made him substantially less inclined to raid the company's treasury in order to support a lavish life style he hoped would impress anyone who knew him. That was fortunate, because Roger's business turned out to be even more cyclical than Larry's. Housing could boom in good times or bust when interest rates rose. With more than 40 percent of his sales coming from professional builders, when they hurt, so did he. The cash that he didn't pull in excessive quantities from his business saw him through the next few downturns in the economy, recessions that otherwise might have bankrupted his company if he had begun to live, as he put it, thinking dreamily about the prospect, "like a Roman emperor."

The money he had—and Larry didn't—caused Roger to be thought of by colleagues as a "brilliant manager," while Larry was viewed as a "brilliant maniac." Again, the real difference was that Roger had the cash on hand needed to ride out normal setbacks, whereas Larry had showered all his available cash on everyone nearby in a vain attempt to make them look up to him. However, this difference in outcome was a result of Larry being a Larry-type, pure and simple; Roger, on the other hand, had remolded his adult personality into a powerful combination of Larry's and Steve's.

HIRING A MIRACLE WORKER

To sum up, most entrepreneurs whose businesses become established and continue to grow will be hit sooner or later with the charge that, "It's time for you to step aside and hire a manager." The suggestion won't be offered until the firm stumbles a bit, but, since every company runs into difficulties of one kind or another, ultimately there is an opportunity to make this seemingly appropriate suggestion.

For some proprietors it is good advice; for the vast majority it isn't. The transition from a creative to a managerial role as the company expands occurs far more smoothly and more often than has previously been recognized. The advice is offered anyway, primarily because we live in an age characterized by service professionals. There is an abundance of people today—doctors, lawyers, psychologists, accountants, and M.B.A.s —who feel quite comfortable saying to someone, "I know what's good for you even better than you do."

Sometimes they are right. However, this aggressive stance is intended to create a market for the services they want to render—assistance that may not in fact be needed. As the United States has moved during the past four decades from a goods-manufacturing to a service economy, a growing proportion of the labor force has adopted this invasive and self-serving position. Without realizing it, that has made them biased against the self-reliant individual who starts and succeeds in his own business. They applaud him in the abstract, yet when confronted with a specific case they immediately assume that they have a contribution to make to his continued prosperity.

Not wanting to appear to be jumping on someone else's bandwagon, eager to maintain their professional dignity, they use a fascinating sales pitch. "I don't need you," they say smugly, and even self-righteously. "You need *me*." Some wind up with a consulting contract. However, even if they aren't trying to find a place for themselves in the entrepreneur's successful operation, the basically hostile public sentiments they are unwittingly echoing in telling him to "hire a professional manager" can be quite harmful.

For, when all is said and done, it is money that he typically needs at this point, not managers or consultants. He knows what he is doing at the office but not on the home front. Having achieved his financial ambitions, his social ambitions move to the fore. They cause him to pull more cash from the business than he should, given the better-established competitors who now see his area as "a ripe opportunity for growth" for themselves.

Swallowing the "remedy" that has been offered, many entrepreneurs do bring in a professional manager. Then they are stunned to find themselves resenting the hefty salary they are paying him. The cost of the medicine would bother them less if it really did cure what ails them. It rarely does. They correctly sense that they are teaching this "veteran" their business and that, worse still, he isn't even pulling his own weight. Unlike someone they hire when the company is doing well and another competent staff member simply must be added to the payroll, this "miracle worker" is brought in to get the company growing again.

The situation is a bad one for both parties, and the most common outcome is for disputes between the two to break out. Once they do, the manager becomes all the more convinced that he is dealing with an entrepreneur who "wants to do it all himself, and can't function any other way." He can always find a receptive audience for this complaint. The owner, on the other hand, usually arrives at the conclusion that, "If he knows so much about how to run this kind of business successfully, why isn't he running his own? What's he doing riding on *my* coattails?" Soon the manager is looking for another job.

The real source of the problem is generally not to be found in the artificial distinction between entrepreneur and manager in a start-up company. An owner who wants to reduce the chance of major business setbacks in the first place needs to look at the problem areas he is used to examining and then add another: his marriage, or, if he is single, the kind of mate who best meets his needs. The wife he selects will be more than just a companion and sex partner. Whether or not he acknowledges it, she will also be a reflection of his social aspirations. Finally, she will have aspirations of her own in this area, even if she hasn't consciously thought about them recently. Their growing wealth generally changes the social focus of both.

Rather than condemning her later for being "a climber," as Larry repeatedly did with Stephanie, it is essential for the entrepreneur to know what his own views about "class" are and how determined he himself is to "move up" on this unavoidably public ladder. Our study indicates that the most dangerous situation—both for him and his wife—occurs when the wife's expectations lead her to press for a pace of upward social progress that can't realistically be met without threatening the financial health of her husband's company. In that case, both the marriage and the business often fail.

Since many of the entrepreneurs we studied (approximately 60 percent) had sizable social as well as financial ambitions, it would have been well worthwhile for them to find an effective method of delaying the switch— the exhilarating moment when they spring from the starting gate announcing that "Now it's time for everyone to see how damned well I've been doing." Postponing this moment isn't easy for anyone who has waited years, perhaps even decades, for it to arrive. And in a period characterized by "buy now, pay later" attitudes, it is hard to come up with a convincing excuse for not participating fully in the good life once one can afford it.

Yet that was what was done by almost all those in our sample who went on to develop truly successful firms, ones that generated more than enough profit annually to allow their owners to live very comfortably without having to worry that their expensive life style was costing their company its ability to compete.

It was revealing to see which excuses the entrepreneurs used to keep themselves from cleaning out the company and going on a personal consumption spree. An overwhelming desire to see the firm grow was among the most effective, but the one that exerted the greatest effect on the lives of those who used it didn't involve the company at all. The most powerful way to delay the moment of uninhibited self-indulgence turned out to be this statement: "I'm building this company for my children."

It isn't said nearly as often in the 1980s as it was in the 1950s. And then, as now, the parents who said it genuinely meant it. However, since it serves so well to postpone into the distant future the urge to splurge, if it didn't already exist as a good excuse, someone would have had to invent it.

CHAPTER
·6·

LIKE FATHER,
LIKE SON?

None of the more than 6,000 men we studied managed to get through adolescence without having at least one "ranking session" with peers. The event had a variety of names at the time but was typically a tense interchange of insults and putdowns, punctuated by laughter, best performed in front of a teenage audience that found it entertaining. The onlookers were especially inclined to giggle since it wasn't *their* egos that were taking a beating just then. Done on stoops, in playgrounds and gym class, or at summer camp, the verbal jousting was as much a device for letting off steam as it was a way of gaining applause from spectators. Most participants found these interchanges nerve-racking and joined in them as little as possible. There were similar, though fewer and less vicious, sessions in college. As time went on, they became easier to avoid.

Courtesy replaced this combative stance once the men finally finished school and found full-time jobs. There they were expected to treat other people's feelings gingerly. Whereas previously they were cheered for their ability to demolish a classmate's image with a humorously hostile remark, now they hoped to gain approval by conducting themselves in a deliberately more thoughtful way. They wanted their good manners to show. Their view was, even if they never put it into words, "Business is civilized."

Is it really? There are few work-related subjects about which people have more schizophrenic an attitude. On the one hand, they see daily examples in the office of face-to-face civility. Hellos are exchanged even by people who don't like each other. On the other hand, precisely because so many of the employees at any company aren't fond of one another, there is a great deal of hushed conversation about co-workers. The behind-the-scenes comments are strikingly different from the self-consciously polite stance most workers adopt.

It isn't that the business world is populated primarily by hypocrites. With so many competing interests clustered together in a relatively small setting, it is necessary to keep people's aggressions restrained. Preventing a free-for-all from breaking out is mandatory if any work is to get done. Giving each worker a formal ranking, a title, and a sense of vertical position in the firm's hierarchy (instead of letting them grapple among themselves, as they did in schoolyards) helps maintain peace, though it also breeds resentment. Their having different jobs to do also helps, but not as much as one might at first have thought. As a result, the device upon which most depend to keep the peace is politeness.

Unfortunately, ambitious men generally come to depend too heavily on this device. Without giving the matter much thought, they merely assume that if they behave in an affable and considerate manner, others will behave the same way—both to their faces and behind their backs. As we'll soon see, basically this is magical thinking, similar in many ways to superstition. By doing x, they hope to ward off evil.

The best evidence that they believe their actions to be not only appropriate but also effective can be found in the comments with which they strongly and repeatedly agree. During the years 1958 through 1986, more than 80 percent of the men in our sample voiced in one form or another the following three statements:

> "Having a good reputation fends off criticism."
> "Your past achievements will come to your rescue when you need them during tough times."

"Being well mannered and looking good help ensure your success."

The comments sound so reasonable it is easy to see why a man who wants very much to do well at work might seize upon them subconsciously. Nevertheless, since so much is at stake, it is crucial to ask: is he just grasping at straws? Does this secret set of guidelines help, or does it in fact harm his chances of eventually attaining success?

People who are employees, rather than entrepreneurs, are significantly more likely to act in accordance with these dictates, so it is this group whose prospects we will be examining most closely. David, the attorney we met in chapter 1, responded in a typical manner when he heard that someone at work had called him a "blowhard."

He was visibly affected by the news, delivered while he was eating lunch with a friend. The situation is more complicated than it seems, because each such blow is actually a double shot. To see why, it is worthwhile to think about how surprised a given man would be if a woman with whom he was quietly speaking suddenly slapped him. The comparison with what typically happens in an office is better if in addition it is assumed that the woman is a tiny, eighty-four-year-old, gray-haired great-grandmother. In that case, the slap may sting, but the shock of receiving one from so unlikely a source may disturb the recipient even more.

David was surprised by the abusive remark he was hearing about, yet is is important to realize that he was equally upset that the remark had been voiced at all. After using for many years the magical thinking discussed above, he was under the impression that he had been suppressing the hostile feelings in others from which such remarks spring, or at the very least, deflecting them away from himself thanks to his charming manner and winning ways.

David wasn't vain enough to have congratulated himself often on his interpersonal skills, yet it is fair to say that—until the insulting remark was repeated to him—he thought he had been doing a more than adequate job of making his co-workers like him. His way of putting it is the same as that voiced by others who share his approach: "I'm good with people. I really am." Even if he is right, our question has to be: What is it costing him? The answer: "Everything. It is radically reducing his chances of attaining either success or a satisfactory personal life."

OVERREACTING—TO THE WRONG EVENTS

The millions of men like David don't want to be boors, so they make the effort to be pleasant even if there is no obvious gain for themselves. Many told us, "I say hello and try to be nice mainly because I think it's the right thing to do. I'm not behaving this way to be manipulative." Be that as it may, the words and actions of such well-meaning men make an impact on others anyway, and if, like David, they are also ambitious, the nature of that impact is worth knowing.

To begin with, let us note that helpful men like David aren't doing what they claim. Ask a large number of them what they envision for themselves ideally in the future and virtually all can spell out what they would like to see happen—an increase in pay, prestige, responsibility, and renown. Since they can describe these long-term goals in such vivid detail, it is natural to assume that they are spending their twenties, thirties, and forties pursuing them.

It therefore comes as something of a shock to see that very little of what they do actually furthers their quest. A careful, day-by-day analysis of their thoughts and actions reveals that they devote most of their time to waiting for someone in their office or profession to do something; then they respond. Another person *acts*; they *react*.

This may seem inevitable in a crowded, complex world in which each person is just one of many players in the game. Watching to see what others do is often a prelude to doing something worthwhile oneself; however, men like David carry this approach to a destructive extreme. Instead of calmly anticipating the best moment to make a move, they wait far more tensely than they realize. The result is that they don't just react, they overreact; and when they do, it is usually to the wrong events, turning their everyday behavior into a strange mixture.

Generally they are well dressed and concerned about their appearance, yet they are so tense that they are jumpy. From the expensive clothes they wear and their attention to good manners, one expects them to be courtly gentlemen—cordial, considerate, bright, and witty—but once they start speaking, the impression is shattered. They seem unable to distinguish between remarks worth responding to and those that should be ignored.

David continually found himself in arguments with his co-workers, conflicts he was certain had developed because others were expressing views that were mistaken. "I can't just sit by," he said to us, wide-eyed, "and let them make statements that are that dumb. I have to speak up." Coiled too tightly to begin with, David regularly challenged almost everyone else's opinions. Ignoring the feelings of others, while paying lip service to how important they were, he bred resentment in most of the people with whom he had daily dealings. In that respect the reactions he elicited were typical: men like David are usually judged the rudest and most insensitive in the firm. That would stun them if they ever heard it (few do), and it would trouble them further to discover that their meticulous appearance makes the biting way in which they respond to others that much more noticeable.

To spell out the paradox these ambitious individuals present to co-workers: on the one hand, colleagues see a man who is fastidious and detail-oriented; concerned about externals, including his own diction and vocal tone; a man trying hard to appear elegant and relaxed. Yet for that very reason, the jerky responses he makes, his tendency to become embroiled instantly in any ongoing argument, and his inclination to turn every conversation into a controversy stand out starkly. Whether he is an entrepreneur or, especially, aspiring executive, he doesn't get very far. His career usually tops out in the middle. No one who gets to know him wants to see him occupy the company's top slot. The judgment rendered privately by David's colleagues is representative: "He isn't the kind of guy I want to see in *any* position of power."

"I'D RATHER BE RICH THAN RIGHT"

The lack of perspective displayed by such men hurts them every bit as much as, if not more than, their practice of alienating co-workers and not recognizing it. Let us grant for the moment David's statement, one he often voiced, that "There are a whopping number of truly stupid people in the world." Sometimes he would add, sarcastically, "And I think I've met more than my share lately."

Even if he had, the key question is, "How many of them should he try to 'correct?'" Their comments may have been error-filled and their behavior in some cases arrogant, but so was David's vigorous attempt to get them to "mend their ways." Men like David frequently claim that they react strongly to someone else's opinions because they sorely want to help set the person on the right road. "My aims are noble," David once remarked. "Of that much I'm sure." Nevertheless, the intensity of these men's responses even to lighthearted remarks makes it apparent that they are out of control.

In spite of the face-saving rationalizations they pin on their own behavior after it has emerged, they don't have tense interchanges on the phone and face-to-face battles to benefit others. They act in this abrasive manner primarily because they can't help it. Like a gun that has accidentally gone off, they find themselves having fired a bullet and now must explain (at least to themselves) why they did it—again.

It is easy to conclude that such men must be psychologically disturbed, and some undoubtedly are; however, the vast majority we studied are simply using the wrong techniques to go about fulfilling their dreams. The connection between their fiery reactions and the men's ambitions becomes clear once we see *whose* opinions they seek to rectify. The bigger the audience the other person has, the more fiercely a David-type is ready to do battle with him. Is he out to "correct" the other person's views or is he really after the other person's audience, hoping to inherit it after he has eliminated this adversary?

Men like David value social acceptance far more highly than money; in fact, their intention is to convert at the earliest opportunity any wealth they achieve into the social acceptance they'd much rather have. Since this is their central if unspoken goal in life, it makes its presence known long before the men have the affluence necessary to put their plan into effect. What is so distressing is that it has a surprisingly disruptive influence on their professional lives.

Larry, too, had towering social aspirations but he was able to shelve them until his financial goals were met. It wouldn't have occurred to him to leap to revise the opinions of his co-workers in a corporation, assuming he had been an employee there. "I'd rather be rich than right," he said more than once, unaware what a revealing comment this was. The attitude of men like Larry is that once they are wealthy, they will be able to *buy* whatever prestige they need. "Everything is for sale," Larry remarked, "even respectability." The words were uttered with an air of cynicism, but he was actually thrilled that this was how things appear to be. David-types, by contrast, don't want to purchase their elegance; they want always to have possessed it—an internal attribute, there since they were toddlers, rather than an external decoration, tacked on later in life.

Men like David want to have been born with a silver spoon in their mouths; men like Larry are happy to have wives who use one, especially in front of company.

AVOIDING HARMFUL OFFICE DISPUTES

How are David-types supposed to improve their own perilous situation? The best method can be described in three words: **learn to disengage.** The men in our sample who stumbled on this technique rate it the most effective solution to what ails them on the job. It is also, they report (and we agree), the factor that has made the greatest difference in their quest for success.

If David could have said to himself, "Sad to say, I turn every skirmish into an all-out war," it would have enabled him to stop himself from doing so, by saying, "Oops, there I go again." Even a momentary pause before yet another fray began might have given him the perspective needed to determine whether, as the saying goes, the game was worth the candle.

Why is it necessary to stop this train before it leaves the station? Because once a quiet difference of opinion becomes an open dispute, it can't easily be laid to rest by such men. Egos become involved, not just issues. It is remarkable to see the intensity with which men like David defend the abundance of emotion they have recently poured into a clearly meaningless argument. Prior to the quarrel they, too, may have considered the topic trivial. However, once they allow themselves to be drawn into a heated debate about the subject—which occurs with frightening ease in their case—justifying their behavior to themselves and others consumes them almost as much as the original quarrel did.

What is particularly damaging is that justifying the argument typically takes considerably longer than the argument itself did. David agonized for nearly three weeks about a hallway battle that didn't last even three minutes. This is what makes the word "disengage" so pivotal. If an ounce of prevention is worth a pound of cure where one's health is concerned—a saying that has become increasingly valid as medical costs have risen—then an ounce of prevention is worth a ton of cure when one's professional life is at stake. Given the rising number of qualified candidates seeking every important position in American business, it is worthwhile for "hotheads" like David (as he was frequently described) to avoid doing serious harm to their careers with mistakes that are far more costly in the long run than a broken leg.

One exercise has proved especially useful in this regard. People who are watching a sporting event, anything from baseball to golf, typically become caught up in it. David considered boxing too brutal but found tennis interesting occasionally. Picking one contestant to root for, the first step in the process, he began to hope that his choice would come out on top. Yet—and this is the key point—the victory of the players he selected was actually irrelevant to David's life. Only to the extent that he came to believe the contest mattered did it in fact matter. Pre-game publicity helps whip up enthusiasm about the event, but unless the public allows its passions to be inflamed, the game has no inherent significance. It is usually just grown men playing a teenager's sport. They play it well, to be sure; yet, whatever the final score, it doesn't change the basic nature of the spectators' lives. Once the game, match, or race is over, the fans go back to being what they were.

That isn't something they want to hear while they are cheering loudly for their favorite player or team. If they are watching a dispute on a TV talk show—an even better place to practice disengaging—they may be equally caught up, both physically and intellectually. However, if they can learn how to stop themselves at will from reaching this tension-filled state—by saying "Time to disengage"—they will have taken an important first step toward being able to do this at the office. There, they have to worry about the added complication that they are participants, not mere spectators, and presumably it is harder to walk away.

Nonetheless, it is actually easier. Whether they realize it or not, most of the fights men like David get into begin as someone else's quarrel—in which *they* become embroiled. Having carefully examined the beginnings, middles, and ends of more than fifteen hundred such office disputes during the last ten years, we can state with confidence that the outcome of the disagreement matters just about as much to the men as does the question of who won the World Series last year.

Since the ambitious men we're discussing aren't fools, one would assume they already know that. Why, then, do they act in so self-destructive a manner? Precisely because (1) they *are* ambitious, and (2) their picture of what it takes to achieve the success they so badly want is appallingly distorted. Regardless of the casual manner they try to project, their behavior indicates that they are using a highly inflexible approach to get what they want. The unwritten rule they are following is "Allow *no* steps backward." Without putting it into words, they truly believe that the only way to attain their goal is the way a soldier marches ten miles: one step at a time until the distance is covered. Yet the fact remains that very few men get to the top of their field in as direct a manner as this; the path is typically much more tortuous.

LEARNING TO HANDLE SETBACKS

There is an irony in our suggestion that David-types learn how to disrupt their own involvement as spectators as a way of enhancing their ability to disengage from a fruitless office fight before it begins. The irony is that, of the four men we met in the first four chapters, men like David tend to be the least athletic and therefore to have the most glamorized picture of what happens to a person who participates regularly and well in sports. They imagine that he experiences a number of victories and that these cherished moments are ones the athlete remembers forever. As David put it, "I would guess they help give him confidence."

They may, but as it turns out, the most valuable moments a high-school or college athlete experiences are not those in which he wins. It is those in which he is virtually handed his head as part of a thumping loss. A narrow defeat he can always dismiss as having been the result of a lucky break or two for the other side. However, a rout—well, that's different. It may make him reassess his performance and improve upon it considerably. The real moral here is, as one champion college football player (now a physician) told us, "You don't learn anything when you win, but when you lose—you better."

What happens in a stadium and what takes place in an office is a study in contrasts. The two settings differ drastically, and not just in appearance, but the quote about setbacks highlights a crucial factor that separates those who go on to succeed at work from those who ultimately fail. It suggests that, first, persistence is essential; and second, that when someone who truly wants to get somewhere is knocked down, he has to pick himself up, brush off the dust, and get back in there—strengthened by the lessons learned from the setback.

To some people that advice is so obvious it doesn't need to be stated.

Others need to hear it again and again, because they aren't even friends with the men who might give it to them. Larry required no such reminders, having acted in accordance with this particular guideline from the time he was a boy. David-types, on the other hand, rarely pal around with men like Larry. As a result, they have to learn from other sources what is highly useful in Larry's business style and what is self-destructive.

"SAVE ME, SUPERMAN"

That is precisely what Ben Cutler did. Although his socioeconomic background and personality profile were similar to David's, he changed over the years in ways that made his approach significantly more productive, both at home and in the office. Moreover, he did it consciously. Some people make major shifts in their interpersonal style without realizing it—for instance, Roger Davis, whom we met in the previous chapter—while others literally force themselves to make modifications that they consider worthwhile.

It wasn't until Ben was in his mid-twenties that he recognized not only that important changes in his life were needed, but also the specific direction in which he should move. As he put it, at twenty-four, "I'm too concerned about what people think of me, too worried that they won't like me." Pausing for a moment, he added, "I'm sure others my age think about it too, but I think about it almost *all day*."

While many men go to Charles Bronson and Clint Eastwood films for entertainment, Ben went to them for lessons. The majority of moviegoers watched enjoyably empty-headed action; Ben, on the other hand, saw eyes that didn't blink, faces that didn't smile, and men who didn't flinch. He began copying them. If he seemed a decade late in doing so ("I was one of the oldest people there who wasn't accompanying a kid"), it was because he had previously rejected the message such seemingly hard-hearted men were sending. "I always thought you were supposed to be sensitive and open, especially when I was in my teens. Now, I'm not so sure. I keep getting my ego bruised and feelings hurt."

That he did. If meek adolescents idolize muscle-bound football players, wrestlers and dragon slayers, it is because the youngsters fear dragons—fear all kinds of things—and want someone powerful to dispel their anxieties. They consider a strong personal protector essential and often imagine the man on the screen rushing to help them when danger arises.

Ben had no such illusions. As an adult, he had come to realize that if anyone was going to protect him, it would have to be he himself. "You can't keep waiting for Superman to show up and save you, just in the nick of time," he said at twenty-five, without despair or self-pity. He knew what he had to do and started doing it.

It wasn't easy. Used to responding to people's every word and emotion, Ben began to ignore some of their remarks and most of their moods. "Playing deaf," a practice that previously would have been as unthinkable to him as it was to David, suddenly seemed a good idea. It was a device that he stumbled upon accidentally, when he really didn't hear what a hostile co-worker had said to him, but he noticed that it served him well as a way of "buying time." Instead of reacting instantly—and too emotionally—he could think about the best reply while the person repeated a comment that may have been a biting one. The device worked. Nasty surprises became fewer as the years went by, because, even though they still popped out of the blue occasionally, Ben made them wait just a moment or two before they bit him.

Interestingly, none of Ben's co-workers whom we interviewed came to consider him as either deaf or rude. They merely thought of him as distracted, lost in thought at the particular moment when they voiced unpleasant news or a personal slam. As Bert Robinson, the most malicious competitor among Ben's co-workers, commented, "I told him he was an ass, and he replied, 'Did you say something? Were you speaking to me?' I just answered, 'Never mind.' You know, it's not the same if you have to repeat it."

Using selective deafness as a shield during unfriendly encounters wasn't Ben's only new technique. He also took a page from Larry's book. Of the four types of men, none is more prepared to enter a verbal free-for-all than Larry. More vocal than Bill, who isn't afraid of them either, a man like Larry may even voice an insult to someone just to make the atmosphere surrounding them start crackling with electricity.

Ben never went that far, but he did indeed decide at some point during his late twenties that "sticks and stones may break my bones but names can never hurt me." Ben didn't take these words seriously until he was nearing thirty. Before then, it is fair to say that he did everything possible to make certain no one called him a derogatory name. They did so anyway, eventually making him realize that he could not ward off this evil merely by dismissing it and would instead have to confront it directly.

RELAXED, READY FOR ANYTHING

Why one person comes to this realization and another who is quite similar doesn't, is hard to say. However, our study leaves no doubt as to, first, the large number of men who in essence are "prisoners of their own politeness" (approximately 19 percent of the white-collar portion of our sample), and second, the high price these men pay for being unable to respond effectively when an interpersonal situation becomes tense or combative. Ben was unusual in sensing both the need for change and then attempting to bring it about in himself. Regardless of how much he learned by imitating "the strong silent type," he learned even more by watching people skilled in repartee. He was determined to be like them, "even though I'm not very glib," he added.

Memorizing a few witty lines, good comebacks that he had seen in classic 1940s movies, was a first step, but it was one that didn't work. When he needed the lines most, he couldn't remember them. Life didn't follow art, and the script of the movie rarely resembled the lines to which he was called upon to respond. It took a while for him to take the next step, yet we noticed that by the time Ben was in his early thirties he had clearly made the decision to "relax and enjoy it." If life inevitably involved some verbal shoving matches, in which civility was set aside for the moment, then so be it.

At work and at home Ben lowered his guard, ready to grapple with anyone—anyone sane, that is—who aimed an insult in his direction. He became noticeably less sensitive to barbs and slights because he had stopped spending so much of each day waiting for them to arrive. Like many men who are overly polite, Ben had married a woman, Jennie Elliott, who had no trouble speaking her mind. If the food they were served in a restaurant was unpalatable, it was Jennie who called the waiter over and said so, while Ben quietly cringed. The changes he made over the years in the direction of becoming more candid and direct would, we suspected, have an impact on his marriage. They did, but, as in the large majority of cases we monitored, the effect was positive.

Instead of fighting more—the expected outcome of his greater assertiveness—the two fought significantly less. At first we concluded that this was because Jennie was no longer annoyed regularly at his meekness ("*He* should be the one telling the waiter the stuff is inedible, not me"). No doubt that was part of the reason for their greater tranquility as a pair, but it turned out to be due mostly to his decreased reactivity. When his wife aimed a gratuitous insult at him, something she was inclined to do, Ben previously reacted with the courtesy that was his trademark, all the while concealing the anger the remark generated. When insult number eight, say, arrived, and he no longer could hold in his accumulated anger, he erupted. Either way, whether holding it in or erupting, he felt foolish. Neither seemed to him the best way of handling the situation.

Thanks to his greater ability to defend himself, developed slowly and haltingly at first, he could more calmly hear her barbs and reply, "What's eating you?" Or, if she persisted, he answered in kind: "Take your hostility and shove it." Letting her know that her anger was *her* problem eventually worked wonders, but, to repeat, it did so mainly because Ben had stopped being so timid—which was frequently what made Jennie hostile in the first place.

By the time Ben was in his early thirties he had stopped walking on eggs and spending nearly every waking moment waiting to be verbally assaulted. He was no longer mortified at the prospect of a bruising argument with someone ("I'll probably get a few black-and-blues, but they will too"). So, for precisely the same reason that well-muscled young men get into *fewer* fights than scrawny ones do, Ben could respond appropriately instead of being the victim. As he put it poignantly, "I don't feel like the patsy, the fall guy, anymore."

That gender wasn't involved here is clear from the fact that the same conspicuous improvement was taking place at the time in his office encounters, whether men or women were involved. Far fewer of them resulted in his flaring up, losing control, and, as he described it, making a fool of himself. Perhaps the greatest compliment he received for deliberately incorporating some of Bill's and Larry's approach to life into his own was a sentence that he never heard. "I used to like picking on him," Carl, one of the office bullies, a wiry, nervous chain-smoker, told us in confidence. "He was so easy to intimidate, especially when other people were around." Wanting him to continue, we asked, "And now?" Carl replied offhandedly, "There are easier pickings. I pretty much leave him alone."

It is small wonder that Ben feels—and his co-workers and superiors agree—that he has been much more productive in recent years.

SELF-PROTECTIVE TECHNIQUES THAT DON'T WORK

It is illuminating at this point to take another look at the three statements cited most often by men like David as the best way to move forward in the world without suffering any reverses. If people were always kind and considerate, David's tense and unbending approach would undoubtedly work better than Larry's "roll with the punches" one. However, people are also gossipy, competitive, envious, self-serving, and at times malicious, and that makes it imperative for David-types to revise the guidelines they have unwittingly been using.

For instance, as we saw earlier, the first rule espoused by these well-meaning men is that "Having a good reputation helps fend off criticism." Actually, it does the reverse, since it makes such a man a target for other ambitious men and women who are seeking to make a name for themselves by besmirching someone else's.

The second maxim David-types live by is, "Your past achievements will come to your rescue when you need them during tough times." It would be nice if that were so, and men like David have no monopoly on this belief. Nevertheless, the evidence indicates that the statement is filled with false hope. In a world that grows more competitive daily, only one's most recent accomplishments count. If David's latest piece of work is good, he can usually count on its being well received; but if it is second-rate, he is kidding himself to think that the senior executives at his firm will say, "That's all right, he has done good work in the past, you know." At most, it will get him a second or third chance to get it right, instead of being fired on the spot.

The third and final belief that men like David live by is, in many ways, the most self-deceiving: "Being well mannered and looking good help ensure your success." This turns out to be so only if one knows when *not* to be well mannered. There is no question that making a good first impression is valuable. Most people are lazier than they care to admit and are willing to take at face value the product or person they see; however, the public becomes less lazy and more skeptical after repeated contact with someone. Then it is especially important for men like David to shift gears and adapt to this more intimate and honest style, one that is characterized by a greater degree of give-and-take.

Unfortunately, few make such a shift at the times when it is needed most. Not only is their image too static, almost a billboard, they also keep presenting it to longtime co-workers who feel they have a right to get beyond this façade of formality. As one of David's colleagues put it, "I almost wish he *would* take me for granted." Said another, "David always makes you feel like he's greeting an old acquaintance he hasn't seen for years, instead of someone he worked with last night—as we did—till 8 P.M."

Many men like David are aware that they spend a great deal of time trying to please, appease, and entertain co-workers. They do so much of this, and it makes them so nervous, it would be hard for them *not* to notice themselves doing it. Some say they feel like firemen, racing from one trouble spot to the next, trying to extinguish a blaze here and a brush fire there. The picture is misleading, for it presents the men in a very active light, moving from one location to another.

A more accurate picture would involve the boy in Dutch myth, with his finger in the dike, staving off a flood. But this time, every hole that David-types plug up only seems to cause yet another leak to appear elsewhere. Trying to attend to them all, men like David can inwardly become quite frantic.

Why does this happen? Because David is spending most of his energies shoring up his guard. If he sets an alarm, he sleeps *less* well that night since he doesn't want to be startled awake. He therefore spends the whole night on edge, trying to make certain he turns off the alarm before it rings. He literally doesn't want to be caught napping—ever. With the lion's share of his time being devoted each day to defense, it is surprising that he can pursue his ambitions successfully at all. Yet the main reason he has to pour so much of his energies and attention into defense is that the self-protective techniques he is using don't work.

Not only do the techniques not work, it is amazing to see them precipitate the very events such a man is afraid will occur. In spite of the considerable effort he makes to placate others, they report feeling "handled," even "manipulated," and don't like it. That inclines them to be more critical of him, not less. Men like David insist that they are attempting to make people like them. We don't agree. What they are actually doing is trying hard to avoid having people *dis*like them, which is another matter altogether. In any event, the approach they use accomplishes neither goal.

David's "Maginot line" mentality—"I've set up a barrier that the enemy won't be able to penetrate"—can also be thought of as a "banker's outlook"—"I'm not going to lose any of what I've accumulated." However it is viewed, this passive, almost cowering approach brings out the bully in others. Fearful that his all-important defense is failing, he overreacts to an erroneous statement someone else makes and becomes engaged in a struggle that harms him—even if he wins.

OUTDOING DAD

Some of the most revealing comments men like David make are about their fathers. While it is commonly assumed that a record proportion of the labor force is currently self-employed, thanks to all the publicity entrepreneurs have received in recent years, the opposite is true. The percentage is actually smaller now (approximately 7 percent) than it was forty years ago (12 percent). For one thing, the stores that lined the downtown streets of American towns and new suburbs springing up in the 1950s were more likely at the time to be run by their owners; now they are more likely to be run by employees. The "mom and pop" luncheonette has been superseded as a fast-food joint and hangout spot for adolescents by a branch of a national hamburger chain.

Most of the children of suburban entrepreneurs, and of workers who commuted to the nearby city, went to college. There they acquired a new attitude, one that was an inherent though unspoken part of the profession they were also acquiring. Men like David's father tried to conduct their business in accordance with the philosophy that "The customer is always right." The men of David's generation adopted the reverse view. "The customer is always wrong," each came to believe. "I'm the pro. The public doesn't know anything."

Whether this approach managed to produce a living for the flood of professionals pouring out of the nation's colleges and graduate schools isn't our concern here. The relevant question is, What attitude did it give these men toward their own fathers?

The answer is an uncomfortable one. The men saw people like their fathers—though not their actual fathers—as "grovelers" and "too accommodating." When shown on film a man whose business behavior closely resembled their father's, they often labeled him "a boot licker" and even "an ass kisser." These men had no intention of being similarly at the mercy of what in most cases were retail customers. The young professionals were going to be able to lord it over their own clients or they would not be in business at all. In short, both for professional and personal reasons ("outdoing Dad"), the men we studied were determined to be classier, if not richer, than their fathers.

The problem with this attitude is that it has backfired badly. The nation is certainly more affluent now than it was three decades ago, and the post–World War II baby-boom generation is the best educated in American history. However, the nature of the U.S. economy has steadily shifted during this period toward services and away from manufacturing. The clash that has developed *within* the minds of each of these men is this: a tug-of-war between providing *service* and gaining *status*.

That is a much trickier pair of goals to achieve than it seems at first glance. It is difficult to say to someone, "I am your humble servant," and in the next breath hit them with, "I am also your social superior." Few Americans handle this one well. In fact, approximately 45 percent of all the ambitious and talented men we studied who failed did so because of difficulties directly connected with the simultaneous pursuit of these two goals. If they had their own company, it failed to flourish; if they worked for someone else, they didn't get to the top—or if they did, were unable to stay there long.

The reason for their repeated setbacks is to be found in the solution the vast majority hit upon to lessen their inner tension. How can someone convince himself that he is humbly serving, to the best of his ability, people to whom he also wants to feel superior? Simple, all he has to do is see himself as providing services to people who are *beneath* him.

Anyone who has ever been served a meal by a pretentious waiter in an expensive restaurant knows what it is like to be on the receiving end of this type of treatment. However, M.B.A.s, doctors, lawyers, librarians, teachers, secretaries, and civil servants actually dispense more of it. What is astonishing is that, although they quickly recognize it when someone else acts this way toward them, they are blind to similar behavior coming from themselves and aimed at their clientele. The price for such blindness is high. Not knowing whether to be humble or arrogant, they alternate unpredictably between the two. Torn between the egalitarian American ethic and their own burning desire for professional eminence and status display, they offend and confuse others. Alienated customers, from whom men like David particularly hope to receive both gratitude and admiration, give them only money—and resent doing so.

Instead of realizing what a major contribution he has made to thwarting his own ambitions, such a man typically takes refuge in the safest and most self-serving of excuses: "I knew it, they really *are* beneath me." While this stance certainly damages his chance for success, nothing hurts him more than his search for a life without setbacks. The stiff demeanor, meticulous appearance, and polite manner aren't sufficient armor against minor or major failures; both are inevitable. Being continually on guard only makes each setback more devastating, a shock when it arrives despite the extensive defenses.

CHAPTER
•7•

BRILLIANT BUT
POWERLESS

"People never give me the compliments *I* want to hear," Steve once said, "just the ones *they* feel like handing out." He has a long list of other work-related complaints—does quite a bit of complaining, actually—and rails regularly against fate. It doesn't take many years of studying such a man to realize that there is a powerful struggle going on inside him. On the one side is a force that compels him to try to be loved "for himself," not for anything specific he is, has, or does. On the other side is an equally powerful force compelling him to be highly skilled in a particular area, so that people will say, "Wow, you really do that well."

While growing up, every boy experiences this internal tug-of-war repeatedly. To be an integral part of a schoolyard baseball team or football game in gym class, he has to demonstrate a well-defined skill. Ideally, that should earn him not only a place on the squad, but also acceptance and friendship from its members. "Do my teammates think of me as just a first baseman?" a sixteen-year-old wearing a baseball uniform asked, repeating our question to him. "Nah, we got past that long ago. We're pals now."

This is the way it is supposed to work, and the Steves of the world are amazed when it doesn't. Resolving their inner conflict about which to be—outstanding in a particular area or loved for themselves—strikes them as easy. The first will lead to the second, they believe, and will do so automatically. They know that each day, as in the episode involving the sixteen-year-old quoted above, there are an enormous number of instances in which the process operates quite smoothly.

Slowly but surely it begins to dawn on men like Steve that, at least in their case, the process isn't working. If this one-two sequence only failed on the playing field, these men wouldn't be so upset. However, they rightly claim that the work world makes the same demand—and holds out the prospect of a similar reward for meeting the demand: developing a special skill will get them a good job that pays well and will also make them an integral and well-liked part of the operation, perhaps even its president.

As they eventually become aware, this rarely happens. It is mathematically inevitable that most of the people who yearn for a top slot won't have one, unless they found their own firms. But men like Steve are justified to some extent in their belief that they are more capable and concerned than the majority of their co-workers. "If anybody has the right to be the chief executive here, it's me," they state sincerely.

Why, then, does the evidence indicate they are *less* likely than their peers to be the ones chosen for these choice positions? If they are ever to hold the top slot, then, like Steve, is each forced to start his own company and appoint himself its chief?

WINNING PUBLIC APPROVAL

Certain stereotypes seem so appropriate that it is hard to believe they might mask more than they reveal. When people are asked what motivates a brilliant scientist, they have little doubt that it is an inner interest: curiosity. "He has a question about the universe and wants badly to answer it," is a typical reply one hears in surveys. Or, "He became hypnotized by a subject he was working on and got lost in it for life."

By the time the scientist is an adult it may be difficult to get beyond this view, since he usually seems to fit it so well. To see what else there is to his story, we either have to watch closely how he behaves when others — colleagues and laymen—are around, or else follow his development from adolescence on. We have done both with more than nine hundred such Steves. Few chose science as their field; in fact, the vast majority became engineers, writers, accountants, musicians, teachers, editors, economists, artists, or securities analysts. While not everyone who enters these occupations is like the people we're about to describe, there are enough of them to make it worthwhile to see what they have in common. As it turns out, their professions differ but their personalities display many important similarities.

The best way to understand how these men behave on a day-to-day basis, and why they go on to do well or poorly in their fields, is to see how they handled rejection in their teens and twenties. Although some things are avoidable, rejection is not. Rich or poor, handsome or homely, men of every description know what this experience feels like. As one put it, "Having lots of money doesn't save you, it simply means you get rejected by a better class of people."

Different men respond differently to rejection. The Bills of the world send it back immediately; aim a cutting remark at them and it is likely to be returned before the initial sentence is finished. They don't take any of it "in," and instead play ping-pong with any insults that come their way. The Davids of the world do the same, yet they worry much more than the Bills do that the remark will compromise their social standing. Totally public in orientation, they continually fear a loss of face. The discovery of a personal flaw doesn't really worry them; each knows he has many but expects others to be polite enough not to point them out. Men like Larry react to rejection by trying harder. Their approach is to "never say die," and if, in their view, it takes twice as much money to earn their way into the inner circle, they are prepared to work tirelessly to get it. Finally, men like Steve (the most sensitive of the four) respond to rejection by recoiling, though it usually isn't apparent to observers. Each insult not only gets in, once it does it ricochets around in their innards, causing even greater damage later. There is something fatalistic about a Steve's reaction. While David-types fret that an abusive comment may knock down the fragile social house of cards they have tried so hard to assemble, men like Steve greet an episode of rejection with surface anger and an inner air of resignation. "I knew it; here is another of my weaknesses being publicly exposed."

Pop psychology has done Steve-types a major disservice in telling them repeatedly that what they need is more confidence. The advice focuses on the symptom, not the source, and actually makes their situation worse. For the real trouble springs from their basically reclusive orientation. The reason they recoil from an insult is that, for them, this is the path of least resistance. To others, watching the withdrawal, it seems as if these men "hole up" for a while, retreat into themselves—angry, to be sure, but intent upon leaving the scene of the confrontation.

Nonetheless, that is almost never the way the men themselves see their response. For instance, shortly after Steve landed his first job, a hostile co-worker called him a "twerp." Bill would have replied instantly with, "Yeah, and you're a bigger one." Larry, who was more feisty and articulate, would have said (and once did), "Why don't we step outside and see if you can say that again with no teeth in your mouth," and, on another occasion, "I don't know what's bugging you, but then again, you're ugly enough for it to be dozens of things." David would have been mortified, since the remark was made with three other people present. He would probably have replied, with an upbeat manner and nervous smile, "That's no way to treat the new kid on the block." Steve, by contrast, only made the hole in which he suddenly found himself deeper, by asking, "Why do you say that?" Fabricating things on the spot, the co-worker then proceeded to tell him.

Steve was wounded by the encounter, as his anger made clear, but his colleagues misinterpreted the few days of irritable withdrawal that followed. Instead of hiding out, men like Steve almost invariably use this time to deepen their commitment to their specialty. To others it may look like a period of hibernation, yet the Steves of the world *more* easily become immersed in their work at such moments because they no longer have to make the effort to be social. In spite of the animosity they feel, as the recipient of a gratuitous jab, they are secretly thrilled at being able to focus on what, in their view, really counts: their work.

This approach is more productive for the men who use it during their teens and twenties than has previously been recognized. In essence, it converts each setback they receive into a step forward. It also explains why the men are so reluctant to imitate Larry, say, and fight back. They know (although no one else around them appears to) that they are making headway in their moments alone, by concentrating on the first of the two-step sequence that they believe ultimately wins public approval for professionals.

LEADER OF THE PACK

Only it doesn't work that way. The logic of the argument of men like Steve is impeccable but the argument is the wrong one. Bright as these men are, it seems not to have occurred to them that to move up they have to become almost entirely different people. "So does everyone else who wants to become a top manager," they might retort. "If nothing else, you have to become more mature." The demand for greater maturity does apply to everyone, yet men like Steve face an extra obstacle: the talents that got them their initial promotions during their twenties and early thirties were technical in nature, whereas skills that more directly involve people become increasingly important for aspiring managers once the men are in their late thirties, forties, and fifties.

That isn't a switch most men like Steve are prepared to make. Why? They don't recognize the pressing need for it in the first place, much less that it will be a hard one to make. *Trusting to the logic of the approach they have been using since adolescence, they remain firmly convinced that if they expand their technical abilities, they are nearly guaranteed acceptance—and even a leadership role—in the group.*

At the first sign that this strategy isn't working, they do something astonishing. Typically the men are in their late thirties or forties by this time, and their expectations of a move into senior management are beginning to grow. They may claim they are happy where they are, especially if the next promotion means they will no longer be doing the work that has gotten them this far. Nevertheless, it is important to remember that, as much as they truly like the technical area in which they have become outstanding, it was always supposed to be a ticket of admission to a more interpersonal and less solitary world. When that payoff isn't received, and they aren't granted the senior executive position for which they have been waiting, they feel cheated.

Sad to say, very few (38 out of 937, or 4 percent) of the men like Steve we studied who found themselves repeatedly in this situation stated, "Oops, looks like I've been using the wrong approach; time for a different one." Instead, what the vast majority did was pout—and handle the next bit of rejection the same way they had been handling similar setbacks ever since high school: by immersing themselves still further in their specialty. It looked to others as if they were recoiling from yet another failure at work; however, as the men themselves knew, they had been liberated. Blocked in one direction, they returned to the sole area of their lives that offered them solace. It calmed their anxieties, erased their frustration, and soothed their bruises. Here, and only here, they felt at home.

If they had then said to themselves, "This is where I feel best, so this is where I'll stay," all would have been well. But they were still guided by the logic they had been using for decades: by embedding themselves yet again in their specialty (forgetting for the moment their motives for doing so), they further increased their technical competence. They therefore expected to be rewarded for the heightened mastery they were ready to display. Paradoxically, each rejection merely wound up making them feel that much more eligible for the promotion and applause they had just been denied.

QUALITY WILL OUT—OR WILL IT?

Smarter than most, brilliant in some cases, the men soon sensed that their careers were going off track. They attempted to remedy what ailed them by using a variety of solutions that were as revealing as the problem itself.

The world makes allowances for talent. Creative people don't have to be as well balanced emotionally as, say, managers and pilots. People who are highly skilled at, for instance, science or art, aren't expected to be as well dressed as maître d's. If not before, most intelligent young men learn this when they attend college. Unlike high school, college demands of students that they perform academically. How they dress doesn't interest the school, and, not surprisingly, it therefore doesn't interest the students much either. Many dress like hoboes and don't give the topic a second thought. Others do think about their clothes, in negative terms; they believe that dressing neatly would make them look like salesmen—"as though I were trying to make a good impression," was how one Princeton physics major put it. It thus becomes important to some students to appear not to be dwelling on the subject at all. The message they attempt to send is, "Can't you see I'm too lost in thought to worry about such trivialities as what I'm wearing?" Some of those walking around in socks that don't match, tattered jeans, and T-shirts that are twisted and too small may be pondering the fate of the universe, and others dressed this way are wearing a costume they hope will convince onlookers that, as the physics student commented, "I'm profound, I really am."

Einstein is the model such men are imitating, and the mimicry goes well beyond costumes to everyday civilities. The attitude is, "I don't have to say hello to anybody if my mind is occupied with matters of great weight." Most know that the switch from campus to corporate life will necessitate some changes, but, especially for men like Steve, the attitude is abandoned much less readily than had previously been thought. That they now put on a suit each morning before going to work isn't as simple an act as it seems.

In fact, this concession, an insignificant one in most people's eyes, is a major one in the view of the men making it. Why? Because Einstein never made it. They have almost his brains, of that much they are certain, and they are also willing to wear an expensive suit. That, they quickly conclude, is a "can't lose" combination. While other men use "dress for success" formulas to improve their chances of getting ahead, men like Steve use them with the supreme confidence that their success is now assured.

Unfortunately, that isn't how things usually turn out. Even if they did, the men would be miffed, for they want to be applauded for their talents, not their clothes. An important rule is being violated, a deeply held belief that "quality will out." Whether the men majored in English, economics, chemistry, or art, they became convinced in school that a brilliant novel, scientific breakthrough, or great painting would create its own prominence. No promotional effort was needed. Yet here they were, fifteen or twenty years later, dedicated to the craft that had become the basis of their livelihood—idealists in the business world, taking seriously what men like Larry peddled cynically—and it wasn't enough. Their true worth remained unrecognized.

Historians of science, owners of art galleries, and publishers of quality works of fiction had some eye-opening things to say that men like Steve needed to hear but didn't. "Every year there are novels published that are outstanding, yet they die on bookstore shelves," the editor-in-chief of a major publishing house told us. Similar comments were heard from the head of one of the best known art galleries. "What good does it do an artist who is long dead before his work receives the critical acclaim it always deserved?" he asked, adding, "And many won't have the acclaim even then—their work will continue to be overlooked." Contrary to popular belief, the same is also true in science and engineering. The timing may simply be wrong; the public may not be sufficiently interested in the achievement at the time. Regardless of the field, there is nothing automatic about the emergence of an applauding audience for a discovery, innovation, or work of art. It has to find a champion, someone of stature who proclaims it worthy of attention. Even then, as the gallery owner reminds us, a favorable outcome is by no means guaranteed.

Men like Steve are used to sneering at marketers of art and literature, marketers of all kinds, and view them as unnecessary. Instead of nodding their heads in agreement when the gallery owner and publisher quoted above spoke, they would have termed each explanation a self-serving excuse for the failure to grant a great artist his due—a situation with which they identify easily.

They are especially sensitive to this situation because they are doing more than artists or scientists; they are dressing up and even making polite conversation daily with people they would prefer never to talk to. As a result—and it would stun them to recognize it—when they put on their suits in the morning, they get mad. Many stay remote and resentful all day, which further diminishes the odds that they will eventually be tapped for the top position at the firm.

COMFORTABLE IN GIVE-AND-TAKE

Reversing this downward spiral isn't all that hard for men like Steve, particularly after they become adept at sensing that, once again, they are reacting in an unproductive and perhaps self-destructive manner. Trying to compel the world to give them the recognition they seek—and deserve—is a waste of time, given the tools they are using. Men like Steve may not like hearing it, but it is precisely the Larry-types who hold the key to their problems. Imprisoned in a mentality that generally fails to produce the positive results they think it will, they need to steal a page from Larry's book if they are truly to free themselves, rather than just feeling free (secretly) the next time someone insults them and they run back to the technical aspects of their work.

The real source of the most serious professional setbacks generally experienced by men like Steve is to be found in their tendency to become intellectual recluses. This inclination, which is present at least from their teen years on, makes them the opposite of men like Larry, who can't wait to grapple personally again with a customer, clerk, or business competitor and hope to emerge on top. Small wonder that, in most firms, someone like Larry is the boss and someone like Steve is his prized but uncelebrated lieutenant. Less colorful but more competent, concerned about doing what is right instead of merely what sells, men like Steve have to do one thing above all: become more comfortable around people.

They think they already are, yet the evidence indicates exactly the reverse. For when someone like Steve has a conversation with others, he is likely to cling to his technical knowledge as though it were a life preserver and he a drowning man. Without being aware of it, he wants people to view him through the lens created by his professional expertise. He hopes they will always keep it in mind, and compliment his skill at the same time that they speak highly of him as a person. He fears being without this aspect of himself, worries that if they can't see him as an accomplished expert of some kind, they won't be able to see him at all.

He is wrong, but only by allowing himself to be seen naked— emotionally, not physically—will he ever find that out. This is much less difficult in some ways for men like Steve to do than for those in the other three categories. Larry-types are often deviously clever and would be among the first to admit that they have much to lose if everything in life, and especially business, were conducted in a strictly open and aboveboard manner. "I exploit the nooks and crannies, the stuff everybody else overlooks," was a favorite phrase of Larry's. Men like David are equally reluctant to level with their peers because of their view that, as David once commented, "Life in high society is mostly a fabulous fiction anyway. Who needs honesty? What's so good about it? It's usually a downer." Men like Bill have their emotions buried so deep, the better to arm themselves *for* the rigors of manufacturing goods and *against* servicing people's personal needs, it would probably take a stick of dynamite to loosen some of the feelings they carry internally in inventory.

However, men like Steve are different; they have indeed tried to live their lives in an honorable and helpful manner, it's just that they wanted to do so from behind an invisible shield that would protect them from rejection—in the end, an impossibility. Technical and creative knowhow was to be their modern equivalent of the suit of armor worn by medieval knights. At least initially, the approach works. It gets them a number of pay raises and promotions. But, once they want to rise into top managerial positions, it holds them back. This is even more so if they want to run their own companies successfully. In such settings first and foremost they have to learn how to be quick on their feet, comfortable in give-and-take with a variety of people. The turtle shell no longer keeps insults out, it merely restricts their own upward mobility and thwarts their aspirations.

If they make the effort to be rid of it, the thing they are most likely to notice is the host of thoughtless and abusive remarks people often make. These hurtful and competitive slams, many delivered innocently and with a smile, are an unavoidable part of contemporary life. Nevertheless—and this is a key point—they are also an opportunity. As Larry knows only too well, every arrow that comes one's way can be turned around and aimed at the sender. "People who dish it out usually can't take it," Larry once said. This insightful remark is based on a simple but immensely useful fact: people who are happy don't shower others with insults, while those who are unhappy with themselves do so regularly. The torpedo they aim one's way is generally full of garbage they want to be rid of (psychologists call this "projection"), and it is important not to let them use one's ego as a dumping ground.

The most relevant advice a man like Steve needs to hear if he is to improve significantly his chances of attaining success is this: don't take in *anyone's* insults at work. Learn to send them back in one form or another, and the sooner the better. Verbal abuse makes a Steve-type retreat into his shell, a response that brings out the sadist, not the sympathizer, in others and usually makes them escalate their attacks. Even if it doesn't, it disqualifies a man like Steve in the eyes of bystanders as a serious contender for the firm's top slot.

To repeat, insults are an opportunity to shine, not to run, and for men like Steve, who have much less to hide than most, they should eventually even be welcome. If that sounds unimaginable to someone who has spent virtually his entire life trying to protect himself from barbs, consider the following three facts:

1. The put-downs—voiced or implied—cannot be avoided, particularly as one moves into executive ranks and the crossfire intensifies.
2. One's response to put-downs can either be productive or unproductive; it is unlikely to be neutral.
3. Giving in to one's reclusive orientation, and allowing the wall of technical expertise that is supposed to act as a shield to grow still thicker, makes the damage an abusive remark inflicts last decades instead of hours. It also intensifies the damage, since one hasn't had a chance to rid oneself of the poison it represents.

Our goal isn't to turn the Steves of the world into corporate gunslingers who use every office hallway to restage the final showdown from *High Noon*. Any progress such men made in learning to defend themselves better was repeatedly found to result in a *decreased* quantity of conflict, and the fights that did occur were generally less intense. As things now stand, it is their own hostility—generated by what they feel is their failure to be appreciated—that starts most of the battles these men get into, and as long as this condition prevails, telling them to concentrate on defending themselves more effectively is only a small part of what is needed for a major improvement to occur. Technical knowledge is often fascinating and has become essential to the quality of modern life, but it should never be used as the equivalent of a cave into which one crawls for protection against criticism. That it cannot provide.

A PAST AND FUTURE SELF

So many men have successfully made the transition from being an almost pure Steve-type to a more productive hybrid of a Steve and a Larry that we should look at a few examples. Less than 10 percent of them made the shift consciously, understanding where they were and knowing where they wanted to wind up. The rest made the right moves, but for practical reasons that were more professional than personal.

"I knew I'd be an engineer one day," Alan Green told us during his sophomore year at a large state university. "Even in high school, nothing else sounded right." Obtaining a degree in electronics engineering opened many doors for him ("I had nine job offers when I graduated"), but after nearly a dozen years in the work world he was still moving up too slowly to be satisfied. "I'm being passed over for the good promotions, and getting just little ones," he told us two weeks after his thirty-third birthday. While switching jobs three times during the prior decade had helped accelerate his upward pace, he felt it had also harmed him in certain ways. "Companies like loyalty," he stated uneasily, "and I can't keep job-hopping forever, though some people in this field probably will."

Always reclusive, Alan liked nothing better than to be given a challenging problem and left alone to solve it. He wasn't fond of working in a team and had long been convinced that "the best thinking people do, they do when they are by themselves, not chatting with a group." The idea of "brainstorming in a conference room" seemed to him particularly overrated; he called it "play disguised as work." Alan got along well with his colleagues and superiors, most of whom viewed him as cooperative, not ornery or rebellious. However, few told us that they considered him a serious candidate for the executive positions he wanted so much to hold eventually.

"Grasping at a straw," he labeled it, but during his thirty-third year Alan applied and was accepted into an M.B.A. program at a major nearby university. "My company will pay for it and I think the degree will do the trick." It did, though not for the reasons Alan thinks. Others with comparable backgrounds and an M.B.A. have done much less well than he, and it was fascinating to see why. Neither the credentials nor the knowledge he gained in class, useful as they were, was as valuable as the *excuse* the program gave him to become more assertive.

Even people who know they have to change, and know specifically in what ways, often can't implement the changes because they don't hear a starter's pistol telling them it is time to get moving. Unable to make today seem sufficiently different from yesterday, so that they have a decisive moment at which to begin, they repeatedly postpone making the desired effort. Calling them procrastinators merely adds insult to injury, and is what they usually label themselves anyway. It would be more accurate to think of them as realists, since they are well aware that nothing concrete actually separates the person they have been in the past from the one they want to be in the future.

Be that as it may, every project has to have a starting point, and the beginning of a two-year graduate program leading to a prestigious degree certainly provides it. Alan was typical of the Steves in our sample in using this period as a break in what was otherwise a continuum. This way, he could insist that there really were "an old me" and "a new me." Naturally, he expected the new one to be given the opportunities and praise the old one had been denied.

It worked. He returned to full-time employment more assertive than he had been before. In the course of playing at being a manager in an academically demanding environment he became accustomed to the role, no longer finding it strange or threatening when he went back to corporate life. Alan still liked being on his own, solving problems solitarily, but he was noticeably more at ease handling the people-oriented problems that are a large part of any manager's daily responsibilities. "Some I treat with kid gloves," he told us, "other people on staff I chew out. Everybody needs something different to be at his best." Whether he had actually discovered the most potent motivator for each was far less important than his focusing on the problem in the first place. Previously, he hadn't. Inspiring others, getting them to coordinate their efforts with his and cooperate with him on various projects, was of secondary interest to him.

His personality certainly didn't undergo a radical transformation—that almost never happens—but the point is that it had changed enough in the right direction so that he was indeed being viewed as a "natural" for promotion. The combination of Steve and Larry that he had become gave him a broader range of skills to call upon in the more demanding senior positions in which he has found himself for the last fourteen years.

It is worth noting that our study found that, all other things being equal, Steve-types benefited most from obtaining M.B.A.s. If becoming more assertive was, in itself, of greater value in the holder's subsequent rise than the credentials themselves or the specific knowledge gained, Larry-types would have benefited most (as measured by pay increases and promotions). They didn't. The main reason was that the men like Larry in our sample were often too aggressive to begin with. Getting an M.B.A. made them even more so—in fact, it made them feel they had been granted the *right* to behave in this manner—which eventually caused their credentials to backfire. They were viewed by superiors as egotistical and arrogant, labels that were applied significantly less frequently to Steve or David-types with similar socioeconomic, educational, and professional backgrounds.

THE HIGH PRICE OF PESSIMISM

What Alan Green achieved using a well-defined graduate business program, Michael Warner accomplished using exercise. An English major in college, Mike was never much of a sports fan or participant. Lanky, bashful, and very bright, Mike's favorite activity in high school and college was reading. This he did actively, not passively, and was able to absorb much more material while doing so than most of his classmates. Mike's imagination made the characters in novels as real to him as the people he actually met. In some ways they were even more so, since he knew things about them that his classmates hadn't told him about themselves, and that he was reluctant to ask them about.

His investigative tendencies were confined to obtaining more works by any authors who satisfied his curiosity about people, rather than himself digging into the lives of actual individuals, who might resent his intrusions. Mike called it "safe snooping—I get someone else to do it for me, and keep my nose from getting broken."

The rich world that literature offered him made everyday life seem flat by comparison. Daily events lacked "structure and significance," he observed, a bit morosely, at twenty-four. "So much of what goes on here [at a financial-services firm] is meaningless and silly." The words accurately convey a cultural haughtiness that was present, but they don't capture Mike's genuine desire to do well in the business world with which he was, slowly but surely, coming to terms. As with so many other liberal arts graduates in their twenties, his leftover academic snobbery masked a good deal of ambition that hadn't yet latched onto a specific area which promised commercial success.

Finally, in his early thirties, he realized that marketing was the area of business that most interested him. The only trouble was that, like Alan, Mike was happiest working alone (in this case, on marketing plans). He didn't enjoy what he called "the endless round of marketing meetings" his firm scheduled each month. "They're a complete waste of time." His comments sounded much like Alan's contemptuous remarks about "brainstorming in the conference room" and "play disguised as work."

Without anyone telling Mike outright that he was headed for trouble, given his career-related ambitions, he came to the conclusion that "holing up in a cave isn't going to make me rich." While he saw this as a feasible route for some ("Being in a lab all the time might be terrific for a biochemist trying to win a Nobel prize"), he knew that remedial steps of some kind were needed in his own case. Like Alan, he considered getting an M.B.A. but finally decided instead to become more athletic. In his late twenties he had taken up jogging ("I'm no jock or anything, it just makes me feel good"), and he came to believe that it could help him become the person he wanted to be.

More self-disciplined than Alan, Mike continued his jogging but added regular Nautilus-machine workouts at a local health club. At first he did it because "this way, my whole body gets exercise, not just my legs." After a while he started to expect professional as well as physical benefits from his workouts. "I feel different—my shirts and jackets are too tight; I had to move up a size when I bought new ones." The layer of upper-body muscle with which he had cloaked himself didn't make him more belligerent, it made him more confident. Surprised, and not boasting, he stated something that his co-workers had also noticed: "I'm not as afraid of the *unexpected* when I meet someone new."

That was welcome news to his firm, since its top officers were looking for people not only to develop new financial products and services, but also, as one put it, "to test the waters"—that is, get out and sell them. Thanks to Mike's self-discipline, he had embarked on a physical training program that had the same effect on him as Alan's entrance into a formal educational program leading to a graduate degree. Both had found a magical cutoff point separating past and present, as well as a method (or, more accurately, an excuse) for remolding themselves into an amalgam of Steve and Larry.

Was it worth the bother? Fortunately, we had enough people in our sample, and followed them for a sufficiently long period of time, to measure the effect of this shift. Taking 304 people who were more like Steve, whom we'll call "Reclusives," and another 304 who were more like Larry, whom we'll call "Marketers," and keeping in mind that the 608 had similar socioeconomic and educational backgrounds, our results can be summarized as follows:

TABLE 1. Financial Returns from a Marketing Orientation*

	Reclusives	*Marketers*
1975	$27,790	$27,640
1977	30,230	30,910
1979	32,990	34,860
1981	35,780	39,110
1983	38,530	44,240
1985	41,050	50,560
1986	42,770	55,050

* All figures are medians. Data compares people who were at the same career levels in 1975 and had similar socioeconomic and educational backgrounds. Total sample size in the financial services field was 1,216. Those labeled Reclusives constitute the lowest quartile, while Marketers were the highest quartile, of scores determined by measuring (1) the respondent's stated interest in sales and marketing and (2) a three-year average of the portion of each day that respondent stated (during his thirty-first, thirty-second, and thirty-third year) he was willing to spend working with strangers. The data from this portion of our study is analyzed by the author in greater detail on pp. 7–9 of *American Banker*, October 20, 1985. The smaller percentage increases granted in 1986 were primarily a result of lower inflation rates and decreased earnings at financial services firms.

Obviously, there is a monetary as well as personal payoff here. What the data make clear is that Mike, whose salary history for the past dozen years has approximated quite closely the column on the right, was able to boost his earnings by an extra 29 percent as a result of making the switch from the Reclusives' end of the spectrum to that of the less fearful Marketers. Similar results appeared in the data we gathered from every other major industry, in addition to financial services, during the past two decades. Like the other men we monitored who made this transition, none changed completely; they didn't abandon a previous personality and adopt an altogether new one. Instead, they achieved something more attainable and worthwhile. They grafted onto their old approach a number of new techniques that enabled them to take better advantage of key opportunities that arose for themselves and their firms.

One important measure of any progress made by men undergoing this transition is a decrease in the quantity of daily complaints they voice. While a certain amount of griping is normal, since the world is far from perfect, chronic complaining usually indicates that the men feel they have sustained yet another defeat. However, once they stop playing target for everyone else's barbs, they feel less like a pincushion. Avoiding face-to-face confrontations no longer seems to them so essential. Men like Steve become used to writing memos to others, or letters to the editor, as a way of expressing annoyance. Anger once removed appeals to them, especially since it gives them a chance to use their titles to help bolster their strength. They sense that in person, instead of in print, such niceties are not that effective. Nevertheless, Steve-types should forget about their own titles and credentials when seeking to take a firm stand calmly in public or make a point compellingly.

A remarkable bonus results from the changes, one that goes well beyond merely monetary rewards. The Steves of the world are the most likely of the four to give reasons—sound, convincing ones—why something *can't* be done. Men like Larry are the opposite, and are the most likely of the four to give reasons—often harebrained ones—why something *can* be accomplished.

In men like Steve the three destructive tendencies that we have been discussing are intimately linked: their pessimism, their sense of being repeatedly defeated, and their habitual avoidance of direct confrontations with colleagues. These are the main ingredients in a downward spiral that causes the vast majority of such men—typically the best intentioned of the four types—to have their careers top out in the middle, as their earnings curve levels off early and the relative rate at which they are fired steadily climbs. Snapping the spiral at any of the three points usually causes a significant improvement in how well the men do, in their own estimation and that of the people with whom they live and work.

CHAPTER
•8•

INCORPORATING
THE STRENGTHS
OF OTHERS

That David, Larry and Steve had something to learn from one another would probably startle none of the three. However, they might be quite surprised to hear that if their main goal is to increase their chances of doing well both on the job and off, what they learn from Bill is equally valuable. We have no desire to glamorize the Bills of the world. However, the evidence we've accumulated indicates that when two David-types are compared—men who are similar in every way except that one has a certain amount of Bill's personality mixed in with his own and the other fellow doesn't—the one who is the "hybrid" does significantly better both professionally and personally. The same applies to pairs either of Larrys or of Steves.

Each has something different to learn from Bill. Before we examine those aspects of him that need to be incorporated, respectively, by David,

Steve, and Larry, it is important for us to review briefly what we learned earlier about why men like Bill generally behave as they do in the first place.

STARTING FROM THE BOTTOM

Blue-collar men like Bill don't think of themselves as doing anything unusual in mocking the manners of men like David. The Bills of the world simply insist that they themselves weren't raised with the same endless emphasis on tact. "We told it like it was, in my family," they state bluntly. While that is largely true, the point is that men like Bill derive more security from this stance than has previously been recognized. Thumbing their nose at "polite society" makes them feel not only strong but unique.

Since there are many advantages to being part of the mainstream, it is easy to overlook the benefits of remaining outside it. Men like Steve, growing up in an upper-middle-class family, have more of a decision to make about this matter than most. For him, it was a question of either imitating his parents or rejecting their socioeconomic accomplishments and consciously modeling his behavior after that of people with less money. He chose the latter.

Bill wasn't really offered this choice. By the time he was old enough to see the options available to him, he had already made a decision, by default. "I am what I am," Bill said at twenty-two, with an air of pride, not resignation. Through TV, movies, travel, and contact with wealthier classmates he had become acquainted with some of the life styles existing in the United States, but it was too late. Had he set his sights earlier on moving up socially he certainly would have been able to do so. Others he knew, who were less bright and hardworking, did just that.

Nevertheless, Bill made great use of his position as a seeming outsider. Instead of feeling defeated, he considered himself victorious. While the number of men like him may have been shrinking rapidly during the 1970s and 1980s, thanks to changes in the economy, he continued to see himself as the real article and men like David, in particular, as phony. However modern this battle sounds, it is actually centuries old.

For at least the last five hundred years it has been common for people, especially those whose economic situation is improving, to copy their social superiors. "Proper behavior" started on the higher rungs of society and worked its way *down* to the lower—if not the lowest—rungs. The dictionary tells us that the word "courtesy" comes from the word "court." Greetings, gestures, and phrases that are widely used by the aristocracy eventually became widely used by the growing European middle class.

America changed all that. Rejecting the very validity of rule by a monarch to begin with, the United States went on to dismiss more than it realized, as the logic of its new position unfolded. The "common man" became king instead, and (as Garry Wills discusses in *Cincinnatus, George Washington and the Enlightenment: Images of Power in Early America*) did so to an extent that would have surprised many of the Founding Fathers, who weren't nearly as free of elitist attitudes as they thought.

With waves of new immigrants, few of whom were of royal blood, arriving during the next two centuries, the praise given people who were starting from scratch helped ease their quest. That they wanted to improve their own condition was obvious, but their primary goal on these shores was financial gain, not social status. Echoing the sentiments inherent in the national attitude, they wanted material comfort far more than to have their names mentioned on the society page of the local newspaper.

One of the distinguishing characteristics of contemporary America is its powerful bias in favor of "the underdog," but it is important to recognize that this stance represents a disguised form of hostility toward aristocracy. This way, rather than being *against* anyone—kings and queens, for example—the country can claim merely to be *for* the nobility of the everyday person. In the United States, "proper behavior" therefore often starts on the lower rungs of society and works its way *up* to the higher—if not the highest—rungs.

The proportion of men like Bill may have decreased during recent decades but, precisely for that reason, they have become more conspicuous in some ways—as unofficial spokesmen for our freedom. When a group of professionals (say, makers of felt hats) steadily becomes more obsolete, they are likely to be increasingly apologetic, as though they are blocking progress. Like Bill, they also tend to be defensive about their vanishing craft. However, most don't have the same secret stamp of approval that he felt he had from our nation.

Men like him were the ones most likely during the 1960s, and later decades as well, to put a bumper sticker on their cars that read "America—love it or leave it." Somehow they sensed that they were the ones who should be the most vocal defenders of the democratic faith.* As a group, they were receiving a steadily diminishing place in the national limelight, yet the subconscious encouragement each got in rooting for a successful "underdog" in any contest (particularly a sporting event) gave him a great deal of private satisfaction.

STRENGTH THROUGH STUBBORNNESS

As in earlier centuries, men like Bill are inclined to brand their social superiors "superficial," "pompous," "hollow," and "insincere." However, the main source of these men's sense of self-assurance comes from an unwillingness to reshape their personalities to get along better with a variety of others. *In this stubbornness lies a kind of strength.* By contrast, David employed the full range of cordial comments he knew in any situation that allowed it, and did so gladly. He wanted to be at home in a wider world, one in which he could never be certain whom he'd next encounter.

In place of politeness, Bill usually uses silence. Men like him have frequently been characterized as existing in a more homogeneous universe—"all the people they know are just like them." They are also viewed as being more xenophobic—"They don't really want to meet anyone new." However, the real difference between the interpersonal style of the two groups is this: David-types are willing to leave their opinions and, especially, their personalities fluid enough to allow room for someone else's. They are prepared subconsciously to let the other person be an anvil and bend themselves during the conversation to fit that shape. *In this flexibility lies a kind of strength.* Bill, who not only meets but has to work with a greater range of others, uses a different device to accomplish the same end, one for which he has received much abuse and none of the credit it actually deserves: he *erases* his personality, instead of continually deforming it the way David does. With his personality gone, Bill in essence is able to say to co-workers, "Look, I've taken my likes and dislikes, tastes and distastes out of the picture, now you do the same.

* Cf. David Halle, *America's Working Man* (University of Chicago Press, Chicago, 1984), and Jonathan Rieder, *Canarsie: The Jews and Italians of Brooklyn Against Liberalism* (Harvard University Press, Cambridge, 1985). These two books, read as a pair, help us understand how this peculiar situation developed and why there was indeed so much frustration and bitterness mixed in with the patriotism of older blue-collar workers.

Then we'll work together like two mechanical marvels and accomplish miracles."

In short, men like David, who play corporate chameleon, changing tint to better match their surroundings, turn out *not* to have a monopoly on meeting co-workers halfway. Being far more verbal than the Bills, David-types have self-congratulatorily characterized these constant reshapings of their personalities as strenuous and fatiguing, and no doubt they are. Yet Bill's less well advertised way of achieving the same goal is even more strenuous, since it requires continual self-suppression, usually an exhausting and irritating experience.

What men of every description can learn from these two is how easy it is to keep using, in one's private life, a technique that has proved effective in one's professional life—and ought to remain there. Men like David carry their awesome adaptability into their personal and social relations and often make a mess of both. Friends see a man like David being vigilant (when they want to relax) and looking for yet another anvil on which to mold himself (at a time when they want to be unstructured, and hence are unsuitable for the purpose), and they end up feeling estranged from him. Paradoxically, in spite of his overwhelming desire to be ac-commodating, they find him too demanding. He isn't the kind of person they want to be with in their leisure hours.

Men like Bill, on the other hand, also bring home what in this case is the stoical and taciturn stance that served them so well on the job. It shouldn't be surprising that people who do manual labor for a living have a bit of "stiff upper lip" about them. No matter how skilled they are at their craft, the tools and materials they handle daily do sometimes slip and cause injuries. Fortunately, the vast majority of cuts and bruises are minor, but the hardy manner laborers adopt—a consciously imposed "high pain threshold"—is valuable if they are happily to remain in their field.

As we've mentioned, this attitude is also made to serve a previously unrecognized *communal* purpose when blue-collar workers submerge their own personality in order to get along more readily with co-workers. A catch-22 then snares the men, and for a very good reason: people who are suppressing their own emotions—regardless of the reason—tend to become intolerant of others, including family members, who appear unwilling to do the same.

The "strong and silent" stance that proved so useful at work therefore intensifies at home, the reverse of what one might have expected. Some of these men leave their "hardened hide" at the front door when they return from work, but, precisely because so few do, the increase in grumpiness the rest display at home is conspicuous. Rather than being "the nature of the beast," as some observers (especially their wives) have suggested, this is a negative response to the more free-flowing emotions each usually encounters in his leisure hours. Preventing himself from recoiling in this irritable manner is difficult once the habit is established.

There *is* a setting in which the men allow themselves to unwind. "Give me a few beers," the majority tell us, "and a few buddies to laugh with, and I can get as relaxed as the next guy." Others, however, would rather not budge. "I'm too tired," is the most frequently encountered excuse for "just staying home, watching TV, or puttering around the house." The manual character of their work makes them reject the idea of using their evenings and weekends for exercise, as sedentary office workers often do. As one thirty-eight-year-old plumber put it, "I get all the 'physical fitness' I need on the job." Not as attentive to diet as their more educated peers, these men tend eventually to become overweight. Then they present an odd picture: more athletic and leaner than the college crowd when both are in their teens and early twenties, blue-colar workers frequently become fat in their thirties and, especially, forties, while college graduates are more determined than ever during these decades to stay slim—"lean and mean," in the business-oriented slang they use.

At first glance, the contrast between the two groups could hardly be more stark: blue-collar men seem slothful and self-satisfied to the white-collar crowd, while college-educated workers strike laborers as being spoiled and self-indulgent. Both views turn out to be largely false. It is true that, generally speaking, people who are affluent and educated take better care of themselves. For instance, they are more likely to seek medical attention for a malady, rather than let it persist and proudly bear the discomfort. This much about the "slothful" label usually pinned on men like Bill as the years roll by is accurate. Similarly, even ambitious college graduates in their twenties and thirties frequently see themselves as self-indulgent, feeling that, in the words of one, "I usually buy whatever I want—I can't wait—even if I can't afford it."

THE SEXUAL SERVANT

Nevertheless, although men like David may be fond of parties and status display, they aren't quite the hedonists they usually depict themselves as being (while criticizing the depiction). A key finding indicates why: above all, these men are polite—more so than most of them will ever realize—and *the essence of polite behavior is a willingness to interrupt one's own pleasure.*

How do we know that the people with whom we are having dinner are civilized? Without going down a checklist, we can immediately sense the answer by seeing if, for instance, they pause between bites—to talk to us—rather than just eating nonstop until they have emptied their bowl or plate. These lessons are learned so thoroughly during childhood and adolescence that it wouldn't occur to most people even to remind someone else to "put down your knife and fork and talk to me for a minute," though they might say such a thing to a teenager. Guidelines that are absorbed this deeply are said to be *internalized*. The name is appropriate, since they become as integral a part of us as our liver or spleen and are just about as visible from outside us.

Well, if people who think of themselves as well mannered feel compelled to interrupt their own pleasures, especially when others are present, what happens when such a person tries to have sexual intercourse? The act is more complicated than it seems, and while most men carry it off without undue difficulty, there is much that sits just beneath the surface and does indeed cause trouble. Sex often symbolizes the problems the men have in other areas, and does so vividly.

David's concern about his bedmate's pleasure usually reached such extremes that he was unable to focus on his own. His efforts should have made his partner's satisfaction all the greater, but they reduced it instead, because, as most of the women stated, "He makes me feel I'm on stage, performing for somebody." It was no accident that both his social friends and sex partners voiced the same complaint. Trying to please, he wound up alienating others because they found themselves unable to relax. The spotlight he shone on them, searching intently for clues as to how *he* should behave, made them tense up and finally withdraw.

This only makes the Davids of the world try harder. Their own inability to please is the one failing they cannot tolerate. They themselves might say, "I want everyone to like me," but the truth of the matter is that they want to *win* that liking, rather than simply be given it. They want to rummage around in their tool bag of prestige affiliations and social skills and come up with just the right witty remark or gracious gesture to make the other person praise them.

Situations in which this approach doesn't work merely heighten David's desire to try. Having interrupted his pleasure once, in the service of showing how responsive he is, he finds it easier to do it a second time. Interrupting his interruptions soon takes him sufficiently far afield from his original goal so that it is supplanted totally by another, more interpersonal quest: pleasing his bedmate. Although this has become his sole preoccupation at the moment, he eventually finds himself unable to please either party present. That puzzles him deeply. His own satisfaction he was willing to sacrifice, but why his partner isn't ecstatic escapes him. The simple seesaw picture in his mind—"I'm down, trying to give her a boost, so she should be up"—obviously doesn't fit the facts.

People like David think of their highly social orientation as a real plus, and in many ways it is. However, many men in this category carry their desire to please too far. Then a sense of direction is hard for them to come by. Having cut themselves off from their own baser instincts, in the name of seeming civilized, they lose a crucial inner guide that tells them how next to proceed. All such a man can do at this point is wait for someone else to tell him what to be. In fact, someone has to be present and act as a mirror for him to see himself as anything at all, a secret he sometimes senses and then masks with a deliberately upbeat manner.

A concise way to think of the forces at work here is that *no pleasure (for oneself) leaves one merely producing theater (for others)*. As children well know, performing can be a joy of sorts too, but the situation we've been discussing is different, since we are dealing with an actor who (1) doesn't really know what role to perform, and (2) can't stop the show. It has no well-defined beginning and therefore no specific end; it quickly attains a life of its own. Having stepped on stage somewhere in the distant past (usually somewhere between ages eight and thirteen), he can no longer leave.

Bill can tell him how. The desire for pleasure continually springs anew in each of us, unless the machinery of interruption again revs up and interferes. Preventing such interruptions from occurring *automatically* is the key to improving the situation, and the attitude that facilitates this immensely worthwhile change is the one Bill typically displays. "I don't have to please you, you have to please *me*," he says, at times to no one in particular. What makes this seemingly egocentric philosophy so valuable, when used in moderation, is that it lets the other person not only exist but also flower. Instead of being merely self-serving, it allows others the pleasure of forgetting themselves for a moment and perhaps doing something nice for him, an action he is always willing to reciprocate. Far from being manipulative, it encourages the pair to strike a better balance between selfishness and selflessness, a crucial factor in the health of any long-term relationship.

Our study leaves little doubt about the changes a man like David should attempt to make: to begin with, he is too nervous, and this tension is primarily a result of a chronic inability to allow himself the release and relief he would experience as a result of personal pleasure. He denies himself this basic need because he wants to be admired for his elegance, and cutting himself off from his more "animal" aspects seems to him appropriate given his wholly public orientation. Yet he offends others, both on the job and in bed, since they find him too demanding emotionally.

Ironically, to be truly effective in public he needs to tap the reserves of strength his own private desires offer him. This he can best do by occasionally reminding himself of Bill's motto, "It is time for *you* to please *me*." The very act of (1) consciously making himself the center of attention (and not coyly making it seem a mere accident); and (2) allowing *uninterrupted* pleasure to be the reason for the switch in focus from his partner to himself will probably make him a little giddy and guilty the first few times he does it, thanks to its novelty, but it does indeed help shift the balance in the right direction. Men who fail to do this are typically branded "lightweights" by colleagues and lovers. Small wonder they do much less well over the years on both the professional and personal front than they expected.

PLAYFULNESS AND SUCCESS

Steve would think it silly for anyone to compare him to Bill, yet the two are alike in at least one important respect that sets them apart from David:

once Steve becomes absorbed in something he enjoys doing, he doesn't allow anything to interrupt his concentration if he can possibly avoid it. In fact, from the time he entered college this was the characteristic that most people who got to know him pointed to as a potential source of trouble.

It became an actual source of problems later with friends and lovers who wanted him to go somewhere when he wouldn't. "Not now, I'm busy," he would say, only half present. Although Steve was generally polite, he could become quite annoyed if the others repeated their request that he join them. At such moments, he resembled Bill all the more. In spite of their occasional similarity, however, a deeper difference divides them: men like Bill are used to having their work interrupted (since they usually work as part of a team or crew), but not their pleasures (they take their play seriously). On the other hand, men like Steve don't want their work interrupted (they are used to doing it alone), and work is their only real pleasure.

It makes little sense to talk about Steve interfering with his own leisure-time joys, for they exist in another compartment of his mind and aren't really comparable to what he does for a living. Whether these activities—for instance, playing ball or having sex—are disrupted is a matter of some concern to him, but not much. Once he starts his participation in them, he would like to remain caught up until each event is over. The point is that his degree of involvement doesn't begin to match that which he brings to his work. Amusingly, others who see him so busy with the activity he considers fascinating may label him, and it, "silly," but if *he* takes it seriously, that is all that matters to him. It consumes him. Calling him "driven" is a mistake, since it is a word that, as we'll soon see, better describes men like Larry. What Steve is, instead, is "absorbed," lost in a world of his own making.

What, then, does he have to learn from the Bills of the world? Something of major importance: *he has lost the ability to play.* This seemingly transient aspect of childhood isn't as easily dispensed with, without harm, as men like Steve are inclined to believe. To look at things from their perspective for a moment, they would insist that they *do* know how to be playful and, at least occasionally, are. Nevertheless, when one takes a closer look at these allegedly "playful" events, it turns out that they usually consist of a sarcastic remark made at someone else's expense—in a word, criticism, delivered in a somewhat hostile if humorous manner.

When the remark is funny, the hostility may not be apparent, but it is there anyway.

Not only does this attitude prevent the Steves of the world from relaxing, it doesn't allow them to do their best in the area of their lives that means the most to them: their work. To be specific, men like Steve who our records show made humorously self-deprecatory remarks on occasion about their profession and their own activities within it were nearly three times as likely to become successful in the subsequent ten to twenty years as those who approached their work in a totally humorless manner.

Why is a deliberate refusal to step back, gain perspective, and smile indulgently from time to time about one's work so damaging? Because while men like Bill handle physical materials, men like Steve work with concepts, and we found that new ideas are significantly more likely to occur to men who regularly permit themselves to play with the intellectual raw material on which their profession is based. Juggling and toying with old ideas is a substantial aid to coming up with new ones. The humorless approach does its harm by reducing the chances that the men will ever achieve a novel or even different way of ordering the structure of their field. Their work is typically characterized by co-workers and superiors as "petty," "derivative," and "formal."

Making an idea one's own is anything but easy. It is possible that someone elsewhere came up with it at the same time—or worse, did so years ago and one simply didn't know about it. All this makes one's efforts to come up with it in the first place much like the proverbial reinvention of the wheel. There is a still more embarrassing possibility: the idea was mentioned by someone else but didn't register at the time. Later, forgetting that it wasn't one's own, one may find it springing to mind "out of the blue," as an altogether new thought.

STAKING ONE'S CLAIM

Someone who is striving above all to avoid being influenced by others while trying to come up with something original may feel that the best way to handle the risky possibilities we've been discussing is to severely limit the amount of outside information he receives. He must monitor the source of each item, scrutinize the message it sends him, and decide whether to admit it to his being. Unwittingly, he begins to play border guard for anything that might enter his brain, even music.

The same hypervigilant stance may be used about substances that enter his body. Food may be examined carefully when it is on his plate and even more so while still in the package or can. Reading labels, becoming knowledgeable about esoteric chemical ingredients, may suddenly seem essential to him. Health and hygiene are the excuses he gives himself, but what he is really doing is shoring up his walls. He worries most about what he can't see, so germs are frequently on his mind. However, we found that hypochondria is usually a fear of being influenced, not poisoned. It isn't so much his lungs or blood as his thoughts that he is subconsciously trying to keep from being contaminated.

People who describe Steve as "obsessive" are using a label that fits, but it isn't a very illuminating one. Rather than being a merely neurotic condition, his obsessiveness is one of many consequences of a strongly reclusive orientation combined with a burning desire to come up with something original in his field. During his late teens and twenties he wanted to make contact with the larger world, but only to see what it prized and what he could learn from it. Then—and this is the tricky part—he wanted to take a piece of this larger picture and make it his own, much like a miner staking a claim. As we've mentioned, that is much more difficult to do with ideas than with material objects. Nevertheless, his reclusive orientation is the most powerful part of his personality and it isn't about to stop pressuring him to drag something worthwhile back to his cave.

Precisely because an idea is part of its time, a strand in the cultural and social fabric of the period, a man like Steve has to leave his deliberately restricted arena of activity and make repeated forays into the larger one. If only to stay up to date and see what others are doing, he must burst the confines of his own self-imposed isolation from time to time. Such occasions fill him with anxiety, for he has voluntarily pierced the walls surrounding his bustling inner city and gone into the uncharted hinterlands, where he is uncertain about who and what he'll meet.

What he really fears, without realizing it, is that he might meet people with whom he will work, play, and laugh—all three simultaneously.

Instead of being the pleasure most others would consider it, the prospect troubles him, and for a good reason. Laughter and play cause people to *share* an experience, and a man like Steve wants to make a name for himself for work he has done alone.

"MINE, AND ONLY MINE"

What can someone like Bill possibly have to say that would be of use to such a man? At first glance it appears that nothing relevant carries over from the manual to the mental world, and therefore all the analogies between them would be strained or synthetic. Yet regardless of the excessively intellectual way in which men like Steve view the territory they have staked out for themselves, there is indeed a *product dimension* present, and ignoring it is costly to their careers.

Books, journals, magazines, films, TV and movie scripts, designs, plays, poems, and computer programs—the primary areas of involvement for men like Steve—are material objects much like a chair. The overly cerebral approach of such men to their field is no accident, for it enables them to feel that they have made a piece of it their exclusive possession. But the feeling is a dangerous illusion. The piece to which they have laid claim is still an integral part of the field, as it must be if it is to be relevant to other professionals or the public at large.

In imagining that ideas are more ethereal than they actually are, the men overlook one of the most critical factors separating those who eventually become outstanding from those who are equally talented but who go on to do poorly. Those who don't do well are convinced that, first, they have seized a portion of this amorphous intellectual substance and made it their exclusive possession, and second, that they therefore must vigorously defend what they think of as their "turf," even going so far as to agonize continually that someone else will make contact with their property and compromise their sense of public ownership of it.

Nevertheless, someone else—in fact, many others—must touch it and even reshape it so that a *product* can be offered to one's colleagues or the world. It is here that Bill's attitude is especially valuable: "Of course other people are going to get involved in what you're doing. So what? It's still yours." His product orientation is one of the pillars upon which his sense of self-assurance rests. Men like Steve could also have that productive peace of mind, but they have carried too far the attempt at exclusive possession of an intellectual concept.

Ironically, disconnecting themselves from the material aspects of their profession (money and goods)—in order to put first things first and tighten their grip on a piece of intellectual turf—causes Steve-types to be done in eventually by their own anxieties, which mushroom whenever they see the output of a competitor. Other people's books, journal articles, designs, theories, computer programs, or scripts upset them unduly, each piece of work from a rival seeming more like a hand grenade than a treatment of the same or a related theme.

In short, as physical objects, these articles, books, or programs are almost certain to be sufficiently different from one another so that men like Steve, who have done their work well, don't need to feel so threatened and therefore defensively angry. However, pointing out differences and discussing them logically doesn't help most Steves (as friends or wives who've tried doing so are surprised to find). This pivotal problem exists on a more subterranean plane in each. His nervous and guarded reactions make it seem that he is worried most about his body's boundaries, whereas it is the boundary around his professional territory that he is actually afraid will be punctured. He has somatized this recurring nightmare, using his skin as the symbolic border around his turf. We know this because men like Steve, after suffering what they see as a setback, are significantly more likely than the other three types of men to complain of a physical ailment. Viewing the world in a more realistically commercial light, with a product orientation more closely resembling Bill's, would dramatically lessen such fears.

The most important work-related insight such a man has in his entire life may be that his prized ideas must first become embodied in a product before they can truly be considered his. Not only does this make them more tangible and visible, it also allows *other people* to say, "This is Steve's." Until then, since the idea may exist in others' minds as well as his own, competitors may well say, "This is mine." As things now stand, ownership feuds seriously reduce a typical Steve-type's ability to function at his best, particularly because the arguments take place mainly in his mind ("I'm not showing this to *anybody*") and make him chronically tense. Only a product—the very item at which he so frequently sneers when others produce one—can resolve the quarrel, for it alone provides the thing men like Steve want most: undisputed title to an original idea.

THE POWER OF PERSONAL POSSESSIONS

In the minds of some observers Larry and Bill already have so much in common, it would be appropriate for Larry to become *less* like Bill. He is indeed trying, for the Larrys of the world often have men like Bill for fathers and want the differences between father and son to be apparent. Even when their fathers are more middle class and have a touch of David in them as well, the Larry-types have little trouble understanding what motivates the Bills of the world.

Nevertheless, men like Larry typically feel compelled to put a substantial amount of distance between themselves and someone like Bill in order to make their own progress up the social ladder visible. Flashy jewelry, expensive clothes, prestige cars, lavish offices, and spacious mansions are part of a pattern of conspicuous consumption that they hope will demonstrate that they have "arrived," have "made it," and are now "on top," to use some of their favorite phrases.

If ever there was an effort doomed to failure, this is it. The primary aim in life of Larry-types is to impress others, and the primary way they intend to accomplish this aim is through the things they buy. Call it "the power of personal possessions." Men like Larry subconsciously believe in this power above all other.

Money, too, is used for the purpose, in the form of tips, gifts, loans, and even bribes, but while a great deal of ceremonial and conspiratorial behavior may be present when the money changes hands, men like Larry want their possessions, not cash, to produce the desired effect. Paying someone to do something for them isn't nearly as satisfying as having the person do it voluntarily because he or she is awed by the image radiated by the things a Larry has already bought. In that case the tip is a bonus with which he is especially happy to part.

While some people react the way he wants them to, the number is much smaller than he imagines. Interviews with hundreds of the people whom the Larrys in our sample were attempting to impress made it clear that (1) most resented his unspoken assumption that they could be bought; (2) they felt he was trying too hard to be classy, something that they view as not requiring any effort at all if it is genuine; and (3) his imitation of men like David struck them as unconvincing and at times even ludicrous.

What, then, does Larry have to learn from men like Bill? That, paradoxically, more people would find him impressive if he tried much less hard to impress them. Years ago, major consumer-goods companies hit upon a product that embodies the philosophy that he sorely needs to adopt. Call Larry's present approach "the greasy look"; he in essence is still living in the era of "a little dab will do you." The more recent strategy the companies are pushing is to make one's hair seem tousled and uncombed, neat without having been pasted in place. The "dry look," as they label it, is an effort to make it seem that looking good not only required no effort, it happened quite by accident.

One sees the approach employed in a wide variety of settings: the goal is to appear natural, no matter how artificial the means used to achieve the image. Larry already utilizes this styling technique—and hence implicitly the philosophy—where his own grooming is concerned, and wouldn't dream of looking like a "greaser," as he refers to men with shiny, slicked-down hair. Yet the rest of his demeanor smacks of the same *obvious* attempt to look good that he so bitterly criticizes.

It rarely occurs to a man like Larry that, in the eyes of the audience from which he wants admiration, only the natural man—comfortable with who and what he is—has true elegance. The Davids of the world don't strike this largely business audience as elegant. Instead, he seems to them a fop, a dandy, too concerned about his clothes, table manners, grammar, and smiling sociability. They consider most of his behavior theatrical and have trouble taking him seriously.

That is precisely the description they also give of a man like Larry when they feel that he too has gone too far in an attempt to gain social status or parade any degree of it he thinks he already has. It isn't a coincidence that this wave of condemnation hits a Larry when he is unwittingly trying hardest to imitate the only type of man *he* thinks has class, someone like David.

As we learned repeatedly during our study, Larry-types who, as Bill did, come to terms with their roots rather than rejecting them are significantly more likely to be seen in the positive light to which they continually aspire.

"I'M A WORKING MAN"

To sum up, as long as this country continues to draw much of its music, language, literature, and art from the middle and lower layers of society—everything from Campbell soup cans to graffiti-covered posters, from Bruce Springsteen's song, "I'm a working man" to slum phrases that appear a few years later at cocktail parties—and as long as it continues to strongly favor the "underdog," any man who doesn't have a healthy measure of Bill in his personality is in for trouble. In both his personal and professional life such a man will wind up an object of ridicule, the subject of caustic remarks voiced by men who are certainly not like Bill yet who are continually on the lookout for anything that smacks of pretension. They do this for personal pleasure, to be sure, but also because it is part of their pledge of allegiance to a continuing democratic rejection of aristocracy. Praising the common man is no small matter to them, even as the Bill-types slowly vanish from the scene. They don't want to be labeled arid, effete, or supercilious, and somehow they sense that a touch of Bill in their makeup is precisely what they need to help keep their own feet on the ground.

In recent years, the boundary between "substance" and "style" has grown thin, leaving most of the men in our sample with the belief that they can always make the right impression as a result of the right purchases. Some conversation and even conflict about "class" seems inevitable in the lives of most ambitious men.

This is a subject with a long history, one that allows us to see that what is considered classy in one period may look silly in another, for instance, top hats and waistcoats. One thing on which almost all the members of our sample agree is that it takes money to be classy. However, there is apparently a much greater difference in their minds than they realize between "old money" and new. The phrase "nouveau riche" has been in use for well over a century to describe the difference; it connotes someone who is still coarse and uncultured. As de Tocqueville wrote in 1830 about Americans, "Their manners almost always lag behind their rise in social position. As a result, very vulgar tastes often go with their enjoyment of extraordinary prosperity."

Inherited wealth is therefore socially preferable to a self-made fortune, even though those who start with little and become wealthy have accomplished something worth bragging about. Most of the successful men we studied wouldn't have it any other way. Yet they can't help longing for the subtle but powerful impact the idea of dynastic wealth makes even in an allegedly egalitarian country like this one. Amusingly, having made their own fortunes, these men start presenting it—and themselves—in public as though it had been inherited.

Perhaps the best way to see the central issue here is to look at it through the eyes of a ten-year-old, who is just beginning to become aware of the importance of these distinctions. When George Orwell died in 1950, among his papers was found an unpublished essay entitled, "Such, Such Were the Joys . . ." In it Orwell writes,

> At the age of ten or eleven, I reached the conclusion—no one told me this, but on the other hand I did not simply make it up out of my own head: somehow it was in the air I breathed—that you were no good unless you had £100,000. The interest on £100,000 (at a safe 4 percent) would be £4,000 and this seemed to me the minimum income you must possess if you were to belong to the real top crust. But it was clear that I could never find my way into that paradise, to which you didn't really belong unless you were born into it. You would only *make* money, if at all, by a mysterious operation called 'going into the City' [London's version of Wall Street], and when you came out of the City, having won your £100,000, you were fat and old. But the truly enviable thing about the top-notchers was that they were rich while young. For people like me, the ambitious middle class, the examination passers, only a bleak, laborious kind of success was possible.

Americans value this kind of success far more than the British do, yet they too are by no means free of the allure of "the family fortune." Since the nation's history is itself so short, in the United States money is old if it has been in a family for at least three generations, and sometimes merely two suffice. Ambitious men can't remake their past, but they can do what others like them have been doing for decades: attempt to find their way into the Social Register by marrying "the right woman"; donate to the right charities and civic organizations; purchase the necessary props; and keep up with gossip about the royal family, or anyone else with a title.

The problem is that with so many people trying to do this in the past few decades as the United States has steadily grown more affluent, ambitious Americans have now become quite critical of each other's efforts in this direction. They are especially harsh in their judgment about such "social climbing" in friends and spouses. It is ironic that a man like Bill, who concentrates above all on substance, should be the one that emerges so often in their conversation as having "class" because he is the only one who strikes them as "the real thing." They don't seek to imitate Bill the construction worker, but instead model themselves after a more traditional version of the man frequently encountered in the Old West. While they are wearing thousand-dollar cowboy boots, a pin-striped suit, and driving a Porsche, it isn't unusual to hear them talking with their wives or girlfriends about the latest sexual, financial, or criminal scandal involving society figures.

It was fascinating to notice that the men they were most likely to consider as having "class" were those who thought about the subject the least. Apparently the very effort to attain this goal usually makes it unattainable.

SOCIAL INSECURITY

A brief look at the real basis of "class" can help one escape the perils of this paradox.

Young children find few things disgusting. They play in mud puddles, fingerpaint with their own excrement, and romp with youngsters of other religions and races. It is up to their parents to teach them that certain things are dangerous ("don't *touch* that"). There are other emotions besides fear that can be mobilized in the child for his or her safety.

A primary one is disgust. Youngsters can't see germs; they don't really understand the concept (it took the human race eons to grasp it) and are prone to forget so invisible a threat. Parents can make the point anyway by switching from an intellectual to an emotional reminder ("that's *disgusting*"). Children have their own word for this reaction, a term not found in any dictionary. It might be spelled "ewe" but they pronounce it "ee-you," while scrunching up their shiny little faces.

The approach is indeed effective, but once learned, it quickly begins to serve social as well as medical purposes. Like adults, children want to be superior to their peers. "I'm the best," one frequently hears them say, as, seconds later another insists, "No, I am."

How will they gain this all-important sense of being "better than?" Disgust can allow them to feel both superior and safe. A typical remark by an adult who is using the emotion in this way is "People who haven't had the same [classical] education that I have really aren't educated at all." And, repeating our question, a fifty-one-year-old woman replied, "Why did we move? To be away from the riff-raff." The mildly contemptuous tone in which such comments are usually voiced is intentional. People anxious to impress you with their social superiority feel compelled to find someone to look down on. With so few absolutes, so few givens in any social situation, they consider it essential to highlight their lofty position by pointing to someone else's lowly one. Relatively speaking at least, that makes them "better than."

There is an objective and a subjective side to what they are doing. Given two pieces of glass, say, there might be no doubt in the mind of a technically knowledgeable observer that one is of higher quality than the other, thanks to fewer flaws and imperfections. However, someone looking to rise a notch may add an emotional dimension to the discussion by stating, with visible or hidden pretension, "But I *prefer* the irregularities, as in handblown antique glass, rather than the boring sameness of commercial plate."

To each his own, of course, but the point is that where discussions of "taste" are concerned, our analysis of a total of more than 1,700 hours of such conversations from every region of the United States indicates that disgust is almost invariably involved when the speaker tries to present him or herself as either socially, athletically, or intellectually superior. In each case, something or someone is looked down upon with a strident or subtle sneer.

Anyone seeking to escape the paradox we've been discussing—namely, that in America the effort to seem "classy" usually elicits ridicule rather than admiration—would be well advised to do two things: first, realize that the attempt to elevate oneself socially too often involves putting someone else down. Second, stop doing it. The evidence indicates that it simply isn't necessary.

In fact, it may backfire terribly. People resent it because they realize that in the very next breath they might be the ones who are put down. That causes them to defend themselves against someone else's snobbery even though they haven't yet been attacked. These preemptive strikes can be devastating, for they come as an unpleasant surprise to an individual who was trying to elevate himself and didn't realize that he was saying (or implying) something defamatory about another person or group in the process.

If he associates civility with aristocracy and therefore expects his interpersonal skills and purchases of prestige products to gain him social status, the ridicule may come as a shock. He thought he looked and sounded only elegant. In short, removing the emotion of snobbish disgust toward others from any attempt he makes to elevate himself socially is likely to prove very worthwhile.

·PART·
THREE

PART
THREE

CHAPTER
•9•

EARLY SUCCESS: MAKING THE GAINS ENDURE

In this chapter we want to examine two key questions: which men are most likely to become successful early? And, what price, if any, do they pay for their precocious accomplishments?

The United States has long had an infatuation with youthful achievers, though they have usually been in the cultural area. Piano and violin prodigies, for instance, Vladimir Horowitz and Yehudi Menuhin, were considered much more newsworthy because of the virtuoso musical skills they displayed while still young. In more recent years celebrity status has been granted those who have become outstanding during their teens or twenties in the world of sports or business. That has made many talented athletes and businessmen feel like losers, they tell us, because they are unable to match the achievements of the people they read about and see doing commercials on TV. Nevertheless, enough young men have managed to excel in spite of (some would say, because of) these unrelenting pressures so that we can see what it is that sets them apart from their peers.

We give central place to financial achievement, but only because the person's income or accumulated wealth affords us a quantitative measure of his relative performance. Renown, while also measurable, isn't as readily quantified and involves a subjective judgment on the public's part.

To begin with, we'll look at the results themselves, the data on who really does disproportionately well. Then we'll try to make sense of the often astonishing financial disparities that develop between pairs of men who seemed so similar at the start.

LOCAL BOY MAKES GOOD

Unlike Larry, who made his fortune in the electronics business, nearly one fifth of the men in our study who were able to "get rich quick"—that is, who made their first million before the age of thirty-five—did so in real estate. The process of "gentrification" afforded them the chance they were seeking. During the 1970s and 1980s the number of young men and women coming to major American cities looking for better jobs, as well as a more interesting cultural and social environment, was large enough to push rents to stratospheric levels. Nevertheless, emphasis on commercial construction, with its greater profit per square foot, caused the rate of construction of new residential units to remain low. Ambitious young professionals told us that they often found themselves talking about the high price of apartments even in bed.

This made old neighborhoods that could be rejuvenated ripe for exploitation. The buildings were generally run down and inexpensive but the neighborhood crime rate was high, so making money from such real estate would require more courage than cash. Larry-types were, by far, the ones most likely to notice such opportunities and seize them. Much less squeamish—about everything—than the Davids or Steves, men like Larry frequently told us, "It doesn't bother me to go there. I've been around run-down places before. Hell, I was born in one."

It wasn't true. Such men typically came from respectable, middle-class suburbs, where lawns and living rooms were kept neat by their proud and community-minded owners. The tenementlike buildings that were to form the basis for these men's future fortunes were another story entirely. Neglected by their owners for years, who had attempted to squeeze every drop of income out of them without investing a penny more than was necessary to avoid running afoul of the law, the buildings were sorely in need of repair. Everything from floors, walls and ceilings to plumbing, heating and electrical wiring required attention. Prevailing rent-control laws usually stunted severely the former landlord's willingness to undertake such improvements.

Into the midst of this financial and legal morass stepped men like Larry with a naïve optimism that made anything seem possible. They knew there was tremendous pent-up demand for additional low-cost housing, and not nearly enough was being built. Larry-types were able to reap the riches a setting like this potentially offered because, unlike the Davids and Steves, they got along well with the unionized and moonlighting Bills, whose talents were needed to breathe new life into what in many cases had become a mere shell of a structure. The greater comfort a Larry had while wheeling and dealing or working with a variety of manual laborers was essential in this context. So were his sales abilities, once each project was nearing completion.

Glowing descriptions of the rehabilitated property were aimed at potential customers who needed to be convinced that they were moving into a neighborhood on the verge of turning chic. Their own moderate incomes made them want to swallow this argument, and they eagerly repeated it to friends once they moved in. That helped make a self-fulfilling prophecy of what the Larrys and their customers had been saying. A steadily rising number of people showed up looking for units.

Why did they really do so? Studying animals for clues to the origins of human behavior has largely served instead to show how unlike other animals humans are. Our intellectual complexity and self-awareness, the ability to make voluntary choices and changes, make our species unique. However, certain resemblances are undeniable, especially that aspect of herd behavior usually referred to as "fads." That a large number of other people are doing something becomes justification enough for still more to do it.

This creates many opportunities for ambitious men to become rich in such diverse fields as restaurants, resorts, records, and real estate. Looking at the behavior of people in our sample, it became clear that if a new restaurant was deemed good, the whole neighborhood was suddenly seen as safe for grazing. Even secondary eateries in the area experienced an increase in traffic. Residences, whether they were for rent or sale, were subject to similarly powerful faddish influences. An old part of town could become the latest chic locale in a matter of months, making instant fortunes for those who arrived early or helped give new life to the area.

One of the most powerful forces helping entrepreneurs like Larry to succeed is that people who come to a major city from a distant destination want not only to do well professionally, but also to be accepted socially. They see the city in vertical and horizontal terms, as a mountain worth climbing and as a sea of people who might admire each accomplishment. In short, they want to make it big *and* impress the locals. They don't realize that this goal is usually unattainable, since most locals refuse to be impressed. We learned this by testing more than four thousand people in the major American cities between 1965 and 1987, measuring their reactions to a story of how well someone had done. When they thought the person they were reading about was from the area, they were more than three times as interested in further details than when they thought he was an out-of-towner. Apparently, there is more emotion in the "local boy makes good" theme than has previously been recognized. That makes the worlds of the immigrants and the locals much more separate than they appear at first glance, even if the two groups live side by side and are friendly. In the eyes of the people who were born and raised in a town, recent arrivals never really become locals, though their children might. As we'll soon see, these background factors go far to explain why certain ambitious men become rich and others, who are similar, don't.

"Guest workers," as laborers from Italy, Spain, and Yugoslavia who are employed in German and Swiss manufacturing plants are called, normally send a portion of their earnings home. However, the Americans we're discussing don't think of themselves as "guests" in the city to which they have moved. It is their new home, one that they feel belongs to them every bit as much as to someone who was born there. Be that as it may, *they come to the city to excel, not just to live from day to day, and as a result, they typically set their sights higher than do the locals.* To fulfill these ambitions and gain a sense of membership, too, they feel compelled to try harder. So, unlike guest workers, they earn a fair amount of money in the city—and leave it there.

By contrast, the locals already feel accepted and therefore don't have to spend money to "buy" it. As a consequence, they save more of their earnings and, for the most part, end up leading lives of quiet satisfaction. To them the town is familiar and comfortable, a place they have known ever since childhood. One of their main *dis*satisfactions is that they don't become early achievers. How come? Ironically, it is precisely their greater comfort and contentment with their lot in life that prevents them from, on the one hand, yearning and striving for more—much more—than they now have, and, on the other hand, from seeing how they could strike it rich right in their own backyard.

They know that instant wealth is being created in the area and that they aren't involved in it, except as spectators. They hear and, mainly, read about people living nearby who are becoming young millionaires, yet they aren't participants in the process, even marginally. Why not? Because, although they are reluctant to admit it, they don't like the brashly aggressive, immigrant Larrys who are making it big overnight, nor do they like the patrons of his restaurants, readers of his publications, or customers for his renovated apartments, all of whom strike them as "climbers." By any measure the locals aren't as hungry, and it is this relative complacency that prevents them from seeing the instant fortunes to be made from the enormous number of eager arrivals.

Perhaps the most damaging bit of blindness that afflicts locals who want to (but don't) become rich overnight is that they hugely underestimate the number of talented and dedicated people who move into the city each year. "Where *are* all of them?" some asked skeptically, when the subject came up. "If there are so many people arriving here all the time, why isn't the city ten times its current size?" The answer is that both the majority of successes *and* failures will leave, thereby continually making room for a large number of new arrivals. The successful ones typically marry and move to affluent suburbs; the unsuccessful ones also go elsewhere, though not home again, for they generally view this as too blatant and painful an admission of failure. The city, acting like a rapidly spinning carousel on which they tried for a number of years to ride, hurls them to yet another, less demanding, distant destination to try their luck again.

THE RELUCTANT ENTREPRENEUR

We've been discussing entrepreneurs like Larry because, statistically speaking, more men in our sample from this category—particularly those who leave home and move to another city—have become millionaires than those from the other three combined. Considering that there are so many of them, they receive remarkably little publicity for their achievement, relative to that given to men like Steven, who made millions early in life but at first glance don't seem interested in money at all. How do the successful Steves do it? And why weren't they the ones doing it a century ago, so that someone like them could have become the central figure in a Horatio Alger-style tale intended to inspire generations of youngsters?

In the 1960s a drastic change took place in the nation's priorities. An unparalleled peace-time emphasis was placed on advances in technology, in order to compete more effectively with the Soviet Union on earth and in space. Government spending on R&D as well as product acquisition, boomed. Into this enormous vacuum moved a substantial number of men like Larry, sensing an opportunity to fill a public need and also make themselves rich. However, an even larger number of scientists and engineers tried to convert their technical expertise into instant wealth.

The few who succeeded received enormous attention in the press, mainly because they were viewed as national heroes, helping the nation hold its own against the Soviet Union. That had the effect of (1) making the process seem easy ("from high-tech to high finance," a major newspaper blared), and (2) giving the impression that this was a daily occurrence. This was false, though the public's perception that innovative products could come off the drawing board and quickly be ready for sale to NASA and the armed forces made it feel safe and secure. What matters more to us than this myth is that, for the first time, men like Steve—not Larry—were forcefully being given the go-ahead en masse to try their hand at combining technology and commerce.

For these reclusive men it was a new and unaccustomed role, and throughout the past quarter century men like Steve who became young millionaires have received vastly more media attention than did the statistically more numerous young millionaires like Larry.

In certain respects, this was a new way of making money and a new group of men were benefiting from it. The technique involved a major shift from the personal to the impersonal. In what sense? The approach of men like Larry who have gone on to become successful isn't fancy, and instead depends on their aggressiveness and sales orientation, their ability to be friendly and, above all, persuasive. These are basically interpersonal skills. "I could sell ice to Eskimos," is a representative remark, from one who has three furniture stores in upper-middle-class shopping centers. Men like Steve, on the other hand, have to depend on the technical sophistication of their products if the items are to be declared "newsworthy." So while the Larrys of the world were trying to make things simple and accessible, Steve-types had no choice but to make their inventions appear awe-inspiring and complex.

In any other field, once an item becomes a commercial success, the man responsible is expected to rise to the occasion by building a company around himself and his product line and transforming himself into an effective manager. The company is expected to diversify and grow increasingly profitable. In most cases—but not this one. The public generally denies the Steves of the world this opportunity by chasing them back into the familiar role of dedicated scientists, deeply immersed in their work and shunning all publicity with the fierceness of a Howard Hughes. Unfortunately, what this stereotyping process does is reinforce a reclusive tendency these men had been displaying in excess all along. The upshot is twofold: first, the men become divorced from their markets, and second, they become enamored of every technical decoration— all the bells, buzzers, and whistles—that makes their product seem "state of the art" but actually renders it unaffordable and not geared to customer needs.

Nevertheless, a substantial number of Steve-types do become millionaires at a young age, largely thanks to the public's vast appetite for "the newest and latest." Photographs of these scientific entrepreneurs appear in business publications and their companies become the focus of a great deal of attention in the financial community. A stockbroker or underwriter somewhere is sure to say, "You know, this company just might become another IBM." In a surprisingly large number of cases the fledgling firm goes public, with hungry shareholders buying the *promise* of future performance, not current profits (usually there are none). At the tender age of twenty-nine, the technically minded and reluctant entrepreneur may find himself worth tens of millions of dollars, at least on paper.

The Steves of the world who get this kind of head start in their respective fields clearly have a jump on the competition. It is small wonder that expectations, both their own and those around them, rise to dizzying heights.

Why, then, do so many subsequently fail? Although the public believes that becoming a millionaire is a very difficult feat to accomplish, they are convinced that once someone has reached this level, it is easy enough for him to stay there and continue to make further gains. The data we have accumulated indicates exactly the reverse; more than one third of the self-made millionaires like Larry and Steve in our sample lost the fortunes they had so rapidly accumulated.

BETTING AN ENTIRE FORTUNE

Men like Larry are especially prone to become convinced that they can now do anything. "The first million was the hardest," such men typically say. "The other ninety-nine ought to be a bit easier." Believing that they have an unlimited amount of money (or can get more any time they need it), they start to throw to the wind some of the restraints that previously served them so well. The shrewd judgment they displayed as they were building their initial fortune suddenly seems to abandon them.

In the past, their free-spending ways had an ulterior motive—convincing people that they were already well off. It may not have been obvious, but they were always making judicious decisions about when to act flamboyantly with their money and when to behave as if they had none. This "internal cost-control mechanism" was invisible to the casual observer but it was indeed present and allowed Larry-types to appear as though they always had the money they only later accumulated.

Intoxicated by their successes, and driven by visions of still greater ones to come, the majority experienced major financial setbacks. Caused by? Usually, they undertook a project that stretched their financial resources to the limit. (As we saw in chapter 6, they typically compounded the problem by spending more freely on the home front at this time as well.) Allowing no room for mistakes, much less delays, they blithely assumed that their capital would multiply itself even more rapidly in the future than it had in the past. They were unable to keep themselves afloat in the face of an economic downturn, cost overrun, or a serious underestimation of the time needed for the public to embrace the lavish new condominium project, restaurant, publication, or product on which they had fearlessly bet their entire fortune.

It seems odd to think that success could hurt anyone, but if it does harm to any of the four types, it is to men like Steve. When they work for someone else, as employees, they feel that it is their technical knowledge or achievements that will cause them to be promoted to the firm's presidency, if anything will. By contrast, if they start their own businesses and are fortunate enough to have one of their technical creations catch the fancy of customers and of Wall Street, they typically become quite obstinate. In their view, they now have proof that their approach works. One often hears them say, "This company is technology-driven, not market-driven." The distinction is a valid one in many cases, but, carried to the exremes to which men like Steve are inclined to take it—particularly once they become millionaires—it has damaging consequences that rarely take long to surface.

It is a painful irony that just at the moment when these men feel that their lifelong approach to work—and the world—has been validated, the evidence indicates that they are in the greatest jeopardy of losing the fortune they have made. Why? What we found was that the more publicity a Larry-type is given, the more likely he is to fall in love with his own public image. However, the more publicity given to a man like Steve, the more likely he is to fall further in love with his own gadgeteering.

In a way, that shouldn't be surprising because men like Steve see any Larry-like dimensions in their own personalities as fraudulent. "I don't want to be a huckster," they frequently say. "I want my products to speak for themselves." It is this highly idealistic stance that turns out to be the source of the troubles that eventually cost the men their overnight success. Rather than mere indifference, they begin to display outright contempt for the marketing and sales staff, the very people who become increasingly essential as the firm grows and a larger quantity of goods must be moved each year.

Steve-types have egos that can swell dramatically, making them seem

Larry-like, precisely because *someone else* is now becoming more important to the company. If there is one, crucial mistake made by early achievers that men who become equally successful in their forties and fifties are significantly less likely to make, this is it: young self-made millionaires are quick to conclude that "the public isn't buying my products, it is buying *me*." If that were indeed the case, no sales staff would be necessary. Instead, the man in such a position would be more in need of a manager or bodyguard, much as a rock star might be, so that he could decide how to apportion himself and his time among his adoring fans.

When seemingly instant wealth comes to someone with a comparable personality profile but who is in his forties or fifties, the person typically avoids this dangerous pitfall by realizing that salespeople are like an army about to go into combat. "Inspiring the troops" is a serious matter, since they have to be made enthusiastic if they, in turn, are to make customers excited about the product or service. As one of the most successful fifty-year-olds in our sample, a man who literally started with $10,000 in his late twenties and is now worth more than $10 million, thanks to the success of his consumer-goods manufacturing firm, commented, "Entrepreneurs like to take credit for becoming rich—I see them do it all the time—but *other* people really make your money for you. You have to give them the chance, and the encouragement, to do that." Sneering at his sales and marketing staff, in order to get all the applause himself, would strike him as ludicrous.

Our surveys indicate that the public generally assumes that a man who becomes wealthy after the age of thirty-five already had all the pieces in place while still in his twenties. The frequently heard phrase, "he really has it together," voiced in a tone of admiration by employees and colleagues, means that the man's personality and work seem to be functioning not only harmoniously, but almost magically together to produce a level of quality or originality that is exceptional. The view that his past and present personality are basically the same (and that only his discoveries are recent) is a logical one and certainly valid in a large number of cases. However, when we examined our records, it was clear that another factor was acting to separate people who continued to do really well from those of moderate or transient achievement.

The factor we're talking about is psychological, one that may aptly be characterized as a personality transformation. Until now, we've been assuming, as does the public, that the personality type a young man has is the same one he will have decades later. Not only does this turn out to be a false assumption; in most of the cases of men who become successful, the kinds of changes that take place over the years play a pivotal role in determining the *level* of success they attain. Here, above all, an understanding of the four types of personality—four kinds of quest—that we've been discussing is enormously useful.

Specifically, the Steve-types who managed to add a solid measure of Larry-like qualities to their personalities, and, conversely, Larry-types who blended some of Steve's orientation in with their own, did significantly better than the pure-form version of either. In a similar manner, Bills who incorporated some of David's characteristics and Davids who amalgamated some of Bill's approach into their own did substantially better as a result.

In a large number of cases a man who exemplified one of the four pure forms did manage to achieve a high degree of success—only to lose it later. This was particularly true of the two types of men who we found were most likely to be early achievers in contemporary America, Larry and Steve. A self-induced "hybridization" seems particularly important for men from these two categories, but is critical for those from the other two as well.

Men like Steve who, without realizing it, started evidencing in their late teens and early twenties personality traits that more closely resembled Larry's were more than three times as likely to do well in their thirties. Why? They were rated by colleagues and friends as being more interesting, innovative, and charismatic. It allowed their careers or companies to attain a "second wind," to maintain, and—in their forties—even increase the upward momentum they had established earlier, while men who remained true to type usually lost it.

A STEADILY INCREASING NET WORTH

The topics we're discussing are so important, and the misconceptions about them have caused so many ambitious and well-meaning men real grief, that is is worthwhile for us to look at the subject from a different angle: the public's.

Ask a wide variety of people what it takes to become a millionaire *early* in the business (as opposed to the investing) world and their answers fall into two categories. In the first is the idea of "volume," and they tell us it means that "you have to find something you can sell lots of—I mean truckloads—to just about everybody." As opposed to this "commodity" approach, the other most frequently mentioned route to riches involves "finding something you can get a very high markup on—you don't have to sell a lot of something if you can make a sizable profit on each sale."

There are people in our sample who have done well using each of these distinct approaches. An example from the volume category is a fellow who made his fortune as a lumber wholesaler. "I don't make all that much on each transaction," he told us, "but if you do enough of them, you finally get there." People in retailing express this view even more strongly: "One sale may net only a few pennies, but they really add up if there are plenty of customers." Conversely, an antiques dealer and an art-gallery owner told us, "I don't have all that many clients, and I don't need them, either. I try to find pieces on which I can turn a good profit."

Nevertheless, at first glance it would seem that neither of these routes to riches is a young man's game. It takes many years in a field to be able to buy repeatedly at the right price and sell in a timely manner while making a profit almost every time. A novice might do this occasionally, and may even put together a string of money-making transactions, but years of experience and a veteran's knowledge of the market are apparently required to do this with sufficient regularity to become—and more important, remain—wealthy. In fact, what characterized the overly eager or swelled-headed men in our sample who had been, as they put it, "on a roll," was that they subsequently sustained a major setback that wiped out their long string of modest gains—and then some.

Similarly, overly optimistic businesspeople who bought expensive items that they thought were rare, and on which they expected to turn a huge profit, frequently put themselves out of business instead. Having paid too much for the pieces, and being unwilling (and, in many cases, unable) to take a loss, they became immobilized. Their working capital was no longer available. Again, veterans in the field were usually able to avoid this fate by knowing which pieces were worth tying up a substantial portion of their capital for. While they too stumbled on occasion (we didn't find anyone who was immune), they made such blunders far less often and, as a result, were able to steadily—often dramatically—increase their own net worth.

In spite of the public's widely held belief that people who become rich quickly in business follow one of the two main routes mentioned above— a small markup on a large quantity or a large markup on a small quantity—we were surprised to see that the majority of men who became wealthy at an early age did so by doing both simultaneously: getting a large markup on a large quantity of either the goods or services that they sold.

To choose a few representative examples, they sold "prestige" cookies or "premium" ice cream or chocolates for previously unthinkable prices. What made the products different from those sold by competitors? Basically, the fact that they contained a much higher percentage of fat. Nevertheless, the packaging was fancy and the marketing sufficiently persuasive and elitist so that even men who told us that they were worried about dying of a heart attack in the near future did manage to buy and wolf down many mouthfuls of these coronary-artery-clogging snacks.

The customers' hunger for prestige usually exceeds their appetite for the product, but whether cookies or clothes are involved, opportunities for a fast fortune obviously keep arising as a result.

GOING WHERE THE ACTION IS

To repeat: One of the main ways in which people succeed at an early age is by recognizing a need that the locals do not. While some of these insightful entrepreneurs are themselves locals, the ratio of immigrants (usually from other parts of the country) to locals among the successful in our study was an astonishingly high figure of four-to-one. Furthermore, the specific areas in which these early achievers made their fortunes were likely to involve real estate, restaurants and night spots, service businesses of all sorts, "gourmet" snacks and desserts, and publishing.

The opportunities which these recent arrivals exploit are invisible to the locals. Familiarity breeds contempt. They didn't think a brownstone being offered for $250,000 was worth the price to begin with, so when it sold for $300,000 to a immigrant (who put 15 percent down and obtained a mortgage for the remainder), they sneered. However, he sold it three years later for $600,000. His reasoning, as he expressed it just before making the purchase, was, "I'm a go-getter, and *I've* come to this town. Other people must be coming here too. Either they, or one of the well-heeled locals, will take it off my hands at a higher price."

Over and over again during our study we noticed that it took an outsider to see a void that could readily be filled by a new product or publication. Whereas the locals we surveyed were generally convinced that "there is too much of everything around here right now," it required the eyes of a recent arrival to see room for improvement and shortages everywhere, ones that could be remedied quickly and lucratively. Rather than rehashing or recycling old styles or statements, the very freshness of their approach often made it newsworthy.

While many people look at an ambitious entrepreneur and see primarily greed, his top priority in life is usually to improve his social status (especially if he is like Larry or David), and he knows that it will take money to accomplish this. What other people think of as an end is for him merely a means. Nevertheless, the reason he ends up doing well financially is that he is firmly convinced that he isn't the only person who is trying to make an upward move. As far as he can see, not only are there millions of people attempting the same climb, it is these very people who are the *real* movers and shakers. Far from being "pathetic," as the city's well-established upper crust often labels such people, they strike him as providing the fuel that makes the city pulse with excitement.

The ingenious thing about such a man starting an enterprise that caters to the city's wealthy and socially prominent residents is that the chances are heightened that he will wind up as one of them. To begin with, he gets to rub shoulders with these exceptional people as the purveyor of the goods and services they are buying. (Larry always regretted that there wasn't much prestige in being an electronics wholesaler, but he was convinced his company's sizable earnings would buy him admission to the upper crust's circle anyway.) Second, he gets to determine which ones are given the best table, merchandise, or service, a "power high" that is as important to him as the money he gets from them.

If the business becomes the new "in" spot, it attracts both the city's aristocrats and the much larger number of people who wish they were. The presence of each produces more visits from the other. One celebrity making an appearance there causes thousands of people who would like to trade places with him to start patronizing the place, perhaps months later. Conversely, stars, ever fearful of falling out of favor with the public, go wherever their noisiest fans are assembling.

The main reason there is such a ravenous appetite among the affluent for new places in which to dine, novel sights to see, and innovative gadgets to buy for their homes and offices is that they are surprisingly fickle. We found that they tire easily of most of their possessions, and, looking for something a little different to talk about with friends to give themselves a boost ("I have the latest . . ."), they will try almost anything new as long as it smacks of "class." Any prestige product, service, or establishment is one in which they eventually find themselves interested. At the very least they must have an opinion about it, or risk seeming musty and out of touch. Although they feel compelled to mask it, this chronic restlessness is precisely what creates such a large number of opportunities for instant wealth for ambitious men like Larry.

When such a hot new store, publication, or product succeeds, the bulk of the business is generated by people who are much like the owner—it is the local Larrys who excitedly patronize an establishment owned by someone like them but usually more of a newcomer. The area's celebrities need only be present occasionally and in small numbers: a starlet or two, a local TV newscaster, a Rolls-Royce or polished antique car parked out front once in a while is all that is required to radiate the image that some of the stars—perhaps many of them—are also regulars.

YOU ARE WHAT YOU OWN

One of the main benefits of modern technology is that even families with a moderate income can clothe and feed themselves and furnish their homes quite comfortably. The economies that result from large-scale mass production and distribution are so substantial that prices of household appliances, jeans, shoes, living-room sofas, and lamps have been driven down to a level that the overwhelming majority of people can afford. This flood of impersonal and mass-produced items, however, creates an appetite in middle- and upper-middle-class families for something about which each can say, "This was made especially for me." The desire to differentiate themselves from a neighbor or peer silently gnaws at them and makes them overly responsive to any product that is touted as being "handmade," even if it is of inferior quality to one produced by a machine.

They are reacting to the impression that there was personal involvement by the maker, and second, that greater attention to detail was displayed during its production. This is an especially appealing feature in an era when an assembly line is thought of by the public as a place where such matters are given short shrift. "You know how it is," said one customer in a department store, pointing to a VCR, "a factory somewhere just belches this stuff out without anyone even looking at it before they stuff it into boxes."

During our study we found that it was particularly those with a little extra money who are looking to rise socially who have the view that "I should have the finer things in life. Why? Because I can finally afford them. If I'm not a member of the elite now, when will I ever be?" They therefore happily pay a higher price for products that have prestige and seem scarce. What they seem not to realize is that price, prestige, and scarcity are closely linked.

Something has prestige today largely because it is scarce; on the other hand, because it has prestige, people like Larry can get away with putting a high price on it—which helps keep it scarce. Since much of what people buy is mechanically produced, there is a growing market for products that appear to have resulted from "cottage industry"—a form of production that the modern world, with billions of people to feed and clothe, has been forced to abandon. So handmade soaps can retail for five dollars a bar, and handknit sweaters for three hundred and fifty dollars.

After monitoring the expenditures of upwardly mobile consumers for a period of more than two decades, it became clear to us that they are willing to overpay for items that fall for the most part into two categories: in the first is anything ordinary that has been given a technologically innovative twist—for instance, miniaturized hi-fi equipment and novel kitchen gadgets. Basicallly, what the customers are buying is "high-tech pizzazz," though (in order not to be "shown up" by something they own) they want it embodied in a product they can understand. As we've seen, they are also willing to overpay for handcrafted items because this gives them the "pizzazz" of the personal—and therefore rare. As many of these consumers told us, pointing to homemade sweaters and soaps, "People don't even know how to make this stuff this way anymore—it's a dying art."

Obviously, someone's upscale marketing approach worked, but less obvious is the fact that someone relatively young became or is on the way to becoming wealthy as a result. Two separate routes to riches became apparent during our study where consumer goods are concerned. Large companies, making and distributing products that have become household names, are in a position to pay their senior executives (usually in their fifties) quite well. On the other hand, so many college-educated, affluent consumers are looking for products that are *not* household names, there are many opportunities for entrepreneurs and distributors (typically in their thirties) to earn similarly large—and in many cases, much larger—sums.

"A STRONG AND INSPIRING LEADER"

So much attention has been given in recent years to job and career changes that the real reasons why so many men feel compelled to make such changes have been overlooked. While many of the shifts are worthwhile and allow people to take advantage of a better situation elsewhere, in more than 40 percent of the 6,600 job changes we examined, the stick of "stagnation," rather than the carrot of "an offer I can't refuse," was the men's explanation for the move. Revealingly, men who correspond to one of the pure personality types we've described were more than five times as likely to eventually report themselves feeling "stagnant" or "burned out."

Needless to say, no one told the Larrys and Steves who went on to attain enduring success that they would have to become such hybrids in order to do well. Fortunately, they did so instinctively. However, unless people have some perspective on this process, they are likely to misinterpret what is going on and criticize themselves. Many men in our sample were confused in their late teen years and twenties by what they saw as their own "irregularities" and "contradictions." While their personalities were developing, each tried to simplify his emotional life by attempting to stay "true to type." If nothing else, that would have made him more predictable in the eyes of his family and friends. Many of these young men told us that they puzzled their parents and girlfriends, who described them as "erratic," or "maddening, but never dull." Fortunately for the men, they couldn't heed the advice of their elders to "fall in line" and were able to develop seemingly incompatible facets of their personality, which paid off handsomely later in life.

They made the transformation subconsciously, usually without reflecting for a moment on where they were going and why. Somehow, they sensed that they were on the right road, and battling their reclusive tendencies (in the case of Steve-types) and their promotional tendencies (in the case of Larrys) produced increasing rates of return on the emotional investment they were making in their own growth.

One, previously a very bookish sort, suddenly announced to us at age twenty-three that "the worm has turned," without being aware of the real significance of his remark. In spite of earlier predictions by college classmates that "he will always be a shy and inhibited hermit," he in fact slowly metamorphosed into a capable corporate leader. As one of his former employees recently commented, twenty-one years after his classmates had their say: "I think of him as strong and inspiring."

In an analogous manner, men like Larry who used their early achievements as a way of quieting their ferocious determination to better themselves, and began to spend some time pondering "the meaning of it all," helped significantly to ensure their own success. Far from rendering them passive or even slowing them down, occasional moments of reflection permitted them to think before they acted in crucial situations. Used to basing their actions purely on instinct, they now began to consider the consequences of what they were about to do.

The men like Larry who never took this step, and who instead continued, as one put it, "to brush my teeth with gunpowder and shoot my mouth off," seemed to their associates and intimates as "lacking depth." That hadn't been considered so important by both groups of observers before. However, once someone like Larry achieves a measure of fame or fortune, they expect him to start behaving in a more "statesmanlike" manner. It even scares them a little when they see that he doesn't, for he now has the power to do harm, perhaps, to many other people besides himself. His success brings him influence over other people's lives, and they are remarkably critical of him when he keeps acting like the aggressive urban nomad he once was.

Given that the Larry-types want above all to appear "classy," it is amazing that they overlook the personality characteristics that would help elicit such esteem, and focus instead on externals—prestige props such as expensive cars and clothes.

WHAT DOES IT TAKE?

Early achievers in America now have the mass appeal of show-business personalities. Everyone is intrigued by the seemingly magical combination of luck and skill needed to become rich while they are still young enough to live it up. One of the most fervent wishes of middle-class parents in our sample is to see their children do well early in their careers as a result of having had the "right education," both at home and in school.

However, our study indicates that it takes more than parental love and good intentions to set the youngsters on the path to precocious financial success, or, more important, to keep any gains that are made. After twenty-seven years of monitoring ambitious men who did well, poorly, and everything in between, we have found that most—more than three out of five—who fulfilled their own (or equally often, their parents') dreams of becoming millionaires by the age of thirty-five had the following five characteristics in common:

First, between the ages of fourteen and twenty-one the young men expressed a sense of detachment from their parents, peers, *and* hometown. Some openly admitted to feeling like a "stranger" in their own homes, and most secretly felt themselves to be "different," never really a part of any group in school, no matter how much they yearned to be a member. Although few were aware of how difficult it would be, they were going to have to "make their own world" since they were so little suited to the one into which they had been born.

Second, because they felt so detached from their own childhood setting, it was easy—almost necessary—for them to strike out for parts unknown. The men finished school and, instead of returning home, started over elsewhere, determined at first to absorb and then make an impact on their newly adopted city. They didn't belong to an "in-group" as adolescents, so they were determined to make up for lost time and find acceptance in an even bigger one as adults. They were reluctant to admit it (because they didn't want to hurt anyone's feelings), but they were "holding out for something—and someone—better" than the "hicks" they had grown up with, as they later labeled their mostly suburban classmates.

Although they eventually came to our attention and everyone else's because of the money they made, the men's achievements ended up being both financial and social. For decades it has been a commonplace of social science that adolescents who feel alienated from their parents form tight bonds instead with their peers. They find a sense of family among friends. This observation may fit juvenile delinquents, who want the company of others while they are breaking windows or stealing cars, but we found that it doesn't at all fit ambitious middle- and upper-middle-class young men. *They* typically feel alienated from both—parents and peers—and from the town in which they went to high school. Unable to "go home again" (as far as they are concerned, they never really had one), they have no choice but to stride forward aggressively into an uncertain future. Nevertheless, social beings that humans are, they want later (with big-city "movers and shakers") what they were unable to find earlier (with people they now view as "small-minded and boring").

Third, more than 80 percent of the men in our sample who went on to become young millionaires are egocentric in an important respect: they feel certain that everyone is at least as interested in "making it big" as they themselves are. In this case, egotism leads to wealth because it makes the men try to keep up with a much higher standard than actually prevails. To bolster their view, they focus intensely on anyone who is working hard and doing well, quickly convincing themselves that this is the norm. In some ways this makes them surprisingly tolerant. How so? They tend to overlook the large number of people who are just coasting, hoping perhaps to win a million-dollar lottery jackpot one day. The men who become rich may be driven, but they aren't nearly as hypercritical as the stereotype suggests. Lazy people are largely invisible to them. Thanks to the men's drive, they are constantly looking for angles to exploit, to beat out the competition—who, they assume, never sleeps. So they don't either. Searching restlessly, making good use of the can-do optimism that their outsider's perspective affords them, they find opportunities where locals only find mind-numbing familiarity.

Fourth, they become more involved with their work than the typical local because they usually don't have much else to devote themselves to. This is what they came to the city for, and this is what consumes them. They see it as a magic carpet, capable of flying them anywhere. Yet they want the respect of the "right" social circle, whether it consists of movie stars or other scientists and engineers. Recluses may seem to be permanently so, but our study indicates that with each passing year they are slowly building up a powerful appetite for the social acceptance they have never really had—this time, though, they want it from the audience whose applause means the most to them. The point is that men who pursue both work involvement and public acceptance are significantly more likely to become young millionaires than those pursuing either one exclusively. Men who were too technically oriented, and thought of this as the key to an instant fortune, were usually shunned as too uncompromising; and those who devoted themselves primarily to finding the sense of belonging they didn't have as adolescents didn't find it as adults either. They seemed both to locals and other recent arrivals just a little too hungry for peer group admiration to be admirable.

Fifth, in annual discussions with the friends and families of the boys who would eventually become young millionaires, it was startling to see that the description these people offered was the same as that offered later by the men's colleagues, friends, and wives. Both groups, past and present associates, viewed the men as difficult to typecast, a very revealing finding. For we found that, sad to say, men who are easily described, both as adolescents and adults, do much less well in attaining either enduring fame or fortune than do those who have never fit the two-dimensional images others set out for them. The unpredictable behavior of the latter baffled their parents, many of whom told us that they were relieved that their son's uniqueness didn't keep him from earning a living and getting along with others.

They needn't have worried, and neither should he. If our study taught us anything about ambitious men, it is this: the ones most likely to become successful early—and later unwittingly undo their achievements—are pure-personality types, while those who become successful later and also have a satisfying personal life are those whom we've called "hybrids." However, that was so only when each man was comfortable with the mixture of drives that propelled him, rather than squandering his energy year after year in an internal civil war about which one of the four—originality (Steve), autonomy (Bill), respectability (Larry), or sociability (David)—represented his "true self."

Put simply, it takes one kind of mentality to spot an opportunity, another to exploit it, a third to run the resulting business successfully, and a fourth to enjoy the rewards the business throws off—without wrecking it because its success has become less exciting and even routine. The evidence shows that hybrids make these transformations best, never feeling long like a fish out of water.

CHAPTER
·10·

SEX,
WEALTH, AND
RECAPTURING
THE PAST

Does success influence a man's sexual appetites? Even more interesting, does it cause him to become drawn to a different kind of partner than the ones he previously found attractive?

The best way to answer these and many other related questions is to study pairs of men who are similar in every important respect except that one becomes successful and the other doesn't, both in their own view and that of the people who know them. After more than a quarter of a century of collecting data continuously on this subject, it is fair to say that the results are not what we expected.

It was clear within the first few months of our study that men who are feeling confident, regardless of the reason, are generally more open sexually. There are limits, of course; prudish men don't suddenly become libertines just because they receive a million-dollar inheritance from a recently dead uncle. However, good news of any kind—pay raises or promotions, for instance—not only usually makes the man in question more emotionally expansive, it increases significantly his desire to have sex with his current partner or find one if he doesn't have any at the moment.

Even a major purchase that reflects his higher status may have a similarly stimulating effect. For example, young men who buy a new car (especially a convertible) have been telling us for decades that their sex lives improved, and that this was primarily a result of willing women being enticed by the car. Our research makes this conclusion doubtful. Had each man's mood remained as upbeat and visibly interested as it was behind the wheel, our guess is that he would have attracted an equal number of willing women even if he had been pedaling a Schwinn.

Conversely, major or moderate setbacks, such as being fired or criticized in front of others at work, had the reverse effect. This time, the men knew it. Many were unaware that a victory made them more amorous, but most were conscious of the fact that a defeat reduced their interest in sex. They had something else, more pressing, temporarily on their minds and were unable to switch gears. In short, where the connection between success and "quantity" of sex was concerned, the answer seemed apparent.

However, the question of "quality," especially the *kind* of partner to whom a successful man might be attracted but wasn't previously, had to be a complicated subject for a number of reasons. The first has to do with masturbation. It is important to realize that most men masturbate at one time or another in their lives to a fantasized sexual encounter with a woman they would *not* want to marry or even live with. This has nothing to do with the "virgins-versus-whores" split common in the thinking of severely repressed men, which was mentioned earlier. Rather, it is a consequence of a man finding himself aroused by a comment someone makes or a picture he sees.

We hear so much about "free-floating anxiety," it is easy to overlook "free-floating arousal," which is every bit as prevalent. When anxiety is present, it will often latch onto any reasonable after-the-fact cause for concern. Similarly, when arousal is present, it will often latch onto any reasonable—and, at times, unreasonable—potential sex partner. The process happens in a blink. Inevitably in most cases only a fantasized sex act (one that takes place during masturbation) will result, allowing the man to rid himself of his interest.

The point is that sometimes an ambitious fellow carries the process a step further, and tries to bed the woman in question. For instance, Ed, a thirty-six-year-old, Larry-like manager in our sample, became aroused instantly when an attractive and braless new waitress in a coffee shop near his office brought him lunch. "The top three buttons of her blouse were open," he said, readily remembering the sight, "and so much was showing when she bent over to put the plates down, it wasn't hard to imagine the rest." Within the next few weeks he went out with her twice and slept with her both times.

Who cares? We did, because Ed had just received a $35,000 pay raise (to $105,000 annually) and a promotion as well, and we were eager to see with whom he'd pair up. Divorced at thirty-two after three unhappy years of marriage to his first wife, he was definitely ready to try again. Yet here he was sleeping with a woman who, by his own admission, "isn't someone I'd want as a wife." His reasons were many, not the least of which was that one of the salesmen in his company was also sleeping with her.

It would have been neater if he had done what most men in his position do, which was to forget the initial encounter that he found so arousing or use masturbation to release the energy the image contained in his mind. Life isn't neat, though, and in this instance—and hundreds of others—we had to wait for such "situational arousal" factors to exert their temporary effects before we could see what, if any, deeper and/or more enduring relationships emerged.

PEAK EXPERIENCES

Social and historical background factors also played an important role. The men we were studying had been raised and were living in a particular time and place, and these exerted pressures of their own. An era of sexual liberation began around 1960, as the nation's youngest ever president, Kennedy, replaced Dwight Eisenhower.

That made it all the more startling to discover that for the twenty-five-year period from the late 1950s through 1983, a steadily *decreasing* proportion of the sexually liberated couples we studied were content with their love lives. Specifically, while 62 percent of the ambitious married men we surveyed in 1958 rated their marriage satisfying sexually, by 1968 only 49 percent of a comparable group felt the same way. In 1983 the figure bottomed out, having fallen to slightly more than one third. After that, in the mid-1980s, it rose again (for reasons discussed in the next chapter).

How could this have happened? What went wrong? Among other things, sex, which previously had been merely one of many strands holding a marriage together, was suddenly singled out. No longer an integral part of a package that characterized the couple's intimate relations, it became a topic of paramount importance, a yardstick that was now being used to measure the overall health of the relationship. The tail had finally begun to wag the dog.

The problem, as men who attempt to search for peak experiences using drugs soon learn, is that as soon as one peak is ascended, another, even taller and more enticing, is visible from the summit. There is no end. Like people who become self-made millionaires, only to find that they now feel compelled to become billionaires, the quest feeds on itself.

The new focus had a profound effect on the durability of relationships. Whereas the proportion of men in our sample who said they were terminating their marriages for reasons of sexual incompatibility was only 18 percent in 1959, the figure more than doubled during the following decade, reaching 41 percent by 1969. When the men couldn't find what they were looking for sexually with the partners they already had, they located new ones. At first, most thought they had found what they were seeking; more than 60 percent of those who began having an extramarital affair felt initially that it was providing the satisfaction their marriages lacked. However, the typical affair didn't last very long; a median duration of only seventeen weeks. Far from making the men feel guilty about their transgression, the first one apparently served only to stimulate their appetite for more of the same. (Those who had an extramarital fling were more than three times as likely as their peers to end up having another.) With the momentum building, and carrying them even further afield from the marital bed, they were able to look at their marriages in what they felt was "the cold light of day" and conclude that these relationships were woefully inadequate. In what way? To experience the real joys that sex could provide, they would have to move on, to yet another partner. At this point, the majority of these men were no longer looking for just another affair; instead, they wanted a divorce.

That makes it sound as though millions of ambitious men, in their own minds at least, had scrapped their marriages during the past few decades and become sexual adventurers. Many did indeed do so, though less than 6 percent did it consciously. However, the majority did the opposite, responding to the emotional and erotic alienation they felt toward their spouses by burying themselves in their work. Many didn't see sex as all that important to begin with. They liked having a family, even though they were painfully aware that they and their wives fought much too often. Ignoring the problem, at least for the time being, seemed the best way.

Far from being the end of the story, it was merely the beginning. The millions of women entering the business world made serious affairs (as opposed to one-night stands or brief flings of the kind Ed had) much more likely. Why? Because opportunity is half of what is required for one to take place. Desire is the other half. We wondered, "Where would they find the time, or the place?" As high-school students know very well, even if both parties are willing, sometimes there isn't a safe location readily available for a lovemaking session. It turned out that working adults rarely have this problem, since their greater resourcefulness and incomes allow them to find a solution if they really want to.

The majority of ambitious married men in our sample who had an extramarital affair were attempting to fill a gap that they didn't realize even existed. When an interesting new woman came along, the fullness of their response to her surprised the men themselves. Whether they were feeling love or lust at that moment isn't the issue; the point is that they quickly became caught up in a complex and erotic relationship. As experienced businessmen, they had become used to deciding over the years whether to participate in any number of work-related ventures. Not this time. Their hidden backlog of desires deprived them of the luxury of perspective and the ability to say no to a sexually available woman. Their pent-up appetite for something new and exciting blinded them to the magnitude of the step they were about to take.

Analyzing a large number of such affairs (more than eight thousand), and isolating the underlying factors that went beyond merely situational ("she was willing, so was I, and I haven't seen her since") or historical factors ("everybody else was doing it at the time"), made it clear that there were a number of important patterns to be seen in what at first glance looked like a mass of randomly occurring liaisons.

OLDER MEN, YOUNGER WOMEN

By examining many pairs of Larrys—though the same applies to pairs of Davids or Steves—it eventually became possible to predict with a high degree of accuracy which one of the two was most likely to become enmeshed in this type of erotic relationship. Our most general and unexpected finding is this: *The man who has had little sexual experience during his teens and early twenties, but moves from a modest or middle-class background to a high level of success, turns out to be the one most likely to find himself consumed by such a relationship twenty to thirty years later, often with a woman young enough to be his daughter.*

She may well be a Lolita-type, interested in sleeping with a man who at least in some ways resembles her father, but we found that the men who become infatuated with such a woman have two major reasons of their own for doing so.

The first is a purely sexual one. They want to make up for lost time, by finally experiencing the sensual highs they wouldn't allow themselves even to think about seriously as younger men. Dedicated to achieving professional goals that struck them as more important in some ways than life itself ("If I work myself to death but become famous posthumously, that's okay too"), they relegated any steamy sexual images to the realm of pornography, not reality. Slowly at first, then ever more rapidly, that changed. Scenes they had previously seen solely in erotic movies and magazines—which they used to claim only "losers" ever became preoccupied with—they were now determined to bring to life. That made them view their nubile partner in a very limited light. Transfixed by her evident sexual interest, blithely assuming that she had no other, they swan-dived into the ocean of sensuality they saw awaiting them.

At first they were thrilled. Most felt they really had recaptured the past they had wanted so much for themselves but were too busy to have. They seemed, they said, to have wound up with the best of both possible worlds: they had become successful in their fields *and* were living out their most pulsating sexual fantasies. Better still, as adults, rather than frenzied adolescents, they were able to savor the experience rather than merely gulp it down. They had the immediate satisfactions of a participant together with the vicarious pleasures of a voyeur.

The second chief goal of successful men who tie up with a younger woman is rejuvenation. More aware each day of their own mortality, they subconsciously hope that in embracing her they will find not only ecstasy, but also absorb a healthy dose of the youthful and invigorating essence she gives off.

Sex is one of the few seemingly personal avenues that people can use to bridge the distance between themselves and a stranger. So here, a driven man, fearful of dying prematurely, employs an erotic connection as a way of getting a transfusion that helps him combat the fear. Just being around her makes him feel that he has increased his chances of living longer. Once they have had sex, subsequent transfusions can take place even over a dinner table.

The colleagues of such a man, who see him with a younger woman on his arm, typically comment that "He's going through his second childhood." The evidence flatly contradicts this view. One fact that jumps out of the data is that these men never really had a childhood. They were "middle-aged adolescents," more ambitious than their peers and much more concerned about the future. Now that they have become a success, in large part precisely because they took themselves and their quest so seriously, they want to force themselves to relax a little.

Reversing their focus, looking backward with the same determination they previously looked forward, they try to go back and fill in the gaps in their lives. They want it to be a joyous rather than melancholy journey. Unable to find compelling reasons for continuing to deny themselves such simple pleasures, they do become somewhat adolescent in middle age. Their peers may criticize them roundly for displaying such immature behavior in public and thereby undermining the success they worked so hard to achieve; but it is that very success that gives them the courage and comfort needed to do at last what they have always wanted to.

The basic strategy these men have long used is to pursue a goal relentlessly until they achieve it; then, without doing so consciously, to turn their back on it and go after something bigger, better, or just plain different. This style both helps and hinders such a man once he has done well in business. Having attained the admiration and envy of his colleagues by becoming successful, he often allows himself to be seen in public in unguarded and even occasionally giddy states without caring that his colleagues are now saying, in hushed tones, "He's making a fool of himself." It never seems to occur to them that, having already enjoyed their esteem, he no longer needs it. Now, as in the past, it is only what he doesn't have that truly fascinates him.

"I'VE BEDDED A BIGGIE"

It is the Larrys of the world who are most likely to act this way, or to want to. Approximately 68 percent of the men like Larry in our sample either formed such liaisons once they became a success or wished they could. It is revealing that both the men who had such a mistress and those who didn't, but would have liked to, produced the same description when asked to characterize their ideal partner. She was vibrant, youthful, openly sexual, and typically in her late twenties. As we said at the start of the chapter, one of the key findings of our study is that the less sexual experience a man has while he is between the ages of fifteen and twenty-five, the more likely he is to seek out younger partners a quarter of a century later.

A converse to this also emerged. Men who during their late teens and especially their twenties had slept with a variety of *Playboy* and *Penthouse* centerfold types apparently exhausted their ability later to project raunch into the images of such women. Having pierced the alluring veneer such bedmates usually generate initially, these men had already experienced the dismay that comes from realizing that, as Larry himself commented, "After the appetizer, there is no main course." The power of the allure was great enough to get such men excited to begin with, but the follow-through wasn't enough to keep them coming back for more. At fifty, say, with perhaps a million dollars in assets and a well-established position in their field, they were unable to glamorize the endlessly aroused twenty-six-year-old woman they met who was driving their equally successful but less sexually experienced peers mad. Having had at least one bedmate like her when they too were her age, they felt remarkably little desire to go back and do it again.

It is a man like Steve, whether married or single, who is generally most harmed by becoming embroiled in such a relationship. For one thing, he is more likely to be the pursued than the pursuer. Unlike a Larry-type, who goes searching for an overtly sexual partner to make up for what he didn't have as a hardworking youth, men like Steve are usually a target for young working women who are using sex as a tool to further their own ambitions.

The enormous amount of adverse publicity given to office romances by articles in women's magazines during the 1970s and early 1980s—in which the writer almost always assumed that a woman sleeping with her boss was being exploited by him—masked an important fact: a considerable number of women were far more adept than their bosses at getting such a relationship started and using it for their own purposes.

Men like Steve were (and still are) viewed as particularly appealing by such women because, first, these men seem like "babes in the wood." Their naïveté makes them easier to handle and more likely to believe a line like, "I was only kidding," voiced by a woman after a sexual overture she makes is rejected. Second, such men proved surprisingly willing to go along with—and respond warmly to—amorous advances made by subordinates.

While these men had become successful in large part because they had mixed some of Larry's personality in with their own, becoming more aggressive and market-oriented as a result, they had much less of his natural comfort with physical and emotional intimacy. This showed, once the affair began. They were more ravenous (for them, all this was new), yet more awkward (precisely because it was so new). To make matters worse, they gave in to their old tendency to see everyone— especially the people close to them—in a three-dimensional light. The prospect of sex with so willing a young woman was magnetic, yet it also made them uncomfortable. The most sensitive of the four types of men, the one most inclined to humanize situations that didn't even warrant it, they made major problems out of what would otherwise have been minor ones.

Taking seriously what everybody but them recognized was basically a fling, they treated their new bedmate as if she were now their wife, whether or not they currently had one. Attentive to her every mood and whim, they wound up being manipulated by her to an extent that shocked onlookers far more than the existence of the relationship itself did.

Why were men like Steve more adversely affected in business than men like Larry when both found themselves in this situation? Because Steve-types are more secretive. Their reclusive orientation is among the most fundamental facts about them, and hiding things—often for no good reason—is an integral part of that orientation. In spite of the sensual satisfactions provided by the affair, they were mortified at the possibility that their private actions might become widely known. They were usually right to worry, for their playmate wasn't nearly as inclined to be discreet as they were. Aggressiveness, she felt, had got her as far as she had gotten, and therefore it wasn't to be viewed in a negative light merely because her executive boyfriend felt squeamish about a little publicity. She was intent on taking another step forward and nothing she was doing, as part of her assertive style, seemed wrong to her.

Moreover, she wanted her gains known. In her view, an achievement that no one knows about is no achievement at all. In fact, the more people who know about it, the greater the achievement is. So without consciously broadcasting the news, in more than half the cases we studied the woman in question simply made certain that other people were kept informed. A joke here, an offhand comment there, a series of complaints or observations, made it quite clear to listeners that she had, in the words of one, "bedded a biggie." The feeling of "being on the inside" exhilarated her (even if it netted her no pay raises or promotions) and, ironically, it did so to pretty much the same extent that her Steve-like lover now felt himself vulnerable. Contrary to the tight-lipped approach he had utilized for so many years, this private dalliance turned out to be the subject of intense office gossip. For the first time in their lives many of these men heard the word "hypocrite" used to describe them.

Unlike Larry-types, who didn't really care if their extramarital flings became common knowledge, men like Steve were quite upset to discover that co-workers and colleagues knew about them. This was an audience whose esteem the Steves of the world very much wanted. The sense of loss was as harmful as the actual loss, since here, as in so many other settings, the fear was worse than the fact. By contrast, Larry's greater indifference to a hostile remark voiced by a peer actually helped limit the amount of damage it could do. Although both men insisted that what happened to them in the work world was often beyond their control ("all I can do is try to *respond* well"), the evidence indicates that each, in fact, sets the tone for the way in which those who found out about their discretions reacted to them. Then, for better or worse, they had to inhabit the "climate of opinion" that they had done so much to create.

THE WINNER, BY DEFAULT

Odd as it may sound at first, men like David are usually the least harmed, and may even be helped, by such an affair. To see why, it is worthwhile to compare briefly the reactions of men like Steve and those like David to an involvement of this kind.

The inhibitions of a Steve make it almost mandatory for the woman he ties up with erotically to be more open and aggressive about sex than he is. His abundant restraint makes it difficult for him to have access to his own sexuality without help from an outside party, who becomes caught up herself in bringing these hidden forces to the surface. To her it may be just a game, and she may not be aroused at all while in bed with him and playing guide, yet this is one setting in which theater often passes for reality. As long as she plays the part of the seductress convincingly, Steve can allow his fantasies to move to the fore.

Two goals will then have been reached: someone else will finally have broken through his many layers of repression and gotten him fully aroused, and, second, his partner will now be able to influence him more easily for her own purposes. The two goals may later become part of an open tug-of-war. Unfortunately, a man like Steve may not recognize at the time how dependent upon her he has become; yet she is the only person he knows who is capable of getting him truly excited sexually. That makes her unique. Becoming aroused while looking at a beautiful woman whom he doesn't know isn't at all the same as getting in bed with her and finding the event satisfying. Two people are present, both making their needs felt, not always compatibly. In that sense, the voyeur has it easy; he has no one's reactions but his own to worry about. However, a real-life partner who is able to bring such a reclusive person to a high level of arousal is invaluable, and, not surprisingly, a man like Steve, who "depends on the sexual kindness of strangers" more than he realizes, may clutch at her emotionally—not realizing how estranged they really are. The impact that this has on his professional and personal life is often quite damaging.

A David, by contrast, generally has no reservoir of passion sitting just beneath the surface. He plays at being sexually inhibited but in fact has little lust to hide. Any woman who uses her seductive wiles in an attempt, as one commented, to "wrap him around my little finger" finds that he performs his part in the drama with a lightness and ease that equal hers. Far from being intimidated by his partner's open eroticism, he is able to use it as a basis for a number of witty and entertaining remarks. He may at times be tense while making them but it is the tension of an actor about to deliver lines in front of an audience.

To many of his colleagues a man like David seems vaguely asexual; some may even label him "a closet case." While he may be, in a much larger number of cases sex simply doesn't hold the same thunderous joys for him that it does for the other three types. However, in order to get along better with the Bills, Larrys, and Steves, he has long pretended that he is nearly as lusty as they. He knew he wasn't, and felt badly about it. Now, as the object of the advances of a sexually aggressive woman, he can revel in the proof it seems to offer that he is indeed "one of the boys." He can exploit the situation, rather than being exploited by it, by going along somewhat—but only somewhat—with the seduction before calling it to a halt with a great show of restraint. Always done to impress others, while making it appear as though he is more mature than they, David emerges as a double winner: he is heterosexual after all, people can now assert, and, as he himself can proudly say, "I know how to keep my desires from getting me into trouble." That is more than most men can state, and he knows it.

Many of his colleagues are puzzled when an earthy woman bothers chasing a man like David in the first place, since he seems so little interested in sex. Nevertheless, it is precisely for this reason that he is such a good choice for a woman attempting to improve her position in the world by pairing up with him, if she can. She doesn't have to worry that after she has chased him for a while, he might turn the tables on her and chase her just as energetically. He remains manageable instead, leaving it to her to determine what will happen. Even if he is the "closet gay" some of his co-workers have labeled him, he will try to avoid brushing her off, lest he confirm the suspicions of his critics. As a result, he may have a small handful of such willing women pursuing him simultaneously. Other men may envy his position, but we found it to be a telltale clue, one that means the opposite of what it seems to say. Ironically, a man more interested in women would tell the ones he wasn't interested in to go away.

In short, although it is the sex partner of a man like Steve who is most likely to go public with the news that she and he are secretly a pair, which mortifies him when he hears it, a man like David usually does the broadcasting before his (alleged) partners have had a chance to do so. By not rejecting such overtures, and, in fact, by subtly encouraging them, he can manage to get a sexually open woman to reach out for him just when others are watching and thereby silence the skeptics. Condemning her advances, though never to her face, he can then boost himself still further by appearing to be, as David himself once put it, "holding out for someone with a little more style."

Unlike a Larry or Steve, each of whom at times may be ridiculed mercilessly by peers for "not being able to keep it in his pants," men like David avoid this embarrassment. Lacking the charisma and drive of the other two, David-types are therefore able later on to gain the ground they lost earlier in the race for success by seeming to be the more responsible and wise by comparison. The gap may not only close, it may in fact finally allow a man like David to pull into the lead as a candidate for top position. His record may be undistinguished, but it is also unblemished— an even more important feature at this point, since his firm or organization can move him into the limelight and feel that he has little to hide.

It takes only one skeleton in a person's closet to disqualify him or her from running successfully for public office. Men like Larry have considerably more than one, and know it. Men like Steve always view themselves as having a much larger number than they actually do. It is men like David, whose aggressions weren't great enough to get them in trouble in the past and whose reclusive tendencies weren't strong enough to yank them repeatedly from the mainstream, who therefore seem to the majority of Americans the most suitable of the three for public position.

THE KISSINGER FACTOR

Most people think of themselves as good amateur judges, capable of deciding an issue once they hear both sides of an argument. "The outcome of an event is determined by the facts," many told us, sounding like jurors, and we, too, believed this at the start of our study. However, the evidence we've collected demonstrates convincingly that, where sex between consenting adults is concerned, the public outcome is almost never a simple consequence of the facts.

To be specific, two men who seem similar in most respects may each have an affair, the women also being similar in most respects; yet the effect on the careers of the two men may differ radically. What accounts for the difference? How do the men deal with the "leak" of the news to co-workers (as we've seen, it isn't always accidental)? And what accounts for the difference in the way the men deal with the matter? The answer depends on whether each is more like Larry, Steve, or David. Generally speaking, Larry-types are the least harmed professionally; Steve-types, the most harmed; and David-types, the most helped.

A devil's advocate who insists that the majority of men who are discovered having an extramarital fling will have their reputations compromised—and thus should avoid such liaisons in the first place—is probably correct. However, as the enormous number of smokers or those who regularly eat fatty foods and sugary desserts teach us, people don't always do what is best for them. Finding out who is most at risk, and who least, is the next best thing we can do in a free society.

The damage done differs greatly, depending on how the situation is handled. What makes this finding particularly worthwhile is that such affairs, always more common than most people suspected, have increased significantly in frequency in recent years. The more than 35 million baby-boom females born in the United States between 1946 and 1964 constitute the largest, most affluent, and best-educated generation of women the nation has ever produced, and a record number of them are now in the business world and the professions. So much for the good news. The bad news is that many of the women are unmarried, unhappily married, separated, divorced, or, like many men, married to their work.

Until the mid-1980s these women were inclined to shun office affairs, but (for reasons that will be made clear in the next chapter) they now prefer them to the alternatives. Men who don't want any part of such involvements can obviously avoid them. Nevertheless, a huge number of men—especially those who are ambitious and successful—will be offered the chance to have at least one. That they are reluctant or even unwilling initially may not make all that much difference. Often, such things seem to have a life of their own and occur almost as if they were destined.

What really causes them to occur, and which men are most likely to become involved? As we saw, it is, paradoxically, the men who have achieved the most as adults but who had the least amount of sexual experience during adolescence and their early twenties. But why, one might ask, does this "sexual-experience deficit" take so long to be filled? The answer is that the men aren't viewed, or don't see themselves, as sufficiently attractive until they are middle-aged and wealthy. Rock stars and professional athletes typically achieve fame and fortune while still in their twenties, yet the majority of businessmen don't attain their own version of the same until they are in their forties or fifties. Any groupies they attract are likely to be older, wiser, and more career-oriented.

We don't mean to portray these successful men as innocents caught in a web spun by a sexually assertive woman. No guy who, at forty-eight, brags (as more than one did) that it is "better to be a red-hot lover later than never" has remained innocent, regardless of what he once might have been. Others who, at the age of fifty-six or sixty-two, told us that the affair they were having made them feel like "hot stuff," also weren't exactly babes in the wood any longer. Nevertheless, the shift in the past few decades has been major: whereas previously men initiated the majority of extramarital affairs, by the late 1980s women were the ones doing so. Especially in the office.

In short, there is a sexual hazard to success. Most men who, when younger, thought of themselves as unattractive, and who therefore concentrated on their work and eventually became wealthy or well known, undergo in the eyes of many working women the same kind of transformation that a caterpillar does in becoming a butterfly. Call it "the Kissinger factor," the sex appeal of power. It was, and still is, commonly encountered in Washington, D.C., New York, and Los Angeles, but has now spread to the nation's businesses, large and small. Some successful men will sidestep the whole issue, but not many. One thing is certain: the outcome of any affairs that develop will depend largely on whether the man involved is more like Larry, Steve, or David.

CHAPTER

·11·

RETURN OF
THE HE-MAN

People who are married don't always see their partners clearly. In fact, it is quite common for couples—especially those who have been together only a few years—to misinterpret one another's behavior. As each comes to know the other better, rude awakenings are typical and so are divorces.

However, even before they pair up, there are some common misperceptions. The most frequently encountered one involving men is this: most women are convinced that men are much more sexually aggressive than they actually are. If this perception is inaccurate, why is it so widespread? Two key factors are responsible. First, in the vast majority of the world's cultures, men are expected to make the initial overture. "If I don't work up the courage and use my hands," Larry once told us, "no one will. *She* sure as hell won't." Second, there is indeed a time when men are likely to display a fair amount of sexual aggression toward a woman they are with. That time is in the later years of high school and early years of college.

Eager to lose their virginity, and convinced that young women are just as eager (but afraid) to lose theirs, young men in the sixteen-to-twenty-one age range are often quite aggressive. If they have already had sex a few times, they want badly to gain more experience and have their date become experienced too. However, the topic is more complex than it seems. Nearly two thirds of the men we surveyed in this age range in 1986 agreed, as had their peers every year for more than two decades, that being obliged to make the first move "often makes me act more forcefully than I want to. It's a no-win situation: if I do nothing—just be polite—I'm written off as a wimp or a closet case, but if I make a move, I may come off looking like a rapist or, at the very least, a bully."

Years later, women with an ax to grind can easily use the impression such an episode makes to condemn all men as "animals," but it was revealing to see that an even larger number are left wondering where this appetite went. As a friend of Stephanie's reported saying to her own husband, "You know, I can remember fifteen years ago when you were twenty-one and couldn't get *enough* of my body. Now it's once a month, if I'm lucky."

Whether women view the decrease in a positive or negative light, or fail to notice it at all, the decrease does indeed take place. In fact, it does so significantly once the men are out of school or approach their mid-twenties, whichever comes first. Then their attitude typically becomes, "Look, if you don't want to meet me halfway, forget it."

Rather than reflecting a physiological change, an abruptly diminishing sex drive, the new approach reflects an increase in civility. It occurs almost automatically in college graduates, and did so in every decade of our study—the fifties, sixties, seventies, and eighties—always to pretty much the same extent. The men were still willing to chase a woman in whom they were interested, but not nearly as far. Someone could readily accuse them of being lazy, not civil, but there can be no doubt that each had normally reduced his level of sexual aggression substantially by the age of twenty-five. From then on, any woman who gave him the brush-off was written off.

Including the men's wives. We expected leaders of the women's movement who characterized men as "Neanderthals" and "beasts" to harm single women above all, by preventing the vast majority, who needed a man in their lives, from making the effort and compromises necessary to find one and keep the relationship intact. We were surprised to see that a greater degree of harm was done to women who were already married. Nature wasn't pushing them as hard; their search was through, or so they thought, since they had already found a partner.

Once women allowed themselves to believe the line that men have little more than sex on their minds, real trouble began to develop. The erroneous belief that men are essentially sex maniacs led many women to reject a cooperative stance where lovemaking was concerned or to rebuff their partners once too often. Worse still, it made them assume that the typical husband would ignore the obstacles and keep on trying to have intercourse with his wife.

He didn't. Giving up on her (often without realizing it), and starting to look elsewhere (subconsciously), had already become an integral part of his civilized approach to sex. If there was one terrible little secret that some men knew during the 1970s and 1980s that could have made a big difference to the durability of their marriages, this was it. It was one piece of knowledge that few men could tell a woman, especially the one they married. Proud of their erotic abilities and happy to have whatever sexual pleasure they were experiencing, the men would have felt inadequate if they had described their sex drive as fragile.

Nevertheless, fragile it is. The subtle signs of interest in having sex that his partner sends him are every bit as crucial to the satisfaction he experiences as the supposedly all-important inner impulse (his own level of interest and arousal). His antennae are constantly assessing the signals he receives, since he wants the involvement to be mutual, not a wild chase with a sweaty conquest for a reward. The picture of a naked ape, standing upright, beating his chest, and then chasing an unwilling partner, may make women cling together in groups, full of fear and outrage, but it is hilariously divorced from reality.

Labeling all men rapists, when so minuscule a proportion really are, eventually backfired badly. Men in the 1950s who were married to prudish women often chased their secretaries around the desk in the hope of finding in an office fling the sexual satisfactions not available at home. The relationship rarely led to divorce, since the goal was erotic, not romantic, and the prevailing attitude of the time called for the marriage to be maintained at all costs, at least until the children were old enough to leave home.

Once millions of college-educated women entered the work world in the sixties, seventies, and eighties, the nature of these affairs changed.

When an executive in the 1950s, in bed with his secretary, said to her, "My wife doesn't understand me," he meant it; but he didn't really expect his secretary to understand him any better. Basically, he was using as a guideline a Kinsey statistic (one that was widely quoted in the early and mid-1950s) that 30 percent of upper-class and 80 percent of lower-class women had had premarital intercourse. That made him feel that he knew, as one put it, "where the action is" and "who is willing and available."

As the decades passed, the women these men chose were increasingly like themselves—better educated, better paid, and more likely to hold a position comparable to theirs. In fact, working together (usually the two were in different departments) was what allowed them to become involved in the first place. In addition, thanks to the sexual revolution of the 1960s, these women were often *more* sexually experienced than their female peers from poorer homes. These were true affairs, rather than mere flings. Romantic as well as erotic feelings were present this time.

It is useful to view this change quantitatively. Whereas in the late 1950s and early 1960s approximately 81 percent of the male managers we surveyed who had recently had or were having an office affair described it as "based primarily on lust," by the late 1980s nearly 60 percent of a comparable group characterized theirs as "based primarily on love." This shift in attitude of more than forty percentage points had a significant impact on the men's marriages. As before, they often said to the woman with whom they were sleeping, "My wife doesn't understand me." However, this time their lover did. She was no mistress; self-supporting, in the majority of cases she even had her own apartment (less than 30 percent of secretaries did in the 1950s, when most lived with parents or relatives). The upshot: many men made the switch.

How many? Three statistics capture the principal changes that occurred. First, affairs involving men in middle-managerial positions began to last longer (a median duration of nineteen months in 1986 versus seventeen weeks in 1958–1959). In the view of the husbands involved, the affairs were more likely to lead to divorce (0.5 percent ended for this reason in 1958–1959—that is, one out of two hundred—versus 9.3 percent in 1986, a more than eighteenfold increase). Finally, they led the man to marry the woman with whom he was having extramarital relations in two tenths of one percent of the cases (that is, one out of 490) in

1958–1959 versus 4.3 percent in 1986, a more than twenty-one-fold increase.

The second statistic is the most important of the three, since it was common for these men to remain single for an extended period (three to six years) after their divorce. By the time they were ready for another serious relationship they and the woman with whom they'd had the decisive affair had usually gone their separate ways, ending the business association that brought them together to begin with.

"YOU AND MY WORK FIT TOGETHER"

It always takes Hollywood a number of years to catch up with a trend, and by the time films about it are conceptualized, scripted, cast, financed, made, and released, the trend is usually starting to wane. Mid-1980s movies such as *The Color Purple*, which *New York* magazine called "a hate letter to black men," and *The Burning Bed*, which was no less so to white ones, symbolized the mentality of the 1970s and early 1980s. Women were told repeatedly during this period that men were merely savages and wife-beaters, and should therefore be attacked "in return" (preferably legally and financially). As William Randolph Hearst well knew, "the other side fired first" is a time-honored excuse for putting into effect one's own expansionist plans.

Mark Edmonds, a production manager at a printing plant, wasn't interested in hearing it. Not the type to explore people's hidden motives, he took his wife's critical remarks at face value and fought back. When she insisted in 1976 that he too start doing the dishes, he replied, "I'd rather eat off paper plates." Thwarted on that front ("Well, *I* wouldn't"), she found other stones to throw.

They had only been married for three years at the time—both were thirty-one—but their routines as a couple had become well established. "We're like Ma and Pa Kettle," Mark's wife, Louise, told us. "The way we are together—we might as well have been married thirty years." The comment seemed premature the following year, as the strain produced by their diverging paths began to show. Louise, who was working for a packaged-food company and hoping to rise to the managerial level, became more of what she termed a "feminist." Mark realized that the term meant merely that she regularly read a few of the newly founded women's magazines that tried to whip up resentment toward men, which she then aimed at him. "Take your anger and stick it," he told her in front of some friends at dinner, when she called him "sexist" for what he thought must be the fiftieth time in less than a year.

Louise was certain that the no-compromise stance that she had adopted would help her career, even if it obviously was causing her personal life to deteriorate. Mark, on the other hand, decided that if Louise was no longer willing to meet him halfway, either sexually or emotionally, another woman would. "I don't have to take this crap from her—or anybody else," he told us, visibly annoyed, just five weeks before he met Debbie for the first time in 1979.

In Mark's case, as with the majority of other Larry-types who found themselves in this situation, he actually benefited from the growing conflict. For one thing, he began to work longer hours. Sometimes that meant staying late in the office, with Debbie (who was single) also working away nearby on production reports, or he would take work home and simply ignore Louise. "I'd have felt bad about doing this [much work on evenings and weekends] before," he told us, with an air of resignation. "But the way she is now, who cares?"

Had it not been for Debbie's availability, Mark would have cared. Like many ambitious Larry-types, he wanted a woman around, almost constantly. He liked to achieve because it felt good, but also because it gave him something to brag about to the woman who was his main partner at the time. Whether other women also heard about his accomplishments was secondary to him; the listener he cared most about was the one with whom he was then chiefly involved. "If things don't go well," he said, explaining why he would tell her bad news as well as good, "that's okay— that's life. Some ups, some downs."

Louise had originally been drawn to Mark because, in addition to their many social and personal similarities, he seemed to her good-looking, determined, and dynamic. What he found most appealing about her was that she was bright, fun to be with, and flexible. "Louise is game for just about anything," he had commented admiringly, a number of times. Once that disappeared and she became "doctrinaire" instead, the marriage had ended long before the divorce was decreed. With Debbie he still had it and that allowed him to devote himself more intensely to his profession and still have a highly satisfying sexual and personal life. One evening, after making love to Debbie on a desk, he said, only half-kidding, "I just realized how nicely you and my work fit together."

He never sat down and analyzed what he needed, but, like the majority of Larry-types who went on to become successful, Mark seized upon things and tried them out. If they worked, he incorporated them into his life; if not, they soon fell by the wayside. His combination of drive and an endless willingness to experiment almost guaranteed that, with so much sifting going on, he'd stumble upon what he needed most at the moment. In his case, as with so many other men in this category, continual trial and error was more effective than armchair analysis (before or after the event) would have been.

AN ENEMY AT HOME

To Steve-types, analyzing problems isn't optional, it's mandatory. Often they analyze a topic so thoroughly, and feel they know it so well, no action at all is required. Gary Williams watched with growing dismay as his wife, Nina, became caught up in the "men are the enemy" mentality of the 1970s, but his situation wasn't quite the same as Mark's. Within a few weeks of their becoming a pair, Nina had begun making snide comments about men in general and Gary in particular.

He saw no reason to call a halt to the practice because, in his words, "They're just smartass remarks—she's a critical person—makes them about everyone." Gary seemed not to realize that the statement was false; whatever animosity Nina was feeling at the moment was much more likely to be aimed at a man than a woman.

There wasn't any way that Gary could escape being a target of her barbs, but what amazed us was how he reacted to them. Instead of sending them back immediately, as Mark did almost by reflex, he absorbed them. Ruminating on her caustic comments, he frequently sank into a state of despair. He never noticed the direct connection between her put-downs and his depressions.

Finally, it started to affect his work. As editor at a national magazine, Gary needed to concentrate to be effective on his job. That made him resent distractions and interruptions of all sorts once he was working. "I'd like to throw my phone out the window," he said, looking exasperated. "It always rings just when I have to have silence." Those were strong words from this mild-mannered, eminently reasonable fellow who shunned violence (even on TV) and loved literature. We found that, ironically, it was primarily in the marital lives of such men that violence appeared. Characteristically, it was of a verbal sort, but it was present nonetheless.

Articulate as well as literate, Steve-types like Gary could have fought back but didn't. They found battles of any kind a strain, taking much more of an emotional toll on them than they would on Larry-types like Mark. However, even more important, in the '70s and early '80s men like Gary were too inclined to see things from the other person's point of view and to assume that they themselves were in the wrong.

Gary was kidding himself when he told us: "I keep trying to understand the basis of Nina's position, the logic of her attacks." This was little more than a self-congratulatory rationalization for inaction, which left him playing pincushion while she needled him. Had a man been treating him in this way, Gary would have recognized instantly (as he had four years earlier with a co-worker named George) that the person was walking around feeling very inadequate and trying not to let it show. "The best defense is a good offense," Gary himself had said, after listening to George's abusive remarks. It was clear to Gary at the time that George was brimming over with envy and thus sought to cut down the enormous number of people he thought were better than he. "No one who is content with himself acts like that," Gary stated correctly.

Yet he was blind to similar subconscious motives in his wife. A fine-arts major in college, Nina was disappointed that the '70s and '80s were such business-oriented decades. In college, and for many years thereafter, she clung secretly to the belief that she was "too good" for the world of commerce and was destined for something "better." Nina reluctantly accepted a job at a large financial-services firm, then moved to another. The pay was good; in the early years of their marriage she earned about the same as Gary, but as with so many other bright women during these decades, it never made her feel professionally fulfilled.

"Years pass," she once commented, "and except for my paychecks I don't really feel any connection to my company." If she had said that about one firm, a move to another might have solved the problem, but the description fit them all. Nevertheless, money was important enough to her to play a decisive role in her nine-to-five choices. "Without it," she said, "people push you around, keep telling you what to do." This was an odd remark, since her bosses—both male and female—did that anyway, in spite of her $730-a-week salary. At work, though, she was willing to tolerate what she found intolerable elsewhere.

Meanwhile, at home she continued to pelt Gary with questions— "What are you doing *that* for?"—an intimidation tactic that was effective. Bothered that he felt himself walking on eggs when Nina was around, Gary looked for a way out. The solution this already sensitive man hit upon, at the urging of his wife, was to become still more sensitive. Nina's initial reaction was favorable, and she had him demonstrate in front of their friends how responsive he had become, as though he were a trained poodle. However, her underlying feelings soon became evident, for she began sleeping with a man in her office who embodied none of these qualities. Ironically, having pushed her Steve-like husband to become even more so, she then turned to a Larry-type to provide what she actually needed emotionally and sexually and was no longer available at home.

Gary's work suffered because he began to feel inadequate even before arriving at the office. His level of defensiveness had increased on the job as a result of the inferiority feelings his wife was saddling him with. This caused him to overreact to a criticism from his boss, a remark that, in retrospect, didn't seem very severe. "He came into my office and wanted to know where a file he needed was," Gary later explained. "I couldn't remember—maybe I had taken it home—but I don't recall what I have at home anymore." Rapidly becoming frantic, wanting mainly to buy time, he instead told his boss, "I can't look for it now, I've got too much else to do." Gary's boss simply said to him, "Your papers sure are a mess." Gary snapped, "I don't need to hear this. Why don't you go pick on someone else." The interchange cost Gary his job. Two weeks later he was fired as part of a "departmental realignment." A dedicated and earnest editor, Gary found another position without great effort, yet the toll on his nerves during this period was high.

That was nearly a decade ago, and things haven't changed much at home. Unlike Mark and Louise, Gary and Nina have stayed married and have even had a child, but the relationship seems to satisfy only Gary's need to "see the other person's point of view" while being privately and publicly pummeled, and Nina's desire to see how far she can bully him. More than once, their friends have winced at what passes for "casual conversation" between the two.

In short, Mark's ambitions were helped and Gary's hindered by their personal relationships. Mark sensed that his wife had stopped providing what he required to be at his best, so he turned to someone else to have it again. Nina did the same, shunning Gary and turning to another partner when her husband had become useless to her. In the process Mark's career flowered and Gary's withered. That, we found, was typical of the outcome seen in hundreds of similar cases. There were quite a few instances in which a woman helped make a man successful, but there were many in which she prevented him from realizing his ambitions by literally stunting his growth.

ADVERSITY PLAYERS

If, generally speaking, men like Larry overachieved during the decade in which women declared men the enemy, while the Steve-types who were married to women with this attitude underachieved, David-types were the least affected of the three. When Phillip Atkins married Diane Nelson, we were certain that they were right for one another in dozens of ways. What we hadn't noticed was that Diane was slowly adopting the same mentality that affected Louise and Nina. It was so thickly in the air at the time, and its adverse consequences—for women—hadn't yet surfaced, many female professionals absorbed the message without realizing they had.

The deep and enduring differences between a Steve-type like Gary and a David-type like Phillip can be seen in the way they handled criticism. Neither was happy about it (few people are), but Phil's greater verbal skills usually came to his rescue. At times it amazed Phil himself that he opened his mouth and coherent sentences came out. "If I arrive late, and I'm not even sure of the subject [under discussion]," he once admitted, in an unguarded moment, "I tune in fast and start talking—and people listen and respond! I might as well have been there for an hour, rather than just a few minutes."

For us, as researchers, these candid admissions were invaluable, since we always wanted to know what action made a particular man say to himself, in the words of a young attorney, "I *did* it. I didn't think I could, but I did. Somehow, without planning it—without even *thinking* about it—I was on automatic pilot—I came through with flying colors." These tense moments that afterward gave way to an inner sense of victory were revealing because they helped let us see what was truly important to the person. The giddy feeling that Phillip had about his ability to handle himself well in conversation (the feeling wasn't always there, of course, since it could hardly have made him giddy every time) reflected a desire to excel on this front. The spoken word had long represented his strong suit, and he naturally turned to it when attacked.

Once Diane adopted the "let's whip up some anger and aim it at men" attitude prevalent in the '70s and early '80s, the frequency and kinds of arguments the two were having changed. At a dinner out with two other couples she started telling Phillip that "men are power freaks—all they think about is manipulating women." Phillip had a reply ready as soon as she finished her sentence: "No one, my dear, manipulates as well as a woman. She just doesn't know how to make as much *money* doing it as men."

Like Mark, he was having none of her attacks. However, while Mark, a Larry-type, took every insult that came his way and slammed it back with a ferocity that nearly knocked his opponents over, Phil was content to make light of it all and emerge the winner by being obviously more witty. Fire a spitball at Mark and a cannonball came back; fire one at Phil and a brightly colored one returned.

In contrast to these two, Gary gasped when attacked verbally by a friend or intimate. He was used to handling written abuse ("That's what *literary* criticism is," he once punned), because even if he was its target, there was time for him to compose himself and a reply. In arguments with his chronically dissatisfied wife—or anyone else, including his boss—no protective medium surrounded him and offered the luxury of time. Few could reply faster than Phil, but Gary responded best when a thought was delivered to him on a page and left, hours or even days later, the same way.

What it boils down to is that Larry-types such as Mark did better than we expected in the '70s and '80s because they are "adversity players," who thrive on hard times that compel them to rise to the occasion. Difficult situations seem to inspire rather than upset such a man because they give him a chance to shine. Well, these two decades provided plenty of adversity, in both the economic and marital arenas. Foreign competition usually gave him a good deal to worry about at work and domestic competition gave him still more to be concerned about at home. The

solution most men of this type in our sample hit upon was to rid themselves of their hostile partners, find more loving ones, and concentrate on
doing well professionally.

So many individuals were forced to go it alone, it is hardly surprising
that, by default, entrepreneurs were among the most celebrated figures of
the time. The business world's equivalent of the Old West's lone rider,
they symbolized accurately the status of millions of people who were
dedicated solely to their work because they had no enduring intimate
relationships.

Steve-types, on the other hand, generally did worse than expected
occupationally after marrying a woman who saw men as the enemy. Not
only was such a man inclined to stay married to her, instead of scrapping
the pairing and finding a more suitable partner; he also didn't fight back
sufficiently often at home. His nervousness and insecurities therefore
surfaced in the worst possible place—on the job—where a difficult economic climate had reduced margins of profit and of executive tolerance.

Finally, David-types during this period were reminiscent of the wealthy
Park Avenue resident who told us that she "didn't even know there was a
Depression [in the 1930s] until I read about it in a history book published
just before World War II." A man like David could talk excitedly for
hours about any subject, and thereby appear to be interested in it, yet be
miles away emotionally. That served him well during this era, if he was
at all involved with his work. Little happened on the home front to thwart
his ambitions.

ARMS AND THE MAN

In spite of the many differences that exist among Larry-, Steve-, and
David-types, the majority of men we studied are convinced that the
picture they have of themselves is the same one they'd have had if they
had been born any time during the past two centuries. Each is aware that
in time of war, he would have been expected to be a bit more combative,
while in time of peace he should be more of a gentleman. But these are
seen as minor variations on a theme, a bit more emphasis here, a bit less
emphasis there, with the overall picture of appropriately masculine behavior remaining largely intact.

The 1960s made it clear that the connection between masculinity in individuals and military involvement by the nation is by no means simple and direct. For the connection to fully emerge the war the nation is fighting at the time has to be popular among young men, and unlike World War II, the one in Vietnam wasn't. The free-loving attitudes that burst forth in the early 1960s gave men the green light they had been waiting for to be more sexually aggressive without feeling that they also had to be physically intimidating. Making love and making war were by no means inextricably linked in their minds.

When a business-oriented militancy among women emerged in the 1970s, it therefore ran into little opposition among men, whose "war-based, military-preparedness" version of masculinity was dormant at the time. Men were much more interested in exiting one theater of conflict, in Southeast Asia, than in getting ready for another theater, anywhere else. This temporary imbalance (which lasted until Americans generally became fed up near the end of the decade with Carter's passive presidency) had a revealing effect on how males viewed their own bodies.

Whereas in the '50s and '60s the majority of our sample who were interested in getting in shape told us that they intended to concentrate equally on developing their arms and legs, in the Seventies men concentrated almost exclusively on their legs. They claimed to be focusing above all on their hearts and were using jogging as an aerobic exercise to prolong their lives. The evidence that it does so is at best controversial, but the point is that exercise involving their arms could more readily have been used for cardiovascular conditioning purposes.

It wasn't until the late '70s that an increasing proportion of health-conscious men began to break free of this excessive concentration on their lower bodies. Fearful of being labeled animals, they had unwittingly let their upper bodies lie dormant, even atrophy. There are fashions in body styles, as art historians have long reminded us, and it made perfect sense for men to neglect their upper bodies. After all, in the 1970s there was almost no heterosexual "market" for muscular middle-class males.

With the coming of the '80s men again returned to a better balanced, whole-body approach. Working out with weights, Nautilus equipment, and rowing machines became as "in" during the decade as jogging was during the Seventies. From 1978 on, an increasing proportion developed their shoulders and upper arms without any of the hesitation that usually accompanies the violation of a taboo. They no longer felt that well-rounded biceps, lats, and pecs would make them look like someone about to beat his wife. None of these shifts, first to the lower body in the 1970s, then, later, back to the upper body, occurred consciously to the typical man we studied.

Nevertheless, what men were doing in concentrating on particular muscle groups in their body provided, in microcosm, a picture of what they were also doing in their marriages. Trying hard to be accommodating during the 1970s, they had virtually strapped their arms to their sides. However, at the same time, many ambitious career women were feeling anger and using it to fuel their pursuit of career success. Some of them were the wives of these men. The process backfired. Instead of becoming calmer, the women found themselves still more annoyed at the end of each workday and on weekends. Why? Because their husbands no longer seemed strong enough to slow them down.

Most of the women would have denied needing any such thing. Having been told repeatedly throughout the decade that they were supposed to be independent and self-reliant, they would have felt very uneasy about making such an admission, even to themselves. They weren't supposed to look to anyone, least of all a man, in order to feel good about themselves. Yet here they were, feeling out of control, and couldn't understand why. They had become so used to mocking what they needed most—a quietly masculine man—they couldn't allow their partner to be one (if he already was) or become one (if he had the makings).

Sadly, their picture of normal masculinity wasn't an accurate one to begin with, and was based instead on the insecure men they had encountered who were looking to make up for their own inadequacies. These men typically were too short, flabby, or uneducated, or viewed themselves as being a bit effeminate and therefore bent over backward to compensate for their failings. What they produced was a caricature of normal masculinity, one in which every gesture was too forced to be really forceful and too practiced to be believable. Few men who saw it bought the act but, unfortunately, many women did, particularly those with an ax to grind. Any woman looking to justify her hostility toward men could single out one of these walking exaggerations and say, "See, this is what they're all like, so why bother with any of them?"

Most heterosexual women who adopted this stance—and many did, during the 1970s and 1980s, for faddish or competitive reasons—wound up harming themselves. Without realizing it, they were criticizing the very thing they most had to have. Rejecting it, even when it was offered them in the more normal version by a real-life partner, left them with nowhere to turn.

If nothing else, that made it easier for a woman bent on career success to subordinate her marriage—in fact, all personal relationships—to her attempts to achieve this goal. Women's-movement leaders told her again and again that she should make sure that her husband not only did half the housework but also shared equally in taking care of the children. The demand was made under the banner of "creating a better balanced and harmonious relationship," but the stridency with which it was made almost guaranteed that nothing positive would result, even when helpful husbands met the demands.

Women who were interested in their careers could rightly claim that household duties stood a chance of slowing their own professional progress, while their husbands' paths were free. Since these women, as latecomers to the business world, felt they had lost decades to make up for, many of them wanted the odds stacked in their favor. Their male counterparts had to be saddled with the same or even larger handicaps to make the race for riches and executive position a fair one. There was no question in their minds that a truly supportive husband would make every contribution he could to their quest for professional success. Conversely, a partner who wouldn't do his share was an anachronism. The same energy and persistence that went into their days on the job were used at night in an attempt to bring their husbands around. With these wives fueled by competitive feelings (a representative remark from the wife of a sample member: "I want him to leave the starting gate with the same weights tied to him that I have"), the search for "justice" in the housework department became a nightly source of conflict.

That the behavior of such women was not motivated by good intentions could be seen by contrasting these couples with others comparable in every important respect (educational and social background, profession, and age) but who were making a serious attempt to pull together. When goodwill prevailed, each could candidly say to the other, "I don't want to do domestic chores, and I know you don't either." Then they could reach the all-important conclusion: "So let's hire someone—even if they come in just once a week—to do them." That went far toward keeping alive the love that existed between them.

What was conspicuous about two-career couples in which the woman was trying subconsciously to do everything possible to slow down the progress of her partner was that the suggestion to hire someone else to handle the housework and child care was rarely heard. Claiming that even with two paychecks they couldn't afford it, although they spent considerable sums on other luxuries, the women insisted that "It's not fair; he *has* to do his share."

Sensing that the demand, though it sounded logical, was actually the result of hostile ulterior motives, the men generally balked. They had no intention of allowing anyone to jeopardize their own career gains, especially someone who allegedly loved them. With every major field becoming more crowded and competitive, the men realized how damaging that could be. Their wives' tone of voice was the giveaway, for it had an edge to it that made the men know it would be unwise to respond positively.

They didn't. It was revealing to see that while in the 1960s 42 percent of the married men in our sample felt it was appropriate for husband and wife to share household duties equally, and acted in accordance with this belief, the figures for comparable groups *decreased* throughout the 1970s, reaching a low point in 1981 of 29 percent. Thereafter, it rose somewhat and by the middle of 1986 stood at 38 percent. By studying a wide variety of individual cases in depth, as well as the overall pattern, it became clear that the more men were pushed, they more they resisted.

VISITING DAY

For decades a substantial portion of the mothers in our sample have been turning children against their fathers, using the youngsters (for the most part, subconsciously) as pawns in the ongoing battles they were having with their husbands. Some of the men we studied recognized that working women were carrying the process a step further in the '70s by attempting to make their husbands again seem like the "bad guys" because they wouldn't do as much housework as they. Needless to say, a substantial number of these couples should not have had children, or even gotten married in the first place, and more than half eventually wound up divorced. However, as we've said, even those who initially seemed a good pair often ended up pointing a finger at each other, rather than utilizing the most effective peacekeeping alternative, which was to hire someone to help with housework. In the face of so relentless an assault from their wives, the majority of men we studied quietly let their marriages fail.

It was only then that the men discovered something startling. They began spending *more* time taking care of their children, thanks to the joint-custody arrangement commonly agreed on, but they minded it *less*. With their strident spouse removed from the picture, they found the activity as pleasant as they had always hoped it would be. That gave them a better understanding of women who were career obsessed than the women themselves had. It is easy for people to convince themselves that their stance is logical and reasonable, but it wasn't until these women had the same experiences with a second husband—or couldn't find another—that some realized how bitter and full of anger their approach had been from the start.

One of the key findings of our study is that even men who stayed with their unhappy marriages, and did whatever they could to be accommodating, found the relationship deteriorating anyway. Eager to please, inclined to take at face value their wives' arguments about "fairness and equality," they were amazed to see the atmosphere at home grow steadily worse. They did almost everything they were asked—everything that seemed "right," even without being asked—yet they couldn't escape noticing that they were essentially an object of scorn. Far from being appreciated for the contributions they were making, they found themselves being taken for granted and a target for gratuitous insults, often in front of company.

Women who were treated in a comparable manner during this period complained loudly about it. At first hurt and puzzled, they finally moved to dissolve the marriage unless a major increase in respect was accorded them by their husbands. Sad to say, men who found themselves the recipient of similarly abusive treatment from their wives frequently did little about it. If anyone was "suffering in silence" during the 1970s and 1980s, it was husbands who tended to be excessively accommodating.

Trapped in the logic of their own view of what a "marriage between equals" was supposed to be, they became more than just hen-pecked. There were hen-pecked husbands in the 1950s and 1960s, too, but at the time they were more acceptable, even to their wives, because neither partner demanded as much of the relationship. It was just one part of a much larger picture that was *family*, the real center of attention. This, above all, changed in the subsequent fifteen to twenty years, so that by the late 1970s the birthrate in the United States had reached a two-hundred-year low point, lower even than during the Depression. No empty statistic, these numbers reflected the decreasing importance of the concept of family to millions of ambitious men and especially to career women. Words and behavior often part company, though, and in the 1970s and 1980s working women claimed to be looking for a warm and enduring marriage to a "secure" man. However, an ongoing examination of the pairings that actually did form made it clear that many were unwittingly doing everything possible to undermine their partner's sense of self-assurance. If that had increased their own, the tactic would have been effective. His loss would have been their gain.

What happened instead is that as the man's self-confidence and masculine self-image eroded, so did the woman's sense of self-assurance and self-worth. Not only did she start to see herself as significantly less attractive and sexy; whatever tranquility and contentment the pair had known steadily evaporated. As it turned out, such a woman was winning the battle and losing the war—she could think well of herself over the long term only to the extent that she thought well of her husband.

Examining nearly fourteen hundred such marriages over a period of more than two decades allowed us to see that the obstacle which most of the unhappy pairs couldn't surmount had to do with the word "sensitive." The women insisted that any man they met, fell in love with, and married had to possess this characteristic. The men certainly tried, and for most it was no effort at all, since this was entirely consistent with the values of thoughtfulness and consideration they had learned while being raised in middle- and upper-middle-class homes. Trying to be "sensitive"—especially since their wives, and women in general, kept harping on the term in the 1970s and early 1980s—seemed normal and natural enough.

Much to their amazement, when the women were interested in having sex, they found their husbands increasingly uninterested. On the one hand, it bothered the men not to be able to perform sexually on the spot, whenever and wherever an opportunity presented itself, since most think of "instant erections" as a normal feature of every truly virile male. On the other hand, the men sensed that their sexual appetite for their wives was steadily waning.

It was revealing to find that even women who claimed to be happy with their own greater aggressiveness and the more timid and gentle manner displayed by their spouses were usually only kidding themselves. The behavior of the women during the workday became increasingly tense, guarded, and hypercompetitive. Something was clearly wrong, though they kept coming up with job-related excuses for their growing discomfort. To see if the excuses were valid, we divided women who were the same in every important respect (age, education, background, and profession) into two groups: in the first were those whose husbands were comfortable with their own masculinity, whereas the husbands of the second were apologetic about theirs—afraid of any hint of their own aggression.

The women in the second group were significantly more likely over the years to become frantic. They might as well have been living alone, and in all probability would have been less emotionally chaotic had they been so. This way, with a man in the picture, automatically creating the expectation that their own need for intimacy would be met, they wound up more frustrated and disappointed than if they had had no one. Without realizing it, they were making certain that their partner was unable to do them any good. In essence, they had disqualified him as a source of strength and comfort that they could respect.

THE SEXUAL MERRY-GO-ROUND

Every six months, for more than a quarter of a century, we have been asking comparable groups of career women, "Would you prefer to be a man?" Starting from the relatively low level in the late 1950s and 1960s of 6 percent (most of whom said men have more fun), the percentage who replied yes climbed steadily in the 1970s and was at 17 percent in 1975 (most of whom said men are more successful). It peaked at 21 percent in 1977 before falling rapidly in the next eight years, reaching 4 percent in 1985 and 3 percent in 1986. Unisex was out. With women once again allowing themselves to become comfortable with the idea of being women, instead of wishing that they could secretly undergo a sex-change operation in order to be better in business, the pressure on men eased. They no longer felt it necessary to defend their gender against envious women who weren't even certain why they were attacking it.

That allowed millions of young men and women to latch on to a distinctly male entertainer and make him a star, without worrying that career women would immediately assail him as "just another chauvinist." It was fascinating to see that the man chosen for the role couldn't be a Larry, David, or Steve; rather, he had to be a Bill, or at least give a convincing performance on stage as one. With his words, gestures, and clothes, Bruce Springsteen, and his songs about "the working man," fit the part perfectly.

To many people it merely sounded like good music and that, if anything was being celebrated, it was the fellow who did manual labor for a living. Nevertheless, what was really being celebrated, after an absence of more than two decades, was the very idea of being a man. That didn't make the majority of males start strutting to and fro like the inadequate-feeling caricatures women loved attacking in the 1970s as "macho." What began to surface in men across the country was a pride in intelligent aggressiveness and quiet strength. Enlistment in the armed forces rose steadily, as men stopped being afraid that they would be ridiculed for using traditional outlets for their energies and aspirations.

Even in the business world, the people who were suddenly idolized had to be at least like Larry, if not like Bill. Since no one who closely resembled Bill in personality sat at the head of a major corporation (or was likely to), it was necessary to choose the next best thing. So Lee Iacocca, and to a lesser extent T. Boone Pickens and Ted Turner, got the lion's share of media attention. Career women now joined men in considering Iacocca's persona attractive, while finding the appearance of a woman who wore suits and ties somewhat dated. In their view, she seemed to be playacting, wearing a costume.

Larry-types generally achieve more financially than the other three types of men—more of them become self-made millionaires. The desire in the 1980s to praise men and money simultaneously led to a general infatuation with the idea of the entrepreneur. People went into their own businesses in the 1970s in record numbers too, and the stocks of small companies significantly outperformed those of the larger ones during this period in the stock market. However, it wasn't until the 1980s that the mixture of masculine assertiveness and the wealth it could produce suddenly captured the public's fancy.

With the coming of the 1980s, women were especially puzzled about what was happening to men. One question concerned them more than the others, namely, "Where have all the good men gone?" During the 1970s they weren't supposed to be looking for men—weren't supposed to need any—even if they were already married to one. Now that this excessively self-reliant stance had softened, and women didn't mind admitting openly that they wanted an intimate relationship with a man to play a central role in their lives, they couldn't find anyone eligible. Since this educated and relatively affluent generation of women had become used to attaining most of the goals they had set for themselves, it amazed them to be able to find so few suitable partners.

What *had* happened to all the good men? Was their disappearance a fiction or a reality? A good way to grasp the answer is to suppose that in the 1970s the United States had a population of only eight adults, all single—four men and four women. The men resembled Bill, Larry, David, and Steve, respectively. Key question: which of the four was the most sexually aggressive? Bill was the most vocal of the four about sex. However, he rarely followed up on his seeming interest when the workday was through, preferring instead to watch ballgames and sports events on TV. While Steve didn't make such comments to begin with, like Bill, he didn't pursue women either, usually choosing to curl up during leisure hours with his computer or a good book. David, by contrast, invited all four women to dinner, but, much to the chagrin of each, slept with none. That left Larry to, as he gleefully described it, "service them all."

Then came the herpes and AIDS scares of the early and mid-1980s, and the sexual merry-go-round slowed down drastically. Larry became more cautious and less active, fearful that he would catch a disease for which at the time there was no cure. The four women also became more reserved, feeling that if they were to become infected by one of these alarming diseases, it was the most sexually active man who was likely to give it to them. Summing up (and going back to the real world now), in the 1960s and 1970s single women looking for a permanent partner usually had sex with a number of Larrys while waiting for a marriage proposal from the Bills, Steves, or Davids whom most preferred. In the meantime, Larry-types distracted and entertained them, making the wait for the man who would eventually become their husband more bearable. In the 1980s, once a man like Larry stopped pursuing them so aggressively, and they in turn started avoiding him, the wait became much less bearable. The lack of interest displayed by the other three, whether married or single, was more striking than ever now. All the "good men" seemed to have disappeared.

MEN: THE NEW ATTITUDE

The message in all this for Davids, Larrys, and Steves is clear. Even before the 1980s began, many a David-type moved to the higher rungs of his organization, only to find himself incapable of handling the other three types of men. This had been only a minor problem before, since he had dealt primarily with people like himself; the typical David was therefore stunned to realize the sheer number of Bills, Larrys, and Steves in the world and the magnitude of the contribution they were making to the economy. They could no longer be ignored merely because they made him uncomfortable.

As a David-type's responsibilities expanded and he became involved in areas previously supervised by someone else, it became essential for him to get along with kinds of men he had formerly avoided, not always consciously. It was a little late for him to begin learning how to handle them adeptly. Even though he tried anyway, his ineffectiveness was apparent. Other top managers who had rubbed shoulders over the years with a greater variety of men, and didn't recoil when it happened, could see a glaring inadequacy in a man like David. Unwilling or unable to describe it, they merely concluded that he was "out of his element."

What the Davids of the world who hope to reach their full potential as leaders should therefore begin doing at the earliest opportunity is not only to gain some confidence in interacting with the other three types, but also to incorporate some of the other three into the makeup of their own personality. That has become particularly important in the 1980s. The 1970s were kind to men like David, since he seemed the most inoffensive and least "macho" of the four. Nonthreatening and social, such a man was frequently latched on to by career women eager to give the appearance of a normal personal life.

All that has changed. While the Davids of the world aren't used to thinking about the subject, the new emphasis on maleness stands a good chance of either making or breaking their success. With both men and women once again currently admiring men who are at ease with their own masculinity, the pressure is on. What for the other three is a relief, thanks to the drastically reduced abuse coming their way because of their gender, is for each David a challenge to which he must rise. It isn't all that difficult, since the world sorely needs the abundant social and verbal skills usually possessed by such a man. The simple realization that he is more likely as a result to become—and remain—a success should be sufficient inducement to undertake this effort at "hybridization." To the most theatrical of the four types, this is one piece of theater that, taken seriously and worked on over a period of years, can gently reshape his personality in the right direction.

While most people think of masculinity in terms of muscles and strength, the message that Steve-types should get from the new attitudes toward men centers on the idea of directness. Throughout the 1970s men like Steve were subtly encouraged to be weak and unassertive. Many acted this way even though, as we've seen, it helped their marriages to fail and their business prospects to worsen. Now, this kind of "Mr. Mom" behavior, whether the man is married or single, looks as dated and ludicrous as a woman wearing a jacket and tie. Instead of thinking of him as admirably nonthreatening, the majority of business people view him as "wimpish and defeated," a broken man. He is hardly a figure to whom they want to hand over the reins of the firm.

Yet high achievement is what the Steves of the world dream about most. Above all, they are certain that their technical skills will catapult them to the top of any firm or organization of which they are a part. When a man like Jimmy Carter was president during the 1970s, the expectation may have seemed more realistic. But someone radiating a similarly submissive image in the 1980s, no matter how nice and well-meaning he may be, is less likely to be viewed as a serious contender for a top slot. Men like Steve are inclined to be secretive and vague, because they don't want to offend anyone and also because they don't want any-one else to know what they are doing.

Now more than ever, that tendency makes him look like a "sneak," both to his colleagues and bedmates. Mixing some of Bill's and Larry's forthright manner with his own would shift a man like Steve in a more contemporary direction and make him more effective personally and professionally. His undeniable technical expertise is every bit as necessary to his company and the nation as the verbal and social skills of men like David. However, Steve-types are likely to labor away for their entire career, underappreciated, unless they incorporate the more candid and less fearful approach of men like Bill and Larry

Larry-types may seem the least in need of personality modification to increase their chances of success, if for no other reason than that these men seem to act the same way from one context to another and one decade to the next. Nevertheless, national trends affect them too, and the major trend during the 1970s called for men of all sorts to get what they wanted in a more subtle manner. "Walk softly and carry a big stick," Teddy Roosevelt's motto, was adopted by many. Feeling themselves under attack, they were inclined to use less obvious ways of getting things done. To these men cash often became king because it made them feel they were more "on their own," as they liked to say, and in charge of their own destiny.

The Larrys of the world are pragmatists, inclined to get a job done any way they can. However, we found that the sometimes sizable effort they make to avoid public scrutiny and accomplish a goal "in their own style" distracts and exhausts them before their aim is fully achieved. The pride they take in being able to camouflage their activities reduces their overall effectiveness. Particularly in an era in which masculine strength and straightforwardness is once again prized, they need to be careful about mindlessly repeating phrases they heard from a hoodlum played so well by Al Pacino.

Many are likely to discover too late that they are no longer being applauded for taking the law into their own hands, having a thriving subterranean business, or, as one put it, "getting away with almost *anything* without anybody being the wiser." Far from being a lecture on morality, this suggestion is offered on the basis of newly prevailing attitudes and reactions. What once elicited applause may now bring forth scorn. For Larry-types, a shift in the direction of concentrating on business, instead of attempting to do so much behind the scenes, can pay substantial dividends. A decade in which a number-one best-selling book is about test pilot Chuck Yeager is not a time to be imitating shady tough guys like *The Godfather*'s Don Corleone.

While the Larrys of the world usually don't need lessons in masculinity, they themselves long for more respect than they are able to get. An easy way for them to obtain it, and to do so profitably as well, is to stop squandering their abundant energies on "trying to put one over on everybody." What is fascinating is that men like Larry tend to be much more open about sex than business. If they would only utilize in their financial dealings some of the same confidence and candor they display where sex is concerned, all would be well.

They may retort that "If I did everything open and aboveboard, I'd make a lot less money and get much less done." The evidence we've collected flatly contradicts this statement. The ability of most Larrys to spot a niche in a market or a widely shared need and to fill it, their involvement with their business, and "hands-on" approach, would be helped, not harmed, by such a shift. Their chances of success would increase, for they would spend more time working and less of it worrying. As an added bonus, each would seem to the public like more of the "class act" he has always wanted to be.

CHAPTER
·12·

FAME AND
FORTUNE

From the admiring comments about wealth that a substantial proportion of young men like Larry voice in their twenties, there is no question that making large sums of money is among their most prized aims in life. For some, it is the only one. Others, like Steve, clearly view the idea of making a fortune as secondary. They suspect that their choice of profession isn't likely to produce great wealth and may permanently rule out living lavishly. Yet in spite of a modest financial future, the Steves of the world often devote themselves to their craft, be it in the liberal or performing arts, or the social or physical sciences, with real diligence, year in and year out. If making money is secondary, what is the reward? Certainly the joy of doing something they love, but also learning to do it well enough to eventually become a recognized expert in their chosen field. Recognized enough to become famous.

The basic goals of the Davids in our sample were not as visible when the men were young. They were quite interested in money—in fact, the life style they envisioned for themselves required lots of it—but they wanted just as much to be well known. When pressed for a definite choice, however, these young men decidedly came down on the side of renown. Questioned further as to what profession would win them this prize, their ambivalent answers told the real story. Unlike the Steves in their class, who expected their work to carry them ultimately to stardom, the typical young David felt himself to be already on the road to fame because of his strong social skills. His personality would get him there, he felt, regardless of how he chose to make his living.

The phrase "fame and fortune" is heard so often it might as well be a single word. Yet as the years went by we were startled to learn that most men want one significantly more than the other and set their sights accordingly. Specifically, about 20 percent of a typical high-school class in the United States is (subconsciously) prepared to chase stardom; approximately one third is interested in making money above all; the rest will enter either blue-collar professions such as carpentry or plumbing, or white-collar ones such as engineering, law, medicine, management, teaching, and accounting.

We anticipated that each of the three types—Larry, Steve, and David— would stay true to his quest until he owned a good measure of what he spent decades longing for, then continue to pursue it, perhaps at a less intense pace—more money for Larry, more professional renown for Steve, and a mixture of fame, fortune, and social success for David. There was, after all, a limit to how much each could achieve in a lifetime. What we hadn't foreseen when the men were still in high school and college was that once they achieved their dreams they'd start trespassing on each other's territory, looking to trade what they had attained for success in fields they had long neglected. As soon as Larry had more money than he ever truly believed he'd have, he became hungry for fame. When Steve was featured in a magazine as a young genius, he was thrilled until he caught sight of the issue in a trash can on the street the following week. Then the glow faded fast. David continued to pursue both, depending upon which of the two he felt most in need of at the moment. Fame and fortune were never as separate in his mind as they were in the minds of Larry and Steve.

WAITING FOR "THE CHANCE OF A LIFETIME"

In the late 1940s and especially the 1950s, young men and women who found the prospect of stardom alluring not only dreamed about Hollywood but also went there. Hoping to be "discovered," they took menial jobs and in most instances suffered indignities that would have been unbearable for anyone who didn't share their optimism. They spoke of "paying my dues" and "trying to be in the right place at the right time." For some, that was exactly what happened.

Nonetheless, so many returned home—or, being too embarrassed to go home, went elsewhere with their tales of frustration and failure—that a subtle but major shift took place. Students in the 1960s developed a more hard-headed approach to this quest, even as a much larger proportion undertook it. Getting all the experience they could while on campus and in the regional theater companies that were springing up across the country, they stopped using the all-or-nothing kamikaze approach of those who a decade earlier had dropped everything and moved to Hollywood.

Most took a much bigger step and began to avoid show-business professions altogether. These fields appeared to them glutted and their pride prevented them from seeing as necessary or even reasonable the emotional abuse would-be actors, singers, and dancers had to tolerate. Having been raised in comfortable middle-class homes, the new aspirants were unwilling to be rejected and humiliated repeatedly, and be paid so little to boot, while waiting for their "big chance" to arrive.

At the time, the decision was facilitated by the rapid expansion of the broadcasting and print industries in America. Old radio and TV stations got bigger, and many new ones sprang up to meet the public's seemingly insatiable demand for entertainment and information. Most people wanted more details about major stories than they could get from TV and radio, which rarely get much beyond the headlines, so they turned to newspapers and magazines. Although it is commonly thought that the print and broadcast media compete for the public's attention, anyone who has monitored the way viewers and readers have actually responded to the development of these two industries knows that this is false. The rule of thumb that best summarizes the situation we found is "a picture *spawns* a thousand words." Instead of satiating the public's appetite, an interesting ninety-second story on the evening news merely stimulates it instead for the kind of in-depth coverage only print can provide. This is especially true of local stories, which rarely make it to network news broadcasts anyway.

With more than two million new jobs created in these professions between the late 1950s and the mid-1980s, a huge number of ambitious men and women were able to find a new field to conquer that offered them all the exposure of a successful acting career but much less of its pain. They could be full-time journalists, publicists, photographers, editors, announcers, script writers, and producers, not marginally employed actors or stage hands, and still be optimistic about realizing their dream of one day being a star. Even if they weren't yet "on camera" or "on the cover," they were closer than they ever would have been taking acting classes in Los Angeles.

"THAT'S WHERE THE MONEY IS"

While many members of a typical American high-school or college class want badly to spend their lives in the public eye, an even larger number want most to be rich. Money means more to them than renown, a fact that is apparent from their behavior. That the bank balances of some grow over a two-decade period as their reputations deteriorate seems to bother them little, if at all. If they think that an unscrupulous business practice will net them a larger income at the cost of their image of respectability, they happily make the trade. They may at times be confused about their ultimate goals, but few who watch them year in and year out at work will share the confusion.

When the notorious bank robber Willie Sutton was asked why he held up banks, he replied, "Because that's where the money is." Men who were interested first and foremost in becoming wealthy aimed at the same target but used a different technique. Armed with college credentials instead of a handgun, they sought to make themselves comfortable in the world of finance in the hope that their own pockets would somehow wind up full. Stockbrokerage and investment-banking firms seemed to them even better sources of instant wealth, thanks not only to the large sums that change hands there each day, but also because the greater excitement surrounding the transactions made anything seem possible.

Unlike some members of their high-school class, who wanted fame but claimed devotion to their "craft" as a camouflage, very few who were committed to making millions felt the need to hide their drive. Not one said, "I'm a broker for the sheer joy of it and don't care whether I earn a little or a lot."

Real estate also seemed to these people an area full of opportunities to grow rich. Becoming a real-estate salesman or broker appeared a good way to cash in on the incessant movement of Americans from one part of town to another, one region of the country to a different one, one marital status to its opposite. The prospect of stumbling upon an undervalued property radiated the same siren song that stockbrokers heard when they thought about undervalued stocks. Just being around people who had enough money to make substantial real estate or stock-market purchases made a fortune of one's own seem nearly inevitable.

As modern economic life grew more complicated, the supermarket concept of "financial services" emerged and became more important each year throughout the 1970s and 1980s. People who were interested in becoming wealthy by "being where the money is" had an ever-widening array of choices to pick from. This labor-intensive industry turned out to be one of the fastest growing during these decades and allowed millions of people who certainly couldn't have been described as "money hungry" to find work within it, frequently in a secretarial or clerical capacity.

Examining the overall pattern of experiences of those who were pursuing either riches or stardom, it is clear that the two roads are more of a study in contrasts than has previously been thought. To begin with, one is a high road, the other a low road, in terms of income. People have gotten used to the notion of the "starving actor," but the main reason that people starve in any major field is that there are simply too many individuals trying to find jobs within it. The same massive influx of eager young men and women that drove down wages on the lower rungs of the show-business ladder had a similar effect on wages for junior positions in print and broadcasting. So many people wanted to be associated with one or the other of these two industries, they were literally willing to work for nothing. Many did just that. They found paying jobs in other fields and spent almost every free minute thinking about or working on a novel or short story whose publication would, they hoped, establish them as a writer. Others, who were more cautious, bombarded magazines and book publishers with query letters and proposals, mailing unsolicited articles and manuscripts when frustrated by repeated rejection. Still others sent tape recordings and video cassettes to broadcasters in the hope of finding themselves overnight on the air.

With so few openings available relative to the number of people seeking them, and with so low a level of wages being paid those who did manage to land entry-level slots, most wound up earning considerably less than they anticipated. Being more "business-minded" had made them pick media companies (in the 1960s, 1970s, and 1980s) over the movies (in the 1940s and 1950s) to begin with, and they thought that this exchange would result in a higher annual income. It did to some extent, but not as much as they had expected, even after they got a few pay raises and promotions. Ironically, even though being associated with celebrities (or becoming one themselves) had been their main goal, they wound up fretting more about their own finances as the years went by than did their peers in the financial-services field.

The work itself had a strange effect on their life's principal dream. Previously, they believed that someone either was or wasn't a celebrity. Like a light switch, the two states, "on" and "off," corresponded to "you are a star" and "you aren't." There was nothing in between; there couldn't be. Slowly but surely people employed at media companies began to notice two things that few members of the public think about—that there are many more near-stars than actual ones, and that most of the men and women who were once in the public eye slip out of it because the audience for their work dwindles. It now became apparent that the whole process of attaining renown—and losing it—was far more volatile than young workers in these fields had suspected.

In school, they studied literary giants and watched movie greats who seemed always to have had immortal status. In class, the also-rans were omitted, or glossed over with a brief mention. It is small wonder that the more ambitious students, presented with this dichotomy, wanted to be counted eventually among the immortals. Yet here they were, with an average of twelve years of broadcasting or print-industry experience, suddenly aware that the whole situation was far more fluid than it had originally seemed. In particular, they were now convinced that many of the men and women who had become celebrities didn't deserve to be; and, conversely, that many people who deserved renown would never have it.

The tremendous amount of movement up and down, with some reputations rising while others were falling, should have thrilled them. After all, with the status of the stars so fluid, they themselves might more readily become one. Since the situation wasn't nearly as static as they had been led to believe in class, and since so many unworthy individuals were attaining stardom in the bargain, surely there was an opening for them, too, somewhere in this public constellation. We expected that insight, once they arrived at it, to make them try harder, since the goal for which they secretly yearned was even more within their grasp then they had envisioned it during their student days.

THE FICKLE PUBLIC

Instead, they become more cynical with every passing year. While the desire to get "behind the scenes" propels millions of people to their newsstand each week to buy magazines containing the latest gossip about celebrities, the people in the business of creating and maintaining a star's reputation ultimately develop a more down-to-earth view of the matter. Then they might as well be promoting a product, not a person, for most talk about their work as though it were much the same as whipping up enthusiasm for a new brand of cornflakes. Even if they themselves aren't directly involved in building or preserving the reputation of a star, they, too, come to know enough about the process to realize that what had once seemed to them as solid as a rock more nearly resembles a house of cards.

The public, each professional soon learns, is fickle and forgetful. He can't help noticing that they presume dead anyone whose name and new movie, novel, or song isn't trotted past them regularly in advertisements and reviews. Conversely, when he watches what happens as large advertising budgets and aggressive promotional campaigns manage to make a second-rate song, story, or movie into a hit, he is disgusted. The business from which he had secretly expected so much—namely, that it would bring him stardom while he was alive and immortality after he was gone—now seems to him full of deceit. Hucksters and con artists appear not only to be prospering, but to be in charge of the very heart of the business.

That makes the starry-eyed innocents these workers once were disillusioned and even angry. Many start using a word which we only later realized means they have come to an important fork in the road: "hype."

Approximately 40 percent of the men in our sample who had chosen the broadcasting or publishing fields were pleased to have their bubble burst. It made them visibly less tense. Like everyone else their age, they had dreamed as adolescents about becoming stars. Now that they had seen how difficult it was to make this happen, and how fragile the state of stardom actually was, the whole effort struck them as not worth the bother because, when all is said and done, it was just business anyway. All the heroes they had idolized as teenagers seemed above worrying about money. Commercial considerations of all sorts weren't on the minds of their favorite greats.

That they had even held such a view in the past suddenly struck them as ludicrous. Their own naïveté irritated and, on occasion, amused them. Almost in a flash they felt they had made the transition from star-struck adolescent to hardened veteran in their field. Having seen the world of the famous from both sides now, from the cheap seats in the balcony as students and (more recently) a choice view backstage during rehearsals, they felt that no one would ever again be able to put one over on them. When their dreams were shattered they lost something, but what they gained seemed to them even more important: a pride in their own professionalism.

For the first time in their lives they felt they could approach their work without any of the illusions that at times had led people like them astray emotionally and proved costly to their firms. Far from feeling cold because their illusions were gone, they viewed themselves as more capable now of distinguishing those who had potential from those who didn't. The realization that they were in "a branch of the celebrity business" no longer had the power to depress them, and instead merely served to give them a more realistic assessment of which "up-and-comers" were likely to withstand the rigors they would be exposed to on the stairway to stardom.

The climb was no picnic, they now knew, and one slip could mean a humiliating tumble all the way back to the bottom. Like executive secretaries who laugh about having had six different bosses who have come and gone, six-figure managers who couldn't hold on to their jobs for more than three years apiece, the disillusioned men we're discussing quietly concluded that it was more fun to be a kingmaker than a king. They would help some people get there and try to prevent others who were seeking renown (but didn't deserve it) from attaining it, but they would stay out of the limelight themselves. For they recognized at last that, whatever else it was, life there was dangerous.

The price to be paid for becoming a star was high, and having seen at close range just how high it was, they weren't sure *anyone* should have to pay it. It had never occurred to them as adolescents that there could ever be a downside to this glittering story. When a "great" died, the whole world mourned, or so they thought. Rhetorically, some asked, "Who wouldn't want that for themselves?" But as the years went by, they could see with their own eyes that when the vast majority of the greats of yesteryear passed away, the world merely yawned. "I thought he [or she] had died *ages* ago," was a typical audience response. No tears, no interest. That made the gut-wrenching upward climb seem like an awful lot of agony to go through for so little—and so late—a reward.

With fame so fleeting and fragile, these men slowly came around to a view that struck them as natural and even inevitable. From now on they would concentrate primarily on making money and not become caught up in all the flimflam and puffery their field continually generated. Living well *was* the best revenge, after all, and it was finally time for them to do so. The low wages they had received during their early years in the industry seemed to them not so much a result of the horde of people trying to enter it—a supply-and-demand factor—but a result instead of their own youthful idealism. As one put it, "My poverty has really been my *own* fault." They were tired of being penalized financially for being so idealistic, for wanting their field to be the embodiment—perhaps the only one—of truth, beauty, and genius. For that reason most had never even noticed that it acted as the lens through which they viewed the world. It gave everything that happened to them a point of reference, a coherence and coloring that was appealing even when the events in question were merely shades of gray.

Rejecting their old stance with disgust, they swore that henceforth nothing would come between them and the real world. From now on, they would see everything as it actually was. If they were in "the *business* of fiction [or film, art, or music]," so be it. They could live with that now, and probably excel at it. More to the point, they might even become rich at it.

Some did. It was fascinating to notice which men in our sample became wealthy and successful in the broadcasting and publishing fields. Much to our surprise, we found that there wasn't an idealist in the lot. While that made many dedicated workers in their twenties and thirties bitter and resentful, the outcome they so resented was by no means an accident.

We divided all the men in our sample who entered these two industries into two groups: one (containing 481 men) which remained attached to a largely purist and noncommercial view of their field throughout their late thirties and early forties, the other (of 305 men) which adopted a consciously realistic picture. That allowed us to see that this wasn't even a horserace. The realists not only prospered, in the sense that they made a median 41 percent more each year by the age of forty-five than their idealistic peers; they also were significantly more likely to move into positions of senior management.

How come? While not doing it consciously, top officers in these industries recognized a certain amount of cynicism as evidence of the distance needed to make a sound decision about a project, one that might involve hundreds of thousands or even millions of dollars and affect the very viability of the firm. Snap judgments that sprang from the passions of an adolescent devotee couldn't be allowed to jeopardize the existence of the company. Yet, and this was the tricky part, top managers knew that the passion couldn't be altogether absent either.

Unlike selling household appliances, the marketing of a movie, song, book, or TV series could be successful only if it captured the experiences of millions of customers, who could somehow see themselves "in" the product. Someone removed from the emotions that were supposed to be present, the feelings that made the film or work "come alive," would be too cut off from the audience to intuit what it wanted.

What are we to conclude from all this? A delicate balance between passion and products, beauty and business, is called for. The slightly cynical stance of someone who previously romanticized the field is a subtle badge that senior officials in the industry subconsciously want to see. They search for it among colleagues whom they'd like to have as friends and also among subordinates they are considering for important promotions. As it turns out, idealists who have lost their cultural idealism and adopted a largely (but not completely) commercial view of the company's products rise to executive positions faster than their "purist" peers.

"CASH—THERE'S NOTHING IT CAN'T DO"

The Larry-types who had been devoting their years to making money in such fields as stocks, bonds, and real estate, and who had managed to become moderately well off, were surprised at how incomplete they felt. Ever since they had left college, the majority of these men (approximately three out of five) believed that "money can make all your dreams come true." So when they found themselves dissatisfied with their lot in their late thirties and early forties, both personally and professionally, their first reaction was to conclude that they simply hadn't made *enough* money. It wasn't that they were on the wrong road, it is that they hadn't yet gone sufficiently far down it.

They did indeed try. The more money the men made, the harder they worked to earn still more. The process clearly fed on itself. Although men who had made half a million dollars by the time they were thirty-five were obviously attempting vigorously to double it and get to the much ballyhooed million-dollar level, men who were already there were typically expending twice the effort to get to two million dollars and validly label themselves multimillionaires. A casual observer might well have viewed the whole quest as mere greed, yet at the time it didn't occur to many of these men that there was any other goal worth pursuing. Money had magic, or so they believed, and the more of it one had, the more miracles it could perform. As far as they were concerned, there wasn't anything it couldn't do.

Nevertheless, they couldn't escape the growing realization that their bank balance wasn't quite the magic lantern they had long envisioned it as being. Their six- or even seven-figure net worth gave many an opportunity to brag casually to others and from time to time feel self-satisfied about how far they had come. Yet even as they said the words, many sensed that something was missing. By their forties, though in some cases it happened sooner, they recognized that they needed help of a nonfinancial sort to make their lives richer. It was only then that they started thinking seriously about the few "media people" they knew.

It is commonly assumed in the United States that everybody wants to know at least one celebrity. Young or old, rich or poor, all these people allegedly hunger for personal contact with the stars. Tens of millions do indeed want to be kept informed daily about the marriages and divorces, victories and setbacks, experienced by celebrities; and magazines, radio, and TV do everything they can to feed this ravenous appetite. In some cases they even create a full-page story or titillating headline from the most innocuous tidbits—or nothing at all. The public often knows that it is being hoodwinked (if not before, then certainly after it reads the story), but it would rather have something that is largely false than silence. However, in spite of this boisterous and widespread interest, there is at least one important group that steadfastly rejects the significance of all such stories, be they true or false.

Many men in their twenties or thirties whose overriding concern in life is making money view themselves as three-dimensional beings and everybody else as two-dimensional. As far as they are concerned, anyone who isn't being paid—and top dollar, at that—for every hour he spends working, is a fool. They find all the talk about "job satisfaction" and "psychic income" ludicrous, little more than a trick some companies or professions play to make members accept a less than appropriate paycheck. Surprisingly, the same mocking attitude is aimed at people who have become well known in the world of show business, and, less surprisingly, at those who spend their time excitedly following the ups and downs of this group. Since many celebrities eventually attain high annual incomes, the bulk of the contempt these men feel is aimed at the fans.

Nevertheless, they generally consider any person who enters the world of stage and screen something of a fool, given that the individual spends years being paid little and has no way of knowing whether the enormous and highly risky investment will ever pay off. (In fact, of 2,147 men— median age, twenty-eight—we surveyed in 1986 who had majored in business administration, finance, accounting, or economics, more than 87 percent—1,869 out of 2,147—felt that acting was "among the hardest ways to make a living," and nearly 91 percent—1,949 out of 2,147—felt that success in the field was "extremely unlikely.") That it turns out well in the end for a few doesn't erase the indignities that, they feel, are suffered along the way by all. This road to riches simply seems to businessmen too indirect and uncertain.

However, once business owners and executives become well off financially, this (in their earlier view) somewhat misguided bunch of showbusiness luminaries becomes quite appealing. Why? Wherever they go, people recognize them, pay them extra attention, and give them the best of everything, often for free. It amazes hardheaded businessmen that a celebrity can dine in an expensive restaurant, be served the finest meal the place has to offer, and not be charged for it. The men are aware that it isn't exactly for nothing, since the publicity generated by a famous patron is worth much more than the check would have brought in.

For the first time in their adult lives these businessmen find themselves envying this kind of subtle exchange, and wishing they could be engaging in it. They have never really wanted anything for free, preferring instead to buy it with their own money. Any other route was charity, or a gift they felt compelled to reciprocate in some way. Their long-held belief that money should play a central role in their lives was more of a philosophical statement than it seemed at first glance. Their unspoken attitude was, "Thinking about everything in terms of cash makes whatever goes on between people neater." Far from viewing money as dirty, it seemed the best medium for keeping all exchanges clean. As some were fond of saying, "With most things in life you get what you pay for, neither more nor less."

BEFRIENDING A CELEBRITY

Abandoning such a hard-and-fast and widely applicable rule wasn't going to be easy, and these businessmen knew it. Not that they thought about the matter consciously, but the majority became increasingly aware throughout their late thirties and forties that money didn't have the omnipotence they had attributed to it for so long. It could buy them respect, of that much they were still certain, but it couldn't buy them something for which they began openly to hunger: fame. Many were puzzled to find themselves even wanting it, for they had gotten used to dismissing it as one of the few rewards that come to people who "have no sense about money" and are foolhardy enough to enter a field that pays the vast majority of its members next to nothing. Yet they did indeed want it and began pursuing it both openly and secretly.

Ironically, what they viewed as their straightforward way of dealing with others (thanks to cash) prevented them from developing the subtle skills needed by people who spend their lives in a profession where incomes are generally low. To businessmen, aspiring actors, artists, and novelists often seem like parasites. Since these would-be performers and writers often don't have the money to pay their bills, some of them keep hoping they will run into a rich patron who will relieve them of that burden. What annoys the typical businessman is that even if he becomes this much-sought-after patron, the artists he is feeding frequently feel compelled to sneer at him behind his back as "vulgar." That makes him recoil from their world without realizing that they are becoming ever more skilled in a way that he too must be if he is to be viewed as more than "merely rich." There is a clash of cultural styles here. He is used to purchasing things *outright*; they have become good at doing favors and giving gifts *with strings attached*.

Acquiring a public persona is never easy, even for people (such as actors and politicians) who devote their lives to it. But those who come to this task late—and wealthy businessmen are the single largest group to do so—find it especially difficult because it involves a personal style they have been deliberately avoiding until then. They like being known locally and want people to think of them as socially prominent, yet, as they quickly discover during their forties, fame—renown on a national scale—is another matter altogether.

It is difficult to acquire vicariously, as businessmen soon discover, inasmuch as they can't think of anything to offer a celebrity that would cement the bond between them. "A dinner invitation won't work," a forty-two-year-old stockbroker told us, referring to a movie star. "I don't think he'll come, or even get the invitation. Besides, he probably has a home every bit as expensive as mine, so that wouldn't attract him." Under the circumstances, the position of agents—the people negotiating contracts for stars—suddenly begins to seem enviable.

In the mid-1980s a book written by one who was the agent for, among others, tennis ace Bjorn Borg, entitled *Everything They Didn't Teach You at the Harvard Business School*, sold more than a half-million copies.

However, the book had nothing to do with the Harvard Business School curriculum and instead in many ways it resembled a typical copy of *People* magazine. Full of gossipy tidbits about sports greats, it drew its appeal not so much from its business wisdom (of which it contained precious little) as from the author's ability to name-drop as an "insider," something many of the book's readers told us that they too would like to be in a position to do.

Since they weren't lawyers, and the few who were weren't agents for superstars, these wealthy men would have to find another way to achieve their new goal. By no means did all wealthy stockbrokers and real-estate developers act this way. Between 1968 and 1986 only 28 percent of those who had a net worth [in constant 1986 dollars] that exceeded $250,000 did so, yet they were the "style setters." Their ability to boast about having an "in" with a celebrity, even when the statement was false (as it usually was), elicited a visible reaction from peers, who, judged by their own replies, would have liked to be able to say the same.

MY COMPANY/MY SELF

Three main routes were used by these moneyed men. The first was to try to get on television any way they could. Talk shows had developed a continual need for new guests, since TV so quickly brings each to the point of "overexposure" and diminishing audience interest. We found that this avenue appealed primarily to men who had previously rated themselves as good-looking or possessing "the gift of gab." Salesmen in many cases, they had refined the latter skill out of professional necessity and often prided themselves on their ability to think on their feet. Thinking in front of a TV camera seemed to them even easier by comparison, since they had a receptive viewing audience.

Entrepreneurs who sold cars, carpets, appliances, or chickens for a living, as well as those who peddled stocks or real estate, carried the process a step further. It was one they especially liked because, as we've seen, they were fond of purchasing things outright, rather than having their transactions be more like favors or gifts with strings attached. So they decided to star in their own TV commercials.

Although the public often hooted and howled at these business owners plugging their wares, and even more so themselves, this was the style that felt most natural to the men. They had purchased a certain amount of air time and said what they wanted to say, and that was that. The transaction seemed to them neat and clean because money was involved. There was an added bonus: that their own name was on the product made them feel more comfortable about promoting both at the same time.

Others, who didn't have the benefit of a company bearing their own name, decided that it was worth whatever effort it took to pal around with media celebrities. There was a preliminary problem that had to be solved, and many of the men therefore took the necessary step: they got a divorce. None thought of it in this direct a manner, yet their actions spoke volumes. Since they were now ready to have their lives enter a new phase, and were determined to be as successful in this arena as they were in the prior one, they started to strip themselves of anything that might compromise the new image they wanted to project. While some thought of their wives as an asset, nearly 40 percent wanted someone more "glamorous" at their side to facilitate their quest. Larry-types were the most, David-types the next, and men like Steve the least likely both to feel and act this way. Those who terminated their marriages (usually for a variety of reasons, not just this one) reported being surprised at how easy it was to "trade up" and find the starlet, model, media figure, or merely good-looking younger woman they wanted as a public companion.

Since the men were skilled at handling money, and often had made a substantial amount of it, one route that struck them as natural was to buy into a media-related business. Acquiring all or part of a magazine or book-publishing firm, movie or TV production company, seemed to them an easy way to get where they wanted to go. It even amused some of the men to feel that they were on the verge of doing with cash what people who had become well-known entertainers had achieved with sweat.

Those who didn't want to be actively involved in the management of a media-related firm often made the decision merely to back a movie, TV series (a "pilot"), or play. In their view, being an "angel" was the perfect combination; it offered the chance to make a killing if the project became a hit (or take a welcome tax writeoff if it didn't), and held out the possibility of rubbing shoulders with the stars.

An equally attractive avenue, for those who didn't want to be directly involved with the day-to-day operations of an organization besides their own, called for them to start thinking of themselves as philanthropists. The cultural institutions of any major city are always in need of well-heeled contributors to offset chronic operating deficits. One millionaire stockbroker, who had been described by two colleagues as having a "tin ear," found himself a trustee of the local opera company once he decided, in his own words, "to become more culturally conspicuous."

THE POWER OF THE PRESS

For every man we studied whose wealth made him feel that he should be on talk shows, do his own TV commercials, be photographed with celebrities, buy into a media business, or do "charitable" work, there were three others who were equally well off but too shy to act in a similar manner. What the majority wanted most was for someone to write their biography. "Even an article about me would be very nice," they volunteered. They weren't quite certain about how to make this happen, but approximately 21 percent didn't mind the idea of "planting" the story themselves.

Instead of chasing after show-business greats, they tried to befriend reporters and editors. Far from seeing themselves as doing anything deceitful, they always attempted to make this gesture appear "symbiotic." It wouldn't benefit solely themselves; the print or broadcast medium had to have an unending supply of new stories and, as one real-estate developer commented ingenuously, "Here I am." They seemed genuinely convinced that their story was worth telling and they were bent on finding someone to tell it.

The first encounters they had with reporters and editors left them shocked. In most cases they had gotten a friend to introduce them in the first place and expected the conversation to be relaxed, friendly, and productive. After all, they were filling a need of someone else's, not just tooting their own horn. Yet their proposal for a story about themselves, even though it was almost always presented in a discreet and roundabout manner, was met with an unmistakable cynicism. They took it personally, not realizing that the senior reporter or editor to whom their friend had introduced them had spent many years perfecting this stance and wore it more proudly each year as an indication that he was a veteran member of his profession. It wasn't something he did consciously, but he could nevertheless sense how valuable an attitude it was.

Approximately 4 percent of the men—17 out of 416—offered him money, while 9 percent—38 out of 416—offered him gifts, favors, or discounts ("a car at *cost*"). There are undoubtedly reporters and editors who have accepted such inducements, but our study turned up only two (out of a total of more than 110 with whom the men had contact during the period 1965 through 1986). In the vast majority of cases the reporter or editor simply brushed the bribe aside, almost as if he were shooing a horsefly. The reasons weren't hard to discover. When a wealthy appliance dealer in our sample died prematurely (by drowning), we asked the magazine editor to whom he had recently offered free use of a summer house on Cape Cod in return for "a feature story" *why* he turned the dealer down flatly. "I'll tell you why," he replied, both surprised and annoyed that we knew about the conversation. "He reminded me of a five-year-old—'I'll let you play with my toys if you'll be my friend.' C'mon, did he really think he was going to get away with that kind of crap?"

Well, as a matter of fact, he did think that. Perhaps the best evidence of how far the men were prepared to go—and how far afield many had wandered in their new quest—was that most thought that merely befriending a radio or TV announcer would enable them to get their names mentioned on the air. That simple. They couldn't explain exactly how it would happen, but they were fairly certain it eventually would. Somehow, right in the middle of reading the news or introducing the next song, they expected the announcer suddenly to say, "You know, Joe Blow is one helluva guy. We're thinking of devoting an entire hour to a retrospective on his life and accomplishments. Don't miss it." As one of the men commented, after describing this Walter Mitty–like fantasy to us, "That would really make my day." Others, to whom we repeated the prospect of such a thing happening, replied, "That would allow me to die happy."

INSTANT RECOGNITION

The sad part of all this is that many of the men *do* have a story worth telling. But while it would stun them to hear it, they are unwittingly doing everything possible to reduce the chances that it will ever be told. Worse still, if it is, they aren't going to be pleased with the version of it that the public gets to see or hear.

What are they doing wrong? To begin with, their subconscious assumption that ditching their "dowdy" old spouse for someone who is more photogenic will help get them on camera is contradicted by the facts. During the past two decades we have asked more than six hundred reporters and editors whether the wife of the man they were writing about—her looks, background, or current activities—made any difference to the slant of the story. Few answered yes. The vast majority replied that, in a typical case, they never got to meet the woman, and in the occasional instance that they did, it didn't color their judgment. When we challenged the statement, a representative response was, "Look, we don't interview *nobodies,* so I know pretty much what the story is going to be about before I ever meet the guy."

However, more than one third of the six hundred stated that a man who had a celebrity for a spouse—or more commonly, a woman he was hoping would be seen as one—made them wary. A typical reply was: "I get very suspicious when I see a man packaging himself and his wife for public-relations purposes."

Few things horrify journalists and editors more than the possibility that they are about to be conned. People who talk about the media being manipulated seem not to realize the lengths to which the members of this industry go to avoid having it happen. Basically, they are inclined to believe that everyone is lying to them—that every statement they hear is false or, at the very least, self-serving. So when a wealthy businessman, hungry to see his name in the news and face on TV, tries to prepackage the story for the press, the press reacts in an intensely skeptical manner.

However guarded the reporter or editor was before, he now becomes much more so. He has no intention of allowing himself to be fooled, if there is any way to avoid it. The years he has spent learning to distinguish between a personal enthusiasm or passing fad, on the one hand, and something truly newsworthy, on the other, are invaluable here. That doesn't mean he always gets the story right the first time, but—and this is a point of enormous importance—even if someone puts one over on him, he is in a better position to undo such a blunder than almost any other professional.

He can write another story, with or without an apology for the first one, and this time tell the truth. Wealthy or ambitious men who trick the press into publishing a flattering profile of them are few and far between; and in the majority of cases we examined, even when they thought they had pulled off such a stunt, they were often appalled at the article that actually did run. Having devoted so much effort to becoming a celebrity, they were amazed at the critical and even harsh tone of the piece.

While personal ethics and a hard-won sense of perspective go a long way to explaining why journalists and editors act as they do, an important reminder keeps coming from the public. The minute the TV audience, for instance, realizes that someone they are seeing on screen bought his way there, they are inclined to sneer. This is one reward they want people to get the old-fashioned way—by earning it. The person's skill or achievements, not a behind-the-scene payment, are supposed to bring him to their attention. Anyone who subverts the process is treated with the same hostility and contempt aimed by spectators at people who rig a basketball game.

The world may seem chaotic in many ways, but one respect in which it is almost predictable is this: people who start out seeking fame, and enter the media-related fields that create and maintain such reputations, are likely to end up becoming increasingly interested in making money— and as a result do better in their profession. Conversely, people who concentrate on making money, and succeed, are likely to end up becoming increasingly interested in fame—and as a result make fools of themselves, thanks to the army of veteran cynics who staff the nation's print and broadcast media.

To people who have become accustomed to solving problems by using a hands-on approach, it will come as something of a surprise to learn that those individuals who make the transition best from a quest for wealth to an interest in renown are those who make little or no attempt to disseminate their own story. What they do instead is concentrate on their work and on giving their lives more substance and satisfaction. With so few wealthy people actually behaving this way, the press eventually finds those that do. *Theirs is a story worth writing about because theirs is a life worth living.*

Can the same be said of the large number of people who have reduced themselves to a two-dimensional copy of a celebrity in the hope that they too might one day appear on such TV shows as *Lifestyles of the Rich and Famous*? What the evidence shows is that the harder they try to achieve this "instant recognition" as a star, the less likely they are ever to become one.

CONCLUSION

CALLING OUT THE RESERVES

From the late 1950s to the late 1980s there was a steady decrease in the amount of formality seen in everyday affairs. A growing proportion of the Americans we surveyed each year agreed with the statement that "we don't stand on ceremony here" in referring to the companies for which they worked. However, the same sentence described what went on at home. A trend toward casualness was evident in their mode of dress and manner of entertainment. The hairstyles of an earlier era always look silly in retrospect, but in the 1980s women's bouffant styles and men's pompadours of twenty-five years ago looked amusingly antique, hardly worth all the bother it took to keep them intact.

Even for those who considered it harmful or boring, physical fitness had become a goal of paramount importance. Sweating during athletics or sex no longer repelled either men or women. The word "natural" was seized on by marketers, who realized that tens of millions of affluent and educated consumers wanted to be free of the many allegedly synthetic constraints and products their parents had lived with. Food, fashions, and relationships were required to be less structured. Only what was spontaneous, not cooked or cooked up, was viewed as wholesome. Even the straitjacket of public opinion was removed, as most of the individuals we studied in their twenties and thirties paid it less attention. Instead, "If it feels good, do it," was a widely used guide.

While all this was beneficial in many ways, since it certainly created more room for people to be "themselves," we found that remarkably few really took advantage of the room. When behavior isn't codified, people are continually "winging it." Without generally accepted guidelines for how men and women should act in a variety of situations—guidelines which both sexes increasingly rejected during this period—they are forced to become good at "thinking on their feet." It is a delightful and continuing challenge for the small proportion who like doing this and are good at it, but the majority find it a chore. They have the ingenuity needed to handle most situations but find themselves walking around with an always present (and sometimes high) level of tension.

How will they react to the next complicated social situation or conflict they encounter, on the job or off? They don't know. But, having been through hundreds in recent years, they usually feel confident about their ability to respond adequately once again—without noticing how emotionally expensive this style is. In short, in the last few decades life in the United States has become much more "free form" than most people realize. In any given situation they usually have to "reinvent the rules."

That has become particularly necessary thanks to a number of important changes that have taken place in the economy. In the 1950s and 1960s it was common for people to think of membership in the major professions as prestigious. Being a doctor, lawyer, or teacher, even a store owner, carried with it a certain measure of public approval. This esteem was available for private use as well, since it was clearly not a fantasy of one's own. While entering the field or starting a company took effort and was usually expensive, once this initial step had been taken one could collect a small, daily dose of community admiration just for staying there.

Their occupation not only served as an umbrella, protecting them from the fallout generated by passing professional fads ("my field is more popular than yours, at least for the moment"), it also was a rich soil from which its members could draw many of the psychological nutrients they needed to think well of themselves week in and week out, both at work and at home.

Much to the chagrin of their members, and of those preparing to become members, these fields have suffered a significant degree of erosion in the esteem in which the public holds them. For one thing, during the past few decades, every prestige profession has become glutted. However, even if hordes of newcomers hadn't been trying to gain entrance to them, thereby driving wages down for those who did manage to land a position within them, our annual surveys indicate that the public was becoming increasingly resentful during these years of high (and still more so, low) inflation about the rapidly rising cost of the medical, legal, dental, and financial services they needed.

They liked living in an economy that was devoted more to services than goods, since they sensed that the world had become cleaner and safer than the old mining or industrial towns were. They were right, as they could see by looking at pictures of old Pittsburgh, or even London, where the air was so thick with fumes from burning coal or factory smokestacks that it cost many people their lives. So much for the good news. Goods, an expensive car or stereo, say, they may have wanted but were well aware they could do without; services were another matter. If one needed them at all, one needed them soon. Whether it involved one's heart or one's teeth, the problems couldn't be ignored for long once they bothered one enough to notice them in the first place. People felt victimized, not always being able to specify why. It irritated their brains rather than their lungs to recognize that they couldn't afford the help they had to have. The result was a widespread antipathy toward physicians, for instance, just at the time when medicine, as a scientific and technical field, was achieving some of its most important breakthroughs.

The public took matters into its own hands and "health food" stores boomed; in fact, any grocery store or fast-food restaurant with a salad bar was suddenly deemed wholesome. People didn't intend to let anyone take advantage of them, and that made them willing to try their hand at being their own lawyers (with the help of paperbacks), doctors (with the help of yogurt, vitamin pills, and unprocessed foods), or financial advisers (with the help of newsletters and cable TV shows). Educated and intelligent individuals allowed themselves to settle for herbal medicines and other medieval remedies in the hope of avoiding dependence on doctors, particularly since many said they could no longer afford them. "Just paying for the insurance has gotten to be a financial burden," was a frequently heard comment in the 1980s. People were willing to turn the clock back centuries and, like hypochondriacs, treat themselves for diseases they didn't even have, all as part of an attempt to dispense with the professionals their parents thought so highly of in the 1950s. A devotion to physical fitness in the 1980s wasn't mere narcissism; it made people feel good because, among other things, it was subconsciously an act of rebellion. Against whom? The label used by the few who sensed their own resentment was "the medical establishment," by which they meant everything from the AMA to the drug companies.

It is hardly surprising that professionals of all sorts in the United States no longer felt respected, and the mushrooming number of lawsuits being filed at the time against physicians served notice on the rest that this view was correct. Since doctors had long ranked at the top of the list in terms of prestige, if *they* could be dragged into court and attacked financially, those who occupied the rungs beneath them also could. It bothered both the doctors and lawyers we surveyed annually during this period that the problem was much bigger than it seemed, since only a small percentage of the people who wanted to file suit against a physician actually did so.

The alleged negligence of manufacturers, carelessness of stores, and malpractice of physicians had become the basis for a new growth industry, one that made millionaires of many. Lawsuits aside, an increasing proportion of the public was becoming skeptical about the competence of the professionals who served them. So much new information was being generated each year, people rightly began to question the ability of anyone, no matter how dedicated, to keep up with this flow. The most important consequence of all the adverse publicity and intense competition from a flood of new entrants to the field was that professionals stopped receiving something essential—the many little psychological rewards they had become used to getting each day. Most complained that patients, clients, and customers were now taking them for granted, no longer even bothering to say "thank you" for work that was well done. A representative remark from a plastic surgeon: "A good job is greeted with silence, a poor one ends up in court and the newspapers."

The effect this had on a huge number of ambitious men was simple: deprived of many small rewards, they began searching for one large one. Not the kind who are inclined to quit, they tried to make up in other areas for what they were no longer being offered—and no longer even expected—in this one. If the people with whom they did business wouldn't applaud them, perhaps the public at large would. They wanted the approval and having, in effect, been evicted from the field emotionally, this wider arena seemed the one place left to attempt to find it. Advertising would previously have been a taboo and superfluous step, since the field looked after its own; now it was necessary, because the people in each field began looking out for themselves. Even doctors began to do the unthinkable, to testify in court against one another. Few noticed that they were doing it, and fewer still stopped to reason why, but many businessmen and professionals in their thirties and forties found themselves once again dreaming about attaining glory, just as they had during adolescence.

The situation they were in was a more difficult one than it seemed. As ambitious adolescents, they had eagerly looked forward to the day when they would obtain a great deal of recognition for doing, as adults, what they were currently doing. The future would solve their most pressing problems, or so they hoped. It hadn't happened, at least not yet, and although most had no idea what was at the root of their dissatisfaction, they blamed their profession itself—the nature of the everyday tasks they had to perform. It troubled them to recognize that they had taken a number of giant steps forward yet were still very far from the goals which they had set for themselves. A shift would have to be made, perhaps a major one. Many changed careers, only to find that the situation was no better elsewhere and their earnings prospects poorer (70 percent of those in our sample who made a career change after the age of thirty became disillusioned and made yet another change within five years).

In the large majority of cases the ambitious men we studied weren't selling a product, they were selling themselves. This was necessary even when a product was involved. Just getting the job required it, as did getting along with colleagues in order to produce and market the item more effectively. Each year of our study the proportion of men dealing primarily with intangibles at work steadily grew. Each year it became a little more accurate to call the United States a "service economy," with ever more of the goods it consumed being produced abroad. In such an economic setting people eager to do well chronically display an "anxiety to please."

Rather than being the psychological problem many think this is, it is part and parcel of contemporary economic life, especially for those who

are driven. The whole idea of being a salesman has had negative con-
notations for more than a century, and admonitions to be wary of "snake-
oil peddlers" had been circulating in America well before that time. Yet
once a country does what the United States did in the post–World War
II period, namely, export a major portion of its industrial base, many of
its workers find themselves engaged in sales-connected activities whether
they like it or not.

Most don't. Since students can't major in this subject in college, and
since many of the best salespeople seem virtually to have been born with
the knack, the field has little prestige. It is too easy to enter; attaining good
results often involves deceit; and people in the profession are generally
viewed as shallow and insincere. Nevertheless, the fact remains that most
workers can no longer overlook the sales dimension of their work. For
example, they may need to inspire in-house salespeople or sales reps, who
then attempt to persuade the public of the product's merits, but dismissing this activity as unimportant and demeaning has brought to a halt the
career of many a rising star. Even doctors and lawyers, who previously
sneered at the very idea of marketing their skills, now pitch their own
services on radio and TV.

What makes the position of so many businessmen and professionals
difficult—much more so than that of the typical salesman—is that they
first have to create a product in order to have something to sell. In a
service economy that product, more each day, is a reflection of themselves. They can speak about its objective merits all they like, but it is
their subjective belief in its quality that must carry the day and persuade
others to give it a chance. Some find this thought exhilarating, but
others—and they are the majority—have a much tougher time of it than
has previously been recognized. Complicating the problem is the fact that
nearly half of the ambitious men we studied (especially those in their late
twenties and thirties) have been torn loose from their moorings, due to
forces that are largely beyond their control.

In a representative case the man's childhood family and friends have
dispersed; the community in which he was raised has a different character
now and is full of old people, low-income minorities, or individuals from
whom he feels estranged; as we've seen, his profession no longer provides
him with automatic daily ego boosts just for being a member; and his
marriage, often a two-career one, has all the emotional stability of weather
in Seattle. Not having these four pillars in place is much like having the

company for which a veteran salesman was working go bankrupt. The urge—the need—to sell is still there in the man, but for the moment he is at a loss to identify just what it is he's selling. Small wonder that *Death of a Salesman* is now studied at many top business schools, such as Harvard.

This goes far to explain why so many dedicated and intelligent men do much less well than they anticipated. Whether the idea pleases or offends them, *they* are what they are selling. At first, when one listens to a wide variety of such men speak, one comes away with the impression that each seems to have a very firm grasp of his stock-in-trade. "I am what I am," he states repeatedly and with conviction. But what is he? Does he really know? Does he understand why it has become so *essential* for him to know?

"TO THINE OWNSELF BE TRUE"

One of America's highest values is the individuality of its citizens. The nation feels that this above all must be respected both politically and economically, with each person being given a real chance to develop it. However, in recent years a new twist has been added. The United States has become a media-saturated, celebrity-crazed country, and merely being an individual is no longer enough. There is enormous pressure to publicly assert one's individuality, to make it visible to others.

This has had the effect of turning almost everyone who wants to get somewhere into a cross between an actor and a politician. Not by accident in the 1980s do we have a two-term president who is a combination of both. The need for everyday people to "take a stand," to express an opinion forcefully, makes it hard for them to back away from what they have said. Anyone who repeatedly changes his mind in public risks being condemned for not only being confused, but also (in an *ad hominem* attack that seems to follow automatically) for being a lightweight, not an important person after all.

Groups form voluntarily at work and during leisure hours, but it is fascinating to watch each of a group's members try hard to differentiate himself from the rest in order, paradoxically, to be a member in good standing. If anyone in the group expresses a strong view, the others— especially those who are ambitious—feel compelled to do something peculiar; namely, express in equally strong terms a counteropinion. Dismissing the initial speaker's comment rather than replying to it heatedly would be less of a strain, but this route generally isn't used for two reasons. First, it gives each an opportunity for an "assertion of self," and, second, a chance to do this in a public setting (at least one other person is present).

Codified responses of any kind, whether they consist of standardized phrases or polite behavior, are therefore unwittingly rejected. Their absence makes social intercourse substantially more difficult; yet conflict has more benefits than peace for those trying to be "public individuals," so the situation isn't likely to change. To sum up, the forces we have been discussing, acting in concert, make it necessary for ambitious men not only to keep "inventing the rules," they must also keep "inventing themselves."

With so much spontaneous behavior, which people then have to defend as appropriate and a reflection of their true selves, clashes develop even between pairs of people who don't want them and, basically, mean well. Each is dancing to a different tune, yet both insist on the rightness of the music they hear, so almost inevitably they end up stepping on one another's toes. Not wanting to be called fraudulent or superficial, both are constantly looking for a deeper, more personal way of reacting to social encounters. The effort is more wrenching than they realize, and frequently exhausts them. They are subconsciously trying to reshape themselves to fit the circumstances, yet still be citizens in good standing by expressing their individuality openly.

To find some structure in their lives and not be torn in half each day by these competing pressures, most settle upon a simple stratagem. Confronted by a new situation, they do the same thing they did last time. In essence, they invent their own traditions. For most Americans, *habit* takes the place of *ceremony* in, say, Japan. Since these habits allegedly spring from an inner source, not a best-selling guidebook on etiquette, they are viewed as deriving from the person's true inner self. Both the speaker and his audience thus accept them as *personality*. With so much uncertainty and instability in their interpersonal lives, most of the men we studied see this as one of the few consistent psychological realities they experience daily.

So they cling to it much too tightly: they can't allow their "personality"—habits, actually—to be changed. Since, by default, it is the main source of emotional stability most have, they use each meeting with a co-worker, friend, or intimate to repeat a past performance. Most want badly to avoid being put through the wringer in every encounter by trying to come up with an appropriate yet individualized mode of behavior, though this is what each does anyway. "I am what I am," they keep repeating, for this alone allows them to justify the wide range of faces that they actually display. "To thine ownself be true," the majority reply when asked to describe a rule of thumb that can be used in the widest range of social situations.

The upshot, and the first part of a key finding: ambitious men are extremely reluctant to change their behavior, even when they sense they should. In their eyes they aren't merely modifying a ceremony, a formal interchange, they are changing "themselves," their "basic personality." This is the underground source from which their behavior is seen as springing, or else it is phony. With so few socially mandated rituals, superficial "rules of the game" that can be modified as needed, people are left to fall back on their own resourcefulness. It should come as no surprise that they often waste as much emotional energy on a trivial encounter as on a major one. To avoid being drained, they do individually for themselves what they refuse as a group to let society do for them: codify their own everyday habits—and stick with them mindlessly, no matter how much damage results.

Then (and this is the second part of the key finding) when things go badly, they have no choice but to look outside themselves for a solution: new jobs, careers, partners, social circles, and cities. The answer to their difficulties lies "out there, somewhere." It might, but it astonished us to find that in the midst of this most fluid of societies there are so many rigid individuals, people who feel forced to take a stand, adopt a platform and a public persona much the way politicians do; and, like them, to ride it to victory or defeat. At least that way, even if they do poorly, they are convinced that no one can call them a fake.

When the vast majority of ambitious men we studied ran into a major setback, they responded by doing what we only realized after many years was among the most destructive things they could do: *they became more of what they already were.* Yet the evidence indicates that in most cases they were too much that way already and that was what was causing them trouble in the first place.

What is sad is that if they were really being true to themselves, they would take advantage of the latitude that is always present in so complex an entity as a personality. Like a heavenly constellation, the pieces of a personality *can* be moved around substantially and the overall configuration still be recognized. But many people don't use this opportunity even though the benefits of doing so have proved enormous. They are afraid to, because they are concerned that it will cost them their "individuality" and therefore their membership in loosely knit groups at work and intimate pairings at home. Making any modifications at all worries them because they think it will disrupt what people see, a devotion to consistency that in some cases is a strength but in a much larger number is a weakness.

The most widely shared daydream among the men in our sample is to stumble upon a fortune by hitting it big in the stock market, in real estate, in business (as an entrepreneur), or in a state lottery. Why does this prospect grip them, and what would they do if it came true? One might imagine that they would use the money to live well, but what most say they want it for even more is to finally be able to tell their superiors at work to go to hell. That indicates to us—and it should also indicate to them—that they are using the wrong approach in an effort both to please and succeed. Precisely because they are laboring under such a continuing self-imposed psychological strain, and are inevitably resentful about it (though rarely is this conscious), they quickly and easily lose touch with what is best in themselves. They aren't developing it fully, day in and day out—either for love or for money. Yet, this is the very thing they should be doing to maximize the odds that they will eventually attain the fame and fortune they are seeking.

THE STUFF OF WHICH SUCCESSES ARE MADE

Let them at last be "true to themselves," by realizing what their true self really is. It begins with the categories represented by Bill, David, Larry, and Steve. *This* is real in a way that anyone who gets to know them well can see.

To repeat, one of our most important findings is that *the majority of ambitious men we studied who did much less well than they (and we) expected did so because they reacted to key setbacks by becoming even more of what they were too much of already—too much like either Bill, David, Larry, or Steve.* For instance, men like Larry who hadn't been successful in using their financial achievements to elicit respect resolved even more strongly to use money to buy it. "The problem," in their view, "is that I haven't yet earned *enough* money." Similarly, when a typical Steve realized that his technical skills weren't moving him up the firm's ladder as quickly as he would have liked, and that he might not make it at all if he didn't do something soon, he locked himself away and sought to deepen the technical skills that had brought him this far. Finally, when the social skills of a David failed to get him what he wanted professionally, he extended his social circle, believing he was making contact with too few of "the right people."

What is the alternative? The lives of Winston Churchill and Theodore Roosevelt provide classic examples of what we found to be a more effective route for ambitious men to realize their dreams. In *The Last Lion: Winston Spencer Churchill, 1874–1932*, William Manchester writes:

> Sickly, an uncoordinated weakling with the pale fragile hands of a girl, speaking with a lisp and a slight stutter, he had been at the mercy of bullies. They beat him, ridiculed him, and pelted him with cricket balls. Trembling and humiliated, he hid in nearby woods. This was hardly the stuff of which gladiators are made. His only weapons were an unconquerable will and an incipient sense of immortality. Beginning at the age of seven, Churchill deliberately set out to change his nature, to prove that biology need *not* be destiny. As a Victorian, Churchill believed he could be master of his fate, and that faith sustained him. He refused to yield to human frailty. In his inner world there was no room for concessions to weakness. He altered his emotional constitution to that of an athlete, projecting the image of a valiant, indomitable bulldog.

Similarly, Theodore Roosevelt writes in his autobiography that during his asthmatic, childhood years, "I was nervous and timid. Yet from reading, I felt great admiration for men who were fearless and could hold their own in the world, and I had a great desire to be like them." Promising his father, "I'll make my body," he adhered to the promise with what Edmund Morris describes in *The Rise of Theodore Roosevelt* as "bulldog tenacity." During his teenage years, Roosevelt writes, "I encountered a couple of boys who were about my age. They proceeded to make life miserable for me." He realized that, in Morris's words, "If he had exercised hard before, he must do so twice as hard now. He must also learn how to give and take punishment. 'Accordingly, with my father's hearty approval, I started to learn to box.' "

The metamorphosis took place slowly. Roosevelt, "not yet sixteen, was still something of a scholarly recluse," yet at Harvard "he managed to get through prodigious quantities of work. Iron self-discipline had long since become a habit with him." Nor would the metamorphosis ever be complete. Other authors agree with Morris in stating that, "There was always something abstract about his social conscience. He 'felt' with his head rather than his heart." However, by the time he was in his mid-twenties and was working on a ranch out west, "Some extraordinary physical and spiritual transformation occurred during this arduous period. It was as if his adolescent battle for health were crowned with sudden victory." When he came back to New York, his friends were astonished "to find him with the neck of a Titan, with broad shoulders and stalwart chest."

What Churchill and Roosevelt did instinctively and at an early age, most men who want to improve their chances of doing well will have to undertake consciously, as adults, and in a direction that may or may not be the same as these two chose. In many ways this makes the task easier. A frail and timid youth may dream of being muscular and powerful because he is repeatedly picked on by his peers. Yet that is not the best motivation for seeking to become forceful in public. The majority of men who look to bigger muscles or a fatter bank account in the future to compensate for derogatory remarks and physical abuse dished out by classmates never achieve the sense of revenge that drives them. We found that for all their effort, they merely get back to zero, at best. Unfortunately, most past hurts can't be avenged.

The man who, as an adult, tries to do what Churchill and Roosevelt subconsciously did while young has the advantage of focusing on a more glorious future rather than dwelling on a painful past. Using a rifle instead of a shotgun, he can concentrate on improving the specific areas of his behavior that are most likely to help him attain success and, equally important, to keep it.

Without this self-awareness, it is too easy to overdo one's attempt to compensate for an alleged weakness. For instance, there are many chronically scared men who constantly try to act tough. Some even swagger and start fights. They think their smokescreen, their blowfish defense—puffing up when feeling threatened—is working. The evidence indicates that they themselves are the only ones who consider their act convincing. People who describe them as "macho" are seeing through the charade and laughing at it.

By contrast, the advantage of, say, a Steve-type trying *consciously* to develop the Bill- or Larry-like facets of his personality is that, first, he is well aware of what he's doing, and that, second, it takes many years of behaving in a particular way before that behavior comes to seem natural. He may feel that he has never matched the picture of his ideal self that he carries in his mind. Still, the benefits derived from making such an effort over a number of years will be there decades later, long after he has said to himself, "I have stopped trying to be like Larry [David, Steve, or Bill]—that's just not me." Typically, he will be among the last to realize how much he has changed in a way that makes him seem more complex and capable to those who know him. Because the shifts take place slowly, and the person living them is the one least likely to notice them, the fireworks he thought would accompany the transformation may be missing. Others, however, have no trouble spotting what he can't see.

Instead of each ambitious man trying to find the magic mixture of, say, Larry and Steve that would bring him success (assuming he is currently more like one or the other of these two men), a more worthwhile route is for him to attempt to develop *all four* of the personalities that we've been discussing throughout the book.

Isn't that just another self-imposed strain? Hardly. People are much more multifaceted than they assume. However, they unwittingly try hard year in and year out to strip away most of what constitutes their normal multidimensional self and attempt to become one-dimensional. They think they have the best of all possible reasons for doing this: it simplifies their lives to lead with what most label as their "strong suit" and therefore improves dramatically their chances of attaining wealth and eminence in their chosen profession.

Well, it may be their strong suit, but it certainly isn't their only one, and as their lives change and different opportunities and challenges present themselves, the other suits may be more useful. They are there, dormant, having suffered decades of neglect. The most underdeveloped territories on earth, those most in need of immediate attention, exist within the personalities of ambitious individuals. People—men, especially—let large parts of their personality remain unexplored because they think they are supposed to present a simplistic picture of themselves, particularly in public. It makes each feel more readily identifiable. "If I'm a different person on different days," many asked us rhetorically, "how will anyone know who I am?"

People aren't *that* flexible; their similarities from one day to the next always far outweigh the differences. Anyone who thinks that he has to have one and only one public personality—just as he has one and only one address throughout life—is sorely mistaken. The goal that is so important to most, namely, being taken seriously by colleagues and friends, isn't facilitated by this relentless effort at self-reduction. It strikes onlookers as affected and stiff—but, sad to say, they rarely, if ever, say so to the person's face.

One thing people don't have to worry about is that in developing their weaker suits, they will lose their strong one. That doesn't happen. In more than a quarter of a century of careful attention to this topic we've not seen it occur even once. The modern work world is so oriented toward specialization—not only of skills, but also of an appropriately stereotypical manner to accompany the skills—that one's strong suit requires no further conscious development. It continues to grow stronger automatically, even as one seeks to strengthen the other parts of one's personality, the very aspects that will be needed most to (1) rise in one's profession and (2) retain the gains.

Specialized skills and an accompanying simplified manner get people their initial positions in a field. But landing senior positions or undertaking large-scale projects in a firm of one's own requires the development of more general skills *and* the diversified personality needed to handle various types of workers, not just those in one's specialty.

Instead of being fearful of one's own flexibility, it is time to utilize it—exactly as the successful men we looked at in chapters 5 through 11 are doing. Using it well means realizing that it falls naturally into four main categories, connected to the four main drives. The world has become too full of credentialed people for that to be the deciding factor any longer in who gets ahead. In such a setting, personal credentials—the ability to use the full range of one's inner resources—become all-important. In a world that grows more competitive and economically unpredictable each day, anyone who hopes to realize his ambitions by becoming even more of what he is too much of already is merely kidding himself. Never has the old saw "Standing still means losing ground" been more valid. There is nothing inevitable about this fate, assuming a man makes the modest effort needed to understand and start changing it. Every person he encounters, on the job or off, provides another opportunity to practice.

Is there a best time for him to undertake such a change? When are the chances greatest that a new, more effective approach will "take"? We found that the two best times are after he gets a divorce and/or changes jobs or careers. No one is suggesting that the man who is eager to deepen and diversify his personality has to terminate a marriage or give up his current position first to enable this to happen. However, without anyone telling them to do so, approximately half the men in our sample got a divorce anyway and more than 98 percent changed jobs at least once. What we're suggesting is that these marital and occupational shifts can, and should, be put to much better use than they currently are. (How about men who, although happily married or relatively content with their business lives, would still like to do better? If their key intimate or professional relationship is as good as they think it is, they should have little trouble making it adapt to the revised approach they feel it is appropriate for them to take in order to develop their dormant personal strengths. Proceeding slowly, so as not to seem like Jekyll and Hyde, is best.)

Unpleasant as these parting experiences often are, they do have a bright side since they provide a perfect context in which to be "someone different" from then on. In fact, some of what is required takes place automatically. After a divorce many of the men we studied said, "I feel free." They meant sexually and were also referring to schedules—"Not having to be anywhere at a given time each evening and on weekends," as one put it. However, what had also come loose was the personality of each; more flexibility was suddenly present since he was no longer stuck in the rigid roles that were part and parcel of what made the previous relationship at home or in the office so unpleasant and unworkable. Making matters worse was that his stances were becoming more brittle and simplistic with each passing year.

Changing jobs or partners causes a breath of fresh air to enter the scene, and it should be utilized well rather than experienced as a temporary high before the person becomes disenchanted by the prospect of having too much time and, more to the point, too much personality plasticity on his hands. Instead, a few moments spent reflecting on which of the four styles he has been overdoing, and which mixture of the other three would be worth adding, can be extremely productive. For men who want to make the most of their ambitions, rather than spending their lives battling them, there could hardly be a better way to turn a seeming setback into a major step forward.

APPENDIX
ON
METHODOLOGY

Stratifying the populations of interest (by profession or, among students, by college major) allowed us to choose sampling units within each stratum that were as comparable as possible, given the psychosocial characteristics discussed in the introduction whose development we intended to monitor. People in business or professional fields are overrepresented (primarily a reflection of the interests of both the study's researchers and its major corporate sponsors), while those in the arts, performing arts, teaching, and civil service are underrepresented. Similar considerations were applied in the selection of a sample of blue-collar workers, where (construction, electrical, plumbing, and trucking) union assistance was solicited and received for 25 percent of the 1,600-man total, that being the maximum proportion of this part of the sample which we felt should have union membership, at least at the start of the study. Latitude to pursue other income or professional opportunities should not, in our view, be limited for sample members by legal and structural impediments that were not directly job-related. Random selection of the remaining 1,200 blue-collar men was achieved using subscription lists obtained from seven national magazines aimed largely at individuals in the categories of interest. Since occupational instability is generally higher for this group than for white-collar professionals possessing graduate degrees, questions about "the media" (newspapers and TV) were used as the primary ostensible reason for our regular inquiries, in the hope that this would limit any embarrassment respondents might feel (due to layoffs, strikes, job actions, slowdowns, or firings) before questions about employment, earnings, and marital status were again asked.

The simplifying assumption of a neat distinction between cohort and period effects, as exemplified in such worthwhile works as G. H. Elder, Jr., *Children of the Great Depression: Social Change in Life Experience* (Chicago: University of Chicago Press, 1974) and R. A. Easterlin, *Birth and Fortune: The Impact of Numbers on Personal Welfare* (New York: Basic Books, 1980), quickly loses much of its validity in an ongoing long-term study using data collected contemporaneously rather than retrospectively. For example, many attitudes and behaviors that first emerged in upwardly mobile college-educated urban groups tended to spread to white-collar and then blue-collar suburban residents, with a mean lag time of 2.8 and 4.1 years respectively for the period 1959 to 1986, a process that is revealingly modeled by a multifocal diffusion equation with an appropriately chosen Green's function. Moreover, as R. C. Kessler and D. F. Greenberg in *Linear Panel Analysis: Models of Quantitative Change* (New York: Academic Press, 1981) and H. Carter and P. C. Glick in *Marriage and Divorce: a Social and Economic Study* (Cambridge: Harvard University Press, 1976) have emphasized, historical factors often exert their most important effects indirectly via changes in the structure of many hundreds of local economic landscapes, not an assumed homogeneous national one (except in anomalous circumstances such as the Depression), an approach that seems particularly valuable given the severe regional dislocations that emerged in 1986 with the collapse in the price of crude oil; and this makes the migratory patterns of sample members a dimension of utmost importance.

Since our focus from the start was on which individuals would succeed (and why) both professionally and maritally—not so much where they did so—changes in residential and occupational setting were anticipated and monitored throughout. The nature of the personal and business relationships terminated or attenuated by a move, and the quality and durability of the new ones established elsewhere, constituted an essential part of our analysis, particularly as they acted to express the differing aspirations of sample members during the various stages of their lives, aspirations that were clearly influenced by an ever-shifting mix of cohort and historical pressures and opportunities.

Random selection of a white-collar sample of sufficient size was accomplished in part using RAND Corporation's computer-generated table, *A Million Random Digits* (Glencoe: Free Press, 1955), and the five-digit account numbers of customers at nine brokerage firms, five national and four regional. Each prospective sample member was told that interviews at regular intervals would be necessary in addition to follow-up questionnaires. In addition to the 2,000 gathered in this manner another 1,500 members were selected from sixteen colleges and graduate schools that represented a cross-section of United States institutions of higher education in 1958–1959. A third sample consisted of 1,518 school-age children of investor families in the sample. A fourth sample consisted of the husbands of the women in the third sample, the school-age sons of the 1,600 manual laborers described earlier, and the post–school age sons of the investor families in the first sample. Altogether, there was a total of 6,981 men in the five samples we selected. Their median household income (in constant 1986 dollars) was $39,400, nearly twice the national figure, and their median age at the start of the study was twenty. The cost savings associated with cluster sampling were not the main reason for making our selections from a total of only approximately two dozen brokerage firms and universities. Although we were aware that almost all varieties of clustering in sample design decrease the precision of sample estimates, since less new data about the population in question is obtained by selecting additional people from the sample cluster than by choosing individuals at random, background similarity was viewed as not necessarily a disadvantage in a long-term study emphasizing differential rates of promotion, pay increases, and marital stability. Initial differences among sample members, although smaller in some cases than we have liked, soon widened and in fact facilitated the study of developmental changes by decade, profession, and personality type.

Attention was paid throughout to inter- as well as intragroup differences, both professionally and maritally. Repeated comparisons, at least on an annual basis, were made between sample means and population means by utilizing, among other sources, College Placement Council, *Salary Surveys*; Endicott, *Trends in Employment of College and University Graduates in Business and Industry*; United States Bureau of Labor Statistics, *Employment of Recent Graduates*; National Science Foundation, *Two Years after the College Degree*; data on "Consumer Income" and "Educational Attainment" from United States Bureau of the Census, *Current Population Reports* on mean earnings of four-year college graduates; United States Bureau of the Census, 1960, 1970, and 1980 Census of Population, *Occupational Characteristics, Earnings by Occupation and Education* and *Occupations of Persons with High Earnings*; United States Department of Labor, *Employment and Earnings*; American Council on Education/UCLA, *National Norms for Entering College Freshmen* (various years); United States Bureau of the Census, Current Population Reports, "Number, Timing and Duration of Marriages and Divorces in the United States," "Marital Status and Living Arrangements," "Fertility of American Women"; United States Center for Health Statistics, Monthly Vital Statistics Reports, "Divorces by Marriage Cohort," "National Estimates of Marital Dissolution and Survivorship," "Trends and Differentials in Births to Unmarried Women," "Births, Marriages, Divorces and Deaths."

While the initial series of questions was intended to elicit information about annual earnings (from employment, inter- and intrafamily transfers, and investment) and growth in company sales and income (among small business owners and the self-employed), or promotions (among employees), as well as dating patterns and levels of marital satisfaction, the respondents themselves were the first to volunteer this information in a career context. For example, sample members in both blue- and white-collar professions often sought to justify what, in certain instances, was a substantial pay decrease, on the grounds that such a decrease heightened the chance of later advancement at another firm or earnings potential at one they eventually intended to start. The number of respondent references to occupation and/or career path was so much higher than we had anticipated in these early interviews, it was clear that this factor could not be omitted in any subsequent face-to-face or telephone interview without risk of offending the respondent who had offered this information as the principal explanation for the financial success or failure that had resulted up to that point from employment or even investment activities.

To ensure consistent data collection from one semiannual interview to the next, each sample member was asked to provide a list of the half-dozen co-workers or colleagues with whom the frequency of professional interaction was highest and/or of greatest importance. The explanation offered for the request was that, to determine the level of job satisfaction experienced during that particular six month period and "the kind of people in this field," brief interviews of the six individuals emphasizing the positive and negative features of each would be useful. Highly critical comments across the board, with no co-workers excepted, did indeed serve to indicate an elevated level of job dissatisfaction, as measured by differential rates of subsequent job change. Be that as it may, the lists turned out to be of great utility in maintaining continuous contact with each sample member. In fact, the sample size would have suffered significantly great attrition (10.8 percent—752 out of 6,981—as of the middle of 1986) had it not been for the lists, which were updated annually if the same occupational position was in effect or within four months after a job or career change. In hundreds of instances, when post office, phone-company records, or residential neighbors were unable to specify the new address, phone number, or institutional affiliation, if any, of a sample member who had moved to an unknown location and thus threatened to become lost to follow-up inquiries, the inner circle of co-workers, colleagues, customers, and clients in each case was able to help us restore contact by offering the name and/or location of the new employer and/or place of residence.

Close co-workers and colleagues, in addition to being what was often the only knowledgeable link between past and present places of employment of sample members, also provided valuable information about factors involved in the move, a subject they were much more willing to discuss freely now that the person in question was no longer with the firm and/or residing in the area. Considerable care was exercised by interviewers to make certain that the inquiries appeared to be off-the-record probes about the firm itself or casual conversation of the "What's new around here?" variety, rather than a series of pointed questions about any specific individual who was no longer employed there. This was necessary since it was not uncommon for sample members (especially those in the white-collar portions of the total sample) to once again find positions at previous employers at a future date. Moreover, the information gathered from co-workers, customers, and colleagues of sample members helped us greatly to determine the overall rate of turnover at the firm in question during the period under examination, a critical reference level against which to measure the frequency of job changes by sample members in that particular industry and company.

Similar considerations applied to changing levels of demand within each occupation, as monitored on a current basis using monthly indices such as *Engineer/Scientist Demand Index* by Deutsch, Shea and Evans, Inc., calculated from want-ad placements. From 1970 on we also used a proprietary index (based on want-ads for nontechnical managerial and professional personnel) that we constructed in order to better assess demand for business and professional people in the specific categories of interest to us. The expansion and contraction of employment demand within any given occupation had a calculable effect on both the professional and personal lives of the members of our sample, one that most were only partially aware of since they tended strongly to localize and then personalize the effects of what were actually national shifts (to the Sunbelt in the 1970s and to the Northeast, for instance, in the mid-1980s) in the top rates of regional economic growth.

A concerted effort was made throughout the study to obtain reliable data on consumption expenditures by sample members, among other reasons to assess the impact of this social/financial factor on career development and marital stability. All 663 of the field researchers we employed during the course of the study (primarily graduate students in the social sciences and statistics) were asked to observe "life-style" patterns whenever possible. Again, sample and stratum means, on the one hand, and population means, on the other, were compared annually, using a wide variety of statistical sources, among them the Consumer Expenditure Series of the Bureau of Labor Statistics.

One effective way to get beyond some of the limitations imposed by the combination of stratified and cluster sampling we employed was to regularly test tentative conclusions by using interested self-employed, employee, and managerial volunteers who were not members of the sample. Although here, too, self-selection introduces distortions of its own, which are then frequently compounded by researcher bias, we believe that much information of a practical nature was obtained by proceeding carefully and remaining mindful of the results discussed in R. Rosenthal, *Experimenter Effects in Behavior Research* (New York: Irvington Publishers, 1976); R. A. Jones, *Self-Fulfilling Prophesies: Social, Psychological and*

Physiological Effects of Expectancies (Hillsdale: L. Erlbaum Associates Publishers, 1977), and J. Cohen, *Statistical Power Analysis for the Behavioral Sciences* (New York: Academic Press, 1977).

Studying a sample of this size over a prolonged period would have been prohibitively expensive had it not been for a Variable Rate Monitoring (VRM) procedure we used, in which individuals who made relatively more changes in location, jobs and partners were contacted more frequently, while those who made fewer changes relative to these three medians for the sample as a whole were interviewed less often. Also, since the blue-collar portion of the sample was being utilized largely for comparison purposes and was not the primary object of our study, its members were interviewed an average of once every 15.2 months, whereas the corresponding figure for the white-collar portion was 5.3 months.

INDEX